The Killing Consensus

The Killing Consensus

Police, Organized Crime, and the Regulation
of Life and Death in Urban Brazil

Graham Denyer Willis

UNIVERSITY OF CALIFORNIA PRESS

University of California Press, one of the most
distinguished university presses in the United States,
enriches lives around the world by advancing
scholarship in the humanities, social sciences, and
natural sciences. Its activities are supported by the UC
Press Foundation and by philanthropic contributions
from individuals and institutions. For more information, visit www.ucpress.edu.

University of California Press
Oakland, California

Library of Congress Cataloging-in-Publication Data

Denyer Willis, Graham, 1979– author.
    The killing consensus : police, organized crime, and
the regulation of life and death in urban Brazil /
Graham Denyer Willis.
        pages cm
    Includes bibliographical references and index.
    ISBN 978-0-520-28570-5 (hardcover : alk. paper)
    ISBN 978-0-520-28571-2 (pbk.)
    1. Homicide—Brazil—São Paulo. 2. Homicide
investigation—Brazil—São Paulo. 3. Police—Brazil—
São Paulo. 4. Organized crime—Brazil—São Paulo.
I. Title.
    HV6535.B73S26266 2015
    364.1520981'61—dc23

                                        2014044815

24   23   22   21   20   19   18   17   16   15
10   9   8   7   6   5   4   3   2   1

For my parents

Contents

PART THREE. DEBATE

Illustrations

Foreword

On January 24, 2014, my wife and I welcomed our second child. This baby—a boy—arrived in a private hospital room in Canada, surrounded by a midwife, a midwifery student, an obstetrician, a pediatrician, a medical student, at least three nurses, and his dad. He arrived in a secure and safe world, with exceptional care paid for by a tax regime favorable to those with low income, beginning a life defined in large part by his citizenship, his skin color, his gender, and the capacity of his parents and extended family to "make" money. He is, in many ways, the picture of privilege.

Not that it had to be quite that way. For seven of the nine months he spent in his mom's tummy, this baby existed in a Brazilian slum—a *favela*—on the outskirts of Rio de Janeiro. There he was surrounded by a much different world—one defined by poverty, by historically deadly police, organized crime, a drug trade run amok, and a public health system that could scarcely be worse—unless one found oneself abandoned by the handful of tireless and resourceful workers that nonetheless exist in places within it. It was a community with a per capita household income of around $200 USD a month, standing in contrast to Rio's lagoon and beachside neighborhood of Lagoa with its per capita household income of $2,700.

While his mom carried out her own doctoral research, his dad wrote most of this book, and his sister played with the neighborhood kids, he grew slowly and, thankfully, soundly. Not that we were sure. At least one of our friends from the neighborhood lost her daughter under questionable circumstances five days after a premature childbirth at thirty-four weeks. After the baby died, the mother was kept in the same shared room in the maternity ward surrounded by the consistent arrival of new lives and laughter, until someone determined she could leave the ward and go home days later.

Six weeks after the birth of our boy, I participated in a workshop in São Paulo on comparative security sector reform. For a couple of days, my colleagues and I talked about most of the things that this book is about—violent police, prison gangs, shifting homicide patterns, and what can be done to improve the conditions of people who suffer under the brutal disparity of urban violence.

At the end of the workshop, a small group of us visited a local women's penitentiary on the outskirts of the city. This penitentiary was semi-open, serving to house women with short sentences, as well as those transitioning from months or years in maximum-security units. Women could go out to work during the day, if adorned with an electronic anklet, as long as they returned at night. In this prison with a little more than a thousand inmates, 95 percent were serving time for drug-related sentences. In the words of the staff, though, these were not the drug traffickers that you may conjure in your mind's eye. Though almost universally from the poorest parts of São Paulo, most found themselves in jail on behalf of someone else—a husband, a boyfriend, a son, a brother, a father—whose engagement in the drug trade had left them holding the bag as mules, scapegoats, or the only person in the house when police raided and found drugs or guns. They are, by and large, the proxy victims of a drug war formulated, carried out, legitimated, and most deadly for men. But though most of these women—thousands of them in São Paulo alone—are defined by the sacrifices they are making for men, most have been abandoned by them. While women line up and wait for hours or days to see their men in prison in order to bring them food, clothes, medicine, drugs, or other contraband stuff like cell phones, visitation lines at women's prisons are virtually nonexistent.

But if these women are guilty by association, their suffering stretches far further. As I write about in the pages that follow, these are the same women that would arrive at the homicide division in the aftermath of a police shooting. They are the ones who welcomed me with food and offers of a room to sleep in during my research in the *zona leste*—the West Side. They are the ones whose red eyes plead with detectives to finish the incident report, already, so they could take the bullet-riddled bodies of their husbands, boyfriends, sons, fathers, or brothers to the cemetery for burial. They are the ones who cheered my daughter on to make her first steps in their living room—which she did. They are the ones who sit for hours in the waiting room at the police station, not exceptionally opposite the police who killed their loved ones, a seemingly unwavering testament to unconditional love. That this book does not come closer to the lives of these women is its biggest failure.

Toward the end of our visit we stopped by the mother and baby unit. There a handful of rooms about ten by twelve feet and split into two, that house women with newborns. On the walls were tones of purple and yellow, bordered with patterns of teddy bears and painted ribbon. The cribs were padded and adorned with colorful and frilly sheets. Under the Brazilian penal code, incarcerated women may keep newborns with them until they are six months old—a policy that while nonetheless tragic puts many Northern countries to absolute and total shame. At six months, the mothers must give their children to relatives on the outside. If none are available, they are put up for adoption—mother willing or not. At the end of the hall, past the group of visitors were a group of mothers with their infants. Some were tiny little boys just weeks old.

This visit was the most emotionally destabilizing moment of my time studying police, violence, and organized crime in and around this city. Perhaps it was my personal sensitivities at the moment, but the tragic condition of these lives seemed much more disturbing than the legitimations of death on the part of both the police and the criminal organization known as the Primeiro Comando da Capital that I had seen for years. In my implicit acceptance of those legitimations—by that I mean, my comparative sensitivity to the innocence of little lives and the lives of women over the lives of young men—I stared back at my own category of valuable life.

This book is not about the hopefulness and innocence of life. I wish it were. But it *is* very much about these babies, especially the fragile little boys. With their current trajectories, these young "men" will be "killable" when my own son is in grade nine, if not earlier. But really, these future men are undeniably already the product of a horrifying configuration of (de)valued life and death. They are already at the heart of a criminalized population, beginning their lives without security, with the "wrong" skin color, without the safety net of wealth or social status and living in a world where citizenship means almost nothing more than voting every four years.

There is no better place to begin building the just society that I have to believe most Brazilians desire than the room at the end of that hall.

Preface

I can't remember what we were talking about when our conversation was interrupted. The tire squealing grew from distant to loud, filling the open window. Craig and I stopped talking to watch as the red hue of flashing lights grew bright on the surrounding buildings, converging from different directions. With sirens in chorus, there was a crashing of metal and concrete, an abbreviated commotion and two gunshots in quick succession. Pop. Pop.

Curious (and certainly reckless), we walked over to see what had happened. Arriving within seconds, we saw in flesh and blood what the sounds had suggested. A vehicle pursuit had ended with police shooting a man. Standing across a residential road, a distance of less than thirty feet, we saw the result. On a street mixed with towering gated apartments and the ornate walled homes of São Paulo's old wealth, a man now lay crumpled on the sidewalk, slumped backward against the glass and brushed aluminum bars of a gated condominium. Beneath him was a growing pool of blood. In front of him, less than ten feet away, was a crowd of Military Police from the Tactical Squad—the Força Tática—mulling around an idling police sport utility vehicle. As we watched, two or three police picked up the man by the arms and legs, carried him to the back of the truck and hefted him into the back section. They closed the door and sped off, lights flashing, to the hospital, presumably.

We hung around for some time just watching the scene unfold. No police cordon went up, even as there were a couple of police directing traffic. There was, in fact, a net loss of police immediately following the conclusion of the chase. Of five or six cars initially involved, only one remained half an hour later. On the other side of the glass and metal wall condominium security guards loitered, rehashing, no doubt, what they had seen. The "getaway car," its front tire burst on a concrete abutment, sat with most of its doors open as if still leaking itself of its contents. Where the others had gone, who knew. We minded our business for the most part—gawkers occupying a space somewhere between irrelevance and graduate student.

Eventually, a military police officer approached us. He wanted to know whether we had witnessed the event. He suggested that we come to the Civil Police station to give a statement—even when we said we hadn't seen it with our own eyes. We'd be welcome if we were willing to understand a couple of things. He gave us a couple of pointers, making sure that two were especially clear. First, there had been three shots, not two as we'd said we'd heard. The .45 of the police sounds different that the .38 that the fugitive was carrying, he said. The .38 is more muted, which is why we didn't hear it. Second, we heard the police shouting for the man to put down his gun before they shot.

Not that this word-in-our-mouths approach was anything all that surprising. I knew from my work in police stations over the years that the streamlining of witness and police statements was standard practice— as long as there was no unavoidable evidence to the contrary, like a video, an audio recording, or a really stubborn witness willing to risk a whole lot. I had no desire to spend the next few hours sitting in a police station on the other side of the "thin blue line"; I would be there later that night anyway.

Nearly an hour on, the detectives and crime scene investigators were nowhere to be found. This was also no major surprise either, really. This case was far from serious, even if the man would die on the Military Police's often deliberately slow scenic route to the hospital. I was expecting to get to the homicide division yet that night. And if the man died, I would have found my way back to this same spot alongside the homicide detectives—since it would then become a mandatory scene visit. But if the man did survive, he'd garner something much less than a diligent investigation. No central investigation would take place. Instead, detectives from the local precinct would eventually show up to take a few pictures for the report with a pocket-sized digital camera to add to the criminal background checks and witness statements that we were being asked to give.

But then, as if to mock my interest in such inane details, the most alarming of things happened. From around the corner, a man and a woman strolled down the street with an impeccably groomed lap dog. Of the social type that wear a sweater over the shoulders, the couple meandered blithely down the sidewalk, chatting under the street lights, their dog stopping at brief moments to sniff corners, telephone poles, or whatever happened to be low and fragrant. They noticed the stationary police car across the street with its lights flashing, a common enough sight that seems to declare a permanent state of emergency in the city. As Craig and I watched, the couple walked right through the pool of blood, brushing past where the man had slumped against the glass. Each of them stepped in the pool, oblivious to their literal and figurative position in the routine bloodletting of the city. The dog, whose fur was almost long enough to take some blood with it, stopped for just a moment longer to smell the edge of the pool, before skipping away to catch up.

For me, this incident was not just a gruesome interruption of my downtime away from the homicide division. It also was a case that reconfigured and sharpened my thinking about police violence and its investigation by detectives. First, this was a comparatively rare example of a police shooting of a citizen in a wealthy part of town, where fear of violence vastly outstrips empirical practice. Almost always, the shooting of suspects occurs in parts of the city that lie far from concentrations of wealth and power, in the worlds of self-built housing and modesty. The routine practice of police shootings of citizens is rendered politically unimportant because of this spatial configuration. As long as violent death occurs on the other side of the glass and aluminum city it remains unremarkable. The image of the man, slumped and dying against the "modern" glass and aluminum of the condominium was odd, irregular, out of place.

Second, this case was a novel—if, like all of my research, unfortunate—opportunity to see what happens before any meaningful investigation begins, either by the homicide detectives I had been accompanying, or—in the event the man did not die—by the neighborhood precinct detectives. Even in cases where jurisdiction isn't in question, I knew it was typical to have a long wait—multiple hours at minimum—between the incident and the arrival of investigators. But the true scope of what this meant, in such a barren and shocking visual, was absolutely something else. I hadn't fully considered how much can happen before someone collects the initial evidence—if they do—how scenes are guarded, from whom—neighborhood dogs?!—and how long it could take for the jurisdictional gap between investigators to be resolved, finally compelling *someone* to act. After all, no one in the local precinct or the homicide division is all that excited about investigating one more case with hours of paperwork. Especially when police get no overtime pay. This incident shed light on a big blind spot in my research: I simply hadn't been able to observe the sheer degree to which investigations can be deeply compromised before they even begin.

To my knowledge, this case never made it to the homicide division. It certainly didn't in the next fourteen hours, when I was there. For the homicide detectives there came no word. So perhaps the man did make it to the hospital alive. And maybe he survived. But I was left asking myself, what would it really matter if he died hours, days, or a week later, when, finally, homicide detectives would be empowered to investigate? They would return to the scene to find a dried puddle of blood. That puddle would have dog and human footprints in it. And who knows what else. That is, of course, if it didn't rain or hadn't been washed off the sidewalk by someone trying to keep the city clean.

Acknowledgments

This book is the product of more than fifteen years of intellectual discovery.

This began with my entry to Brazil as a teenage exchange student in the 1990s and continues through the research that took me to some of the most historically dangerous urban spaces in Latin America—if not the world. Unavoidably, it is a culmination of much more than a doctoral research project. The pages that follow are also a byproduct of the ways I have tried to cope with the moral ambiguity (and moral position) of organized violence in its many forms around the world. Readers who know me may recognize in my writing a struggle to navigate the complex personal histories of those mired in different forms of the victim—perpetrator complex. Conversations with and memories about some of the people and positions of violence that I have come close to in the last decade and a half—refugees with obscured histories, criminal deportees from the United States in prisons in the Global South, international mining functionaries working in (and/or under) subsistence communities—all inform my interpretation of those in the midst of violence in São Paulo. But too often I've been a voyageur-voyeur, viewing the troubling circumstances of others only to leave them behind all to abruptly. I'm the first to admit that this is the case in São Paulo. The city remains a place that I am more or less free to leave when the floor starts to cave in. To those who enrich my understanding of the circumstances of violence, knowingly or unknowingly, in São Paulo (and elsewhere), and almost always with little or nothing of substance in return, thank you. This book, and I, are indebted to you.

I've leaned heavily on many people while completing this book. Most prominent among these is Diane Davis, a mentor and an inspiration of intellect, poise, and pragmatism. I will be forever grateful that Diane bet on the long shot and stuck with it in spite of a move of her own. John Van Maanen's jovial scholarship and support has reminded me that academia need not be grumpy in its brilliance, criticism, or politics—even for those who study the nuts and bolts of unhopeful things like police. Larry Vale has been a supporter for many years, well before taking a more active role in this project in latter years. Many thanks for your thoughtfulness and our city and intellectual explorations. Desmond Arias has been a compass for many years, helping me make some big decisions in educated ways. Thank you for your patience and eagerness.

I'm very grateful to those who were interested in this project from well before it became anything of substance. Paz Buttedahl was central, but left far too soon. To Shirley Case, a friend who gave up everything doing what we all should do, you left one hell of a legacy that I will never overlook. Nancy Cardia, Jorge Nef, Alejandro Palacios, Anthony Pereira, Maria Fernanda Tourinho Peres, and Pablo Policzer all helped me get my intellectual or practical foot in the door. At MIT, special thanks go to Patti Foley, Nimfa de Leon, and Bish Sanyal for going out of their way to bring me in to the SPURS program. For Rajogopal Balakrishnan and John Tirman with the Program on Human Rights and Justice and the Center for International Studies, I'm grateful. I likely wouldn't have gotten through the first part of my doctoral studies without the friendship and support of those in (and around) my cohort in the Department of Urban Studies and Planning at MIT. To Madhu Dutta-Koehler, Onesimo Flores, Jason Jackson, Deepak Lamba Nieves, Alexis Schulman, Shomon Shamsuddin, Mia White, and Yuan Xiao in specific, I hope I returned the favor. To those tireless administrators who put up with me, particularly Kirsten Greco, Sandy Wellford, and Karen Yegian, thank you. To my colleagues during a brief period at the University of Toronto's Centre for Criminology and Sociolegal Studies, Jessica Chlebowski, Kelly Hannah-Moffat, Matthew Light, Wilhelmina Peter, Mariana Valverde, and Lori Wells, thank you. I'm especially indebted to Rosemary Gartner and Scot Wortley. I am excited about what my future holds at the University of Cambridge, where I have already found much support and encouragement from an inspiring new group of colleagues.

With the intellectual journey has come a need for other kinds of support. This project was funded in its different stages by the Drugs, Security, and Democracy Program of the Social Science and Research Council and the Open Society Foundations, the Social Science Research Council of Canada, the Carroll L. Wilson Fellowship at MIT, MISTI-Brazil, and other sources at MIT like the Harold Horowitz Award and the Emerson Fellowship. Particular thanks go to Markus Gottsbacher, David Holiday, Nicole Restrick Levit, Jessica Mack, and Cleia Noia for providing not just funding but an enduring intellectual community that I will engage with for years to come.

A number of colleagues have made this book possible and much better than it once promised to be. Cynthia Arnson, Lucia Dammert, Peter Houtzager, Gareth Jones, Elizabeth Leeds, Julita Lemgruber, Fiona Macaulay, Guaracy Mingardi, Eric Olson, Dennis Rodgers, Ben Ross Schneider, Susan Silbey, Finn Stepputat, Judith Tendler, Phil Thompson, and Orlando Zaccone all contributed in important ways.

Some others contributed by reading and providing feedback on parts or all of the text. Regina Bateson, Kristen Drybread, Daniel Esser, Anthony Fontes, Jeff Garmany, Beatrice Jauregui, Eduardo Moncada, Robert Samet, Kimberly Theidon, and Austin Zeiderman read, commented, or invited me to give talks on parts (or all) of this book. It has been a pleasure working with Mariana Mota Prado on related projects. In Brazil, the people at the Forum Brasileiro de Seguranca Publica served as both welcoming hosts and inspiring scholar practitioners. Thanks in particular go to Samira Bueno, Renato Sérgio de Lima, Ana Maura Tomesani, and Caio Valiengo, as well as to Rob Muggah and Ilona Szabo at Instituto Igarapé. Camila Dias and Bruno Paes Manso have also shaped this work in some vital ways. To friends that I leaned on in many ways (and sometimes for a bed), Nick Barnes, Pedro Henrique de Cristo, Paulo Duarte Filho, Abigail Friendly, Yanilda Gonzalez, Blair Hagman, Tiffany Kearney, Peter Klein, Anders Knudsen, Enrique Pujals, Julia Tierney, Stephanie Savell, Craig Scheutze, Luisa Sotomayor, Theresa Williamson, and Mike Wolff, I'm indebted.

I have presented parts of this manuscript in many places. Thanks also go to all of those who read and commented at the SSRC/Open Society Drugs, Security, and Democracy workshops in Bogota in 2011 and Villa de Leyva in 2012, the 2012 MIT-LSE-Harvard Writing Cities workshop, in talks at the Centres for Transnational and Diaspora Studies and Criminology and Sociolegal Studies at the University of Toronto, American University's School of International Service, the Woodrow

Wilson Center for International Scholars, the Brazil Institute at King's College London, the School of Social and Political Studies and the University of Glasgow and the Department of Geography and Environment at the London School of Economics, as well as at the Latin American Studies Association congresses in 2010, 2011, 2012, and 2013. Special thanks go to the dissertation award reviewers of the Brazil Section of the Latin American Studies Association, the Association of Collegiate Schools of Planning, and the Department of Urban Studies and Planning at MIT for giving a previous version of this manuscript a number of commendations.

I'm indebted to Sasha Polakow-Suranski and Simon Romero at the *New York Times* for their interest in policing and the PCC in São Paulo in late 2012, to Tom Cowan at Open Democracy, as well as to Matt Lord, Nausicaa Renner and others at the *Boston Review* for inviting me to write and creatively explore some ideas.

Three other scholars saw this manuscript through its early stages at the press. Ed Maguire, Peter Manning, and Kevin Lewis O'Neill each provided productive feedback about the substance, direction, and organization of this book. Three reviewers from the *American Sociological Review*, provided very positive and constructive comments on a manuscript that I've taken to heart in this version. At the University of California Press, I thank Reed Malcolm and Stacy Eisenstark for their interest and guidance. I extend gratitude to Michael Bohrer-Clancy at Westchester Publishing Services for editing support. Additionally, I thank Max Horder for assistance with indexing. The usual caveat serves: I alone am responsible for the content and interpretation of this book.

There are a few people who have shaped my life in defining moments along the way. Thanks to Moe and Barrie Reid, Michele Darling and Michael Eagen, Iara and Ovidio and Inês and Marconi, for providing me with space to grow, either by sharing their home, their inspiration, or much more. Marion and Art and Lois and Gordon led humble lives and never went to university, but they gave me one hell of a gift—a passion and a demand to think deeply about the circumstances of others. In the sacrifices you made for others near and far, and in a political lineage, I find myself.

Finally, thanks go to Cathy and Mark, Wes and Judy and Paul. You can't get rid of me now. Sara, you are a model of calm. To my parents: Mom, you pushed me to get out of the small town in the first place, and I barely came back. You handle it with such grace and love. I have the sense that we grow together. To my stalwart father of few words, I have six for you: Could I ever be so good? To Arden and Jude, I hope you don't read this book until your teenage years, though you've both already existed rather close to some of these very difficult realities. Most of all I thank Laurie Denyer Willis, my partner on this ongoing personal and intellectual journey. You are the foundation and inspiration of what I do. This book is as much yours as it is mine. Onward we go.

PART ONE

Surviving

Sovereignty by Consensus

It is forbidden to kill; therefore all murderers are punished,
unless they kill in large enough numbers to have the trumpets
play behind them: that is the rule.

—Voltaire, *Dictionnaire Philosophique*

"The Brazilian people can go fuck themselves," was all Henrique could muster.[1] We had just returned from a murder scene, and this police detective was boiling over. On the steps of the Civil Police headquarters in downtown São Paulo, he watched—but not really—as media vans and camera people shuffled on the street in front of us.

The murder scene had been a mess. The walls were littered with bullet holes and pools of blood seemed to be everywhere. Beat cops and police detectives were swarming the place looking for answers. But the answers they were looking for were few. A few blocks away on a stainless-steel-topped concrete slab tiled with a black crucifix, was a dead police officer. His body perforated and lifeless. Morgue workers had tied both his hands and his toes together with gauze to prevent them from splaying apart. His right forearm had been blown open, a testament to the frailty of his attempt at self-defense. We had stood silent there. Someone took a few photos for the file. I took two for reflection and this description, which I knew would come later.

We later regrouped with the rest of the team of detectives who had been interviewing his police partner down the hall. The partner was alive against all odds. When detectives had come to see him in hospital he was on the phone with his wife, divvying up his earthly belongings so his kids wouldn't fight over them. He had been shot more times than anyone had cared to tally yet. Doctors said it was just a matter of time. When I asked a detective about his chances, he just shook his head.

The detectives were frustrated. "The media only shows Israel bombing Palestine. We're in the middle of our own Civil War here," said one detective outside the morgue. "This is worse. Much worse," said another. Indeed, it *was* bad. Police and an organized crime group known as the Primeiro Comando da Capital, or PCC, were in the midst of what some have called a blood feud. By the end of that year, 2012, more than a hundred police would be dead. The number of PCC members—or presumed PCC members—dead in the same period was (and is) almost impossible to quantify, but likely numbered in the thousands. This violence was exceptional; it defied the *relative peace* of police-PCC relations in normal times that has defined life in São Paulo over the last fifteen years. But now, the complex but predictable and mutually intelligible ways that police and PCC members have dealt with each other were ruptured. All bets were off. Killing was now the only currency.

And so it was. The media vans and camera people in front of Henrique and I were there not because of the dead policeman or his partner that afternoon. They were there because of a recent case in which a group of police executed a supposed PCC member in cold blood. Faking their story, these police had been caught by someone filming the incident on a cell phone. This was an early example of a commonplace act—PCC members, the police themselves, and different communities using social media in an attempt to promote their various causes and claims. A detective from the Homicide Division was now in charge of the case. The media waited tirelessly at the station because, at some point, these police would be taken from the station to a prison reserved exclusively for wayward police. They would walk in front of the cameras, perhaps slightly obscured by sympathetic colleagues, becoming premium footage to be alternately celebrated and condemned on newscasts and afternoon crime shows for weeks to come.

"Brazilians just want to know about their rights but not their obligations," Henrique finally said in an attempt to make sense of it all. But his concern obviously ran much deeper than the supposed checks and balances of democracy. That Brazilians should fuck themselves was really about a deep-seated feeling of being hung out to dry. As police were being killed left, right, and center—and killing, left, right, and center— there had been little substantial response from the media, politicians, or civil society. To the contrary, that police could (and indeed would) be killed was really quite normal—if not expected. At least fifty per year are eliminated when times are *good*. These police *must be* dirty or corrupt—or so it goes. Almost certainly Henrique could picture himself on that cold table in the morgue, his own forearm a failed shield. That the policeman in the morgue was largely expendable and his death more or less unremarkable, his purported association with the PCC or other unnamed goons trumped up, was the name of the game. Such is the state of policing and sovereign authority in São Paulo, even if Henrique knew it and was tired of it.

How is life and death regulated, and by whom? We hold some powerful and defining assumptions about police. One of the greatest is that they are the only people who may legitimately kill in the name of order. Police, and no other, may take the life of an individual—or individuals—as a means to ensure the safety and security of a population. But the assumption goes further. This unique mandate is paired with an important accomplice and occasional counterpoint—an obligation to regulate all killing.

Much of our knowledge, our assumptions, and our prescriptions for making police better rest on this foundation. And for good reason too. Much policing takes place in contexts backed up by a hegemonic idea and practice of sovereign authority. Sovereignty means control over the right to kill.[2] In the contemporary world, this control is vested in territorial entities known as states that practice a kind of ideal subordination over their populations. These states, by virtue of their sovereign power, uniquely decide the terms of life and death for their populations.[3] Who lives and who dies in routine ways is a derivation from what a given definition and routine practice of (in)valuable life demarcates. Police are the guardians of these definitions, reproducing and consolidating social order in ways that are largely uncontested by violence. Of this there is remarkably little debate.[4]

This book is about circumstances and spaces in which most of these assumptions do not hold. It is about the exercise and everyday practices of *sovereignty by consensus*, where the right to kill is a shared practice and lived experience for police and urban citizens. It is about the ways that the regulation of life and death is carried out by not one but two violent parties. It is about why some cities crumble into violence and tend to stay there, why public security appears so insolvent, when democracy is a pariah, and why police defy almost all expectations—even when we already expect them to defy them.

In the pages that follow, I accompany the world of homicide and other detectives of the Policia Civil in the megacity of São Paulo, Brazil.[5] Homicide police the world over are expected to investigate, solve, and repress the practice of murder. They are expected to examine the evidence, collect witnesses, piece together the storyline, make determinations about motives, submit evidence for analysis, and where at all possible, to find the perpetrators and have them arrested.[6] We expect them to investigate all suspicious deaths as homicides until proven otherwise and to get their "bad guy" at least most of the time. We tend to believe that they are an elite agency of police—if not *the* elite agency—and a primary gatekeeper of public security fighting in defense of the right to life, backed up by technology, a career of knowledge, and with no real shortage of resources.[7] Not just that, they (and we) rarely need consider that these police are in danger from those they arrest. They are safe enough, in fact, that they have been known forget their gun at the office.[8]

But imagine the contrary. In São Paulo, homicide detectives are ill-equipped, lacking anything more than basic forensic analytics; they are devoid of political clout and are the subject of collegial derisiveness and deep suspicion. They are near the nadir of their careers—rookies and tired hands—and usually exert less influence—both in strength and organizational position—than other police units celebrated for their lethality. Only deaths that are obviously—visibly—intentional are considered homicides from the get go. More important, these detectives are inclined to be dismissive of certain kinds—indeed a *normal* kind—of homicide in the city, being less diligent in their investigations as a result. In other words, if we invert our conceptions of homicide detectives learned from research and popular portrayals in Northern contexts, we might actually start to come close to what they are like in São Paulo.

These homicide detectives are mandated to investigate and resolve two kinds of killing. The first is homicides where the assailant is not known.[9] The second is police killings of citizens, know until recently as "resisting arrest followed by death," or *resistência seguida de morte*. But these two kinds of killing also reveal two primary means of ordering social relations via violence. Police in this city kill citizens at a pace of 1.6 per day during *peaceful* times, and the PCC is behind the "quotidian" or "normal" homicide. Every day, and usually multiple times a day, these detectives must visit scenes of violent death caused by one or both of these two violent parties. In an environment of routinized killing, they draw upon their discretionary space to make judgments and evaluations as to the appropriateness of these deaths that underlie the manner and direction of investigation. But, for the most part, the reasons and structures of routinized killing are taken for granted or assumed. This book is about how homicide detectives make sense of these deaths, why their inclination to allow some deaths to be classified as not being homicides makes systemic "sense," and how the cumulative result of these decisions traces a particular formulation of shared governance over the conditions of life and death in this city. A focus on their regulation, then, is not about absolutes or total control. It is about everyday practices of mediation, negotiation, and arbitration in the face of significant obstacles.[10]

This book is also very much about cities, social relations, and the patterns of urbanization common in the Global South. It is, in *some* ways, about "the margins." But these pages will relate how those from the margins have come to define many aspects of the center. Homicides and violence cannot be disentangled from their spatial coordinates, the built environment in which they take place, or their deeply racialized correlates. São Paulo, like other megacities in the South, is defined by two patterns of urbanization: one is built *by* owners—commonly called "informal"—that exists in the relative absence of centralized property regimes, rights, and state regulation; the other is built *for* owners—commonly called "formal"—and regulated by land tenure, building codes, engineers, and the like.[11] Both are deeply historical, reflecting long-standing patterns of citizen-state relations—the latter anemic, the other comparatively strong.[12] These historical correlates of state-society relations are particularly relevant when it comes to policing, public security, and contemporary forms of violence in urban space. While wealthier parts of cities have had public services fashioned from above, others have been left to devise their own from the bottom up. For decades—if not centuries—the focus for many residents on the urban and social fringe has been on collective solutions for survival and getting by.

Urban residents have routinely been left to cobble together their own security solutions as well. In the absence of a more appropriate redistribution of public security over much of the twentieth century, but acutely following the downfall of Cold War authoritarian regimes with tightly held central power, new and decentralized security entities have become powerful producers and regulators of violence, particularly in parts of cities with weak state–society relations. These groups use violence as a means to bring about decentralized permutations of security—even as they may be violently destabilizing to others and draw on illicit economies as forms of revenue—in an effort to achieve order. They range in size and complexity from seemingly spontaneous lynch mobs, to street gangs controlling a few blocks, to sophisticated organized crime groups that control swathes of urban peripheries and entire city-sized informal settlements. These groups usually have little if any political or revolutionary goals. They are made up of and often supported by people who are well past placing faith in democratic or traditional civil society institutions, existing in spite of the state rather than in protest with it—even as they occasionally destabilize cities with startling violence as a form of protest.[13]

The proliferation of forms of self-help security in many cities of the Global South, but acutely in Latin America, is among the strongest example of a broad pattern of statephobic attempts at security.[14] But exactly what the rationale and structural conditions are for these groups is the point of some debate. These new security formulations are sometimes construed as products of recent efforts to restructure economies and governance following a neoliberal model. Grassroots efforts for security are, then, sometimes called "violent entrepreneurs," who act roughly in keeping with the new rules of the game emergent from structural adjustment and economic liberation.[15] Other times, they are understood as an outflow of the disaster of democracy and regime change that followed the Cold War, having proliferated as liberal governments demanded an end to authoritarian security.[16] Some assert that the localized demand for security emerged as Cold War regimes did decentralize, defund, and devalue local security agencies, leaving local public security in cities in disarray.[17] I contend that each of these are true to some degree or another, insofar as they complement, aggravate, consolidate, and criminalize deeply historical modes of urban exclusion along known racial, spatial, and class lines.

Of all of these forms of decentralized security, the presence and influence of organized crime groups is usually the most jarring. I understand organized crime to be a security-oriented collective, often membership and identity based, and usually with subdivisions of labor that are engaged in the provision of goods and/or services deemed illegal by empirically existing states.[18] For the most part, organized crime groups—or similar informal institutions—have been understood as profoundly violent and destabilizing. Yet in recent times and in certain spaces these groups have also occasionally made cities *less* deadly. Truces, pacts, and other implied or formal agreements between multiple groups, or between groups and police or the state, can send a precipitous homicide rate into steep decline virtually overnight.[19] Absent the state's provision of security, many of these groups have taken it on themselves to make a defined constituency more secure and also to tax these constituents in highly bureaucratic ways, much like modern states do.[20]

These groups suggest an enormous empirical and theoretical turn. They are emergent from what has for almost a century been called "the margins," or "marginality."[21] The PCC is a product of this marginality. That much is clear. Poor black and brown men have been—and are—the subjects of the social processes that criminalize bodies and spaces, alternately called structural, everyday, institutionalized, or symbolic violence.[22] This systemic violence is also the terrain from which the PCC builds its support. But today, though, the PCC has its *own* structural, everyday, institutionalized, and symbolic violence.

The margins are no longer simply the subject of violence. They are now an object of it. We need to be able to see groups like the PCC as both marginal and marginalizing. So far, we have not. Notions of the marginal such as "bare life" and the "hyper-ghetto" are marginalizing in their own ways. As Ticktin (2011, 14) has put it, these kinds of conceptual approaches minimize the possibility of "action for those least likely to be seen as political subjects." And yet it is the lack of utility of "the marginal" that makes the category more relevant than ever.[23]

In other words, to paint the PCC as only marginal is to misunderstand both the empirical reality of the city and also to misplace the ways that groups like this have reshaped social relations—and the city itself. The PCC now sits at the heart of the governance of the urban conditions of life and death—while at the same time remaining many of its victims. These "marginal actors" are now inescapably significant, with their own definition, regulation, and practice of life and death in historically violent communities—the populaces historically most targeted by mechanisms of social control. They are a new mode of social control existent within the historical mode. And in their management of the urban margins they provide for those in the center. The margins are now at the center of social control—or so I will argue.

But what does this mean for sovereignty and policing in the contemporary period? Organized crime, paramilitaries, transnational firms, and even NGOs are redrawing the relationship between sovereignty and states.[24] Many empirically existing states, defined by mutually observed or UN-recognized borders, powerful national militaries, and stable national governments, have multiple parties within or transcending them with their own sovereign characteristics or tendencies. Many have argued that today's states are porous entities, with varying forms of sovereign violence and influence transcending, pervading, overrunning, or accompanying their physical and bureaucratic boundaries.[25]

Such decentralized practices of sovereignty within empirically existing states have brought a wide-ranging reevaluation of what it means to
be sovereign in a world of "failed," "failing," and "weak" states. What
is the point of the state and sovereignty, after all? Some contend that sovereignty is more descriptive and abstract then substantive; more suited
to a token nod than to serious debate—especially a debate that is rooted
in empirics. Some have sought to abandon sovereignty as a unifying theory, noting its dissonance with empirical realities of violence and suggesting that the state is dead as a helpful conceptual and actionable
category.[26] The consequence is a repurposing of the idea of sovereignty to
better understand these new empirical forms and patterns of violence.
But the move toward recognizing the shortcomings of de jure sovereignty
in favor of de facto sovereignty is evocative of more than globalization's
ability to perforate states. What exists, according to this school of thought,
are "new" sovereignties that explode borders, push back at Western normative notions of order, and defy (or repackage) the global discourse of
development and governance.

These distinct practices of violence and authority necessarily denote
a novel separateness from states, defying regulation, centralized order,
and the territorial dominion vested in government and states. De facto
sovereignties carry an ability to kill, punish, and discipline with near impunity, in the absence of (or defying) sovereignty grounded in formal ide-
ologies and structures of rule and legality. They are, in other words, popular sovereignties, shadow sovereignties, informal sovereignties, social
sovereignties, phantom states, or parallel powers that cannot be slotted
into modes of formal governance.[27]

Not everyone accepts this position, however. Another body of research
approaches this question from a different direction and with different
conclusions. Looking at abandoned, forgotten, informal, or marginal
spaces of cities, researchers are pushing back at the suggestion that these
spaces are islands cut off from any of the various capillaries of the state
or its practices of governance and authority. These populations are not
separate from states and their agents in the first place, being, rather,
mutually constituted. Organized forms of violence in places like urban
slums or ghettos that can seem so separate—or that are regularly placed
in urban binaries like slum/city or il/legal—are part and parcel of troubled political and social systems. They are impossible to disaggregate, the
city not being the city without its component parts, including the modes
and spaces of exclusion.[28] These new forms of violence are connected
both morally and in everyday practice with states and their mode of gov-

ernance. To use terms like pluralism, shadow or parallel is to apply a distinction apparent more in normative position vis-à-vis certain theories than in lived experiences.

Much of this work does not draw explicitly on theories of sovereignty or contribute to them, however. Rather, they deal with the circumstances of the urban poor and or use conceptual approaches that question actually existing democracy, reform, the failure of supposedly public institutions, and systemic political inequities. Yet since democracy is a conceptual foundation, treatments of security and violence are often decidedly normative and prescriptive in nature. That a state may have a relationship with other organized sources of violence necessarily departs from a perceived ideal. For orthodox democracy theorists, logic dictates that the engagements between these sources of violence indicates a kind of "dirty togetherness."[29]

In addition, such theory generally sees violence as part of a formative process of transformation—and not a chronic condition of some other configuration of governance or stateness.[30] How to deal with the "deviant" or corrupt behavior of states, bureaucracies, and bureaucrats is a constant challenge for what some have called the "democratization school." Incongruent with democratic theory and decades of supposed transition, many states and the practices of their agents are routinely, superficially, and terminally stamped as "corrupt." Fatal in its own normative suppositions, "corruption" is nearly useless as an organizing and analytical concept in such a context.

This same challenge exists for the literature on police and police reform, learned overwhelmingly from countries with Northern patterns and histories of state formation. For the most part, the existence of sovereign control over violence in police studies goes unquestioned, obscuring the structural bedrock of social relations in police work. Instead, scholars have increasingly presumed that democracy is *the* structural foundation, formulating their prophylaxis for troubled police forces on this premise. Unsurprisingly, reform prescriptions rooted in deeply normative concepts like human rights, which are extracted from discourses inseparable from places like the United States, the United Kingdom, and Europe continue to almost uniquely fail, paralyzed as they are by the chronic presence of violence and perceived resistance on the part of police.[31]

The real or implied position that democracy—democratic reforms, processes of accountability, and independent public oversight—can and will centralize authority into states overlooks a critical fact: sovereigns and empirically existing states are *defined by* violence and subordination. Security and democracy are not two sides of the same coin. They are often (if not typically) contradictory. If we suppose that democracy (and more democratic police) comes to pass when institutions function and citizens demand it, we ignore the exceptionally violent elephant in the room. The idea that some states are engaged in ugly processes of monopolizing violence, whether via official policies or in de facto police practice should come as little surprise, both in the way violent crises tend to explode and are dealt with, as well as in the sheer incongruence of the violent response with democratization doctrine. By some consequence what we witness in many police is a performance of democracy but a reality of violence.

If the debate about sovereignty and statehood hinges generally on notions or conceptual logics of separateness or connectedness in everyday life it largely misses the point. Building on tools from both, I argue a third position: there is togetherness that isn't all that dirty, there is (usually) only one sovereign power, and the state is neither conceptually tired nor empirically irrelevant—even in contexts of violence. The main tenant of sovereignty—the right to kill—can be defined and carried out by multiple and seemingly antagonistic actors at the same time, and in quiet, routine, and everyday ways. The simple existence of multiple violent actors does not necessarily denote active conflict or two "sovereigns," but rather, the existence of a "disposable" population that states allow to be preyed on under an acknowledged definition and common denomination of deservedness. Even if routine violence appears uncontrolled, it is only because the definition of life and death is so expansive. This is partly because the relative size of politically important constituencies is small. In other words, the set of appropriate practices and subjects of violence that some states allow appears limitless. The extensiveness of the definition allows for decentralized forms of regulation over life and death to emerge from that same definition. Today these forms are an inseparable part of a single regulatory system and its larger definition of life and death.

If sovereignty denotes security, sovereignty by consensus denotes qualified security with periods of crisis and unpredictability. Sovereignty by consensus is contingent on the recognition and practice of boundaries for violence, which can occasionally be ruptured—and mended. Violent parties that concur most of the time and disagree in others will have that effect. I advance the idea that sovereignty by consensus is marked by distinct moments—one "normalized" and suggestive of a *relative peace* defined by implicit and explicit consensus about the terms of violence, mutual benefit, and equilibriums in everyday interaction. The second is exceptional—periodic moments of crisis where a shared understanding and practice of appropriate and comparatively nonviolent behavior implodes into feud-like violence. In these exceptional moments when the relative predictability of life disintegrates, police and PCC definitions of acceptable killing are remade. Who may be killed (and who is killed) expands.

São Paulo has witnessed two such urban scale moments in recent years—a bloody 2006 feud between the PCC and police known at the Mother's Day Attacks, and a 2012 battle between the same parties that lasted six months. These exceptional moments stretch far beyond alternative explanations, such as civil unrest or riots.[32] When the formats of killing change, police practices shift and reveal both individual and occupational adaptations to the bifurcation of the right to kill. It is these exceptional moments that reveal the normal state of the right to kill—consensus—and its theoretical relevance.

The consensual practice of sovereignty may not be an entirely new phenomenon. Long ago, empires used apparently informal, extralegal, and separate violent actors to surreptitiously augment their authority. The connection between the British monarchy, pirates, and buccaneers is one example we now know to be true. But there are more contemporary examples too. Italy's shared mafia-state governance has long defied theoretical categorization. Different experiences in state "formation" show the possibility of shared sovereignty as an enduring trait. An explanation for this difference hints at certain contextual, historical, and structural factors that shape how and why states came to define, more unilaterally, the conditions of violence. Not abnormally, this processes occurred with the kind of violence we would today term mass killing, social cleansing, or genocide. If the contemporary period is defined by two largely oppositional structures—democracy and security—might we be witnessing a new cohort of states in the Italian "model," where the democratic rules of the game actually sustain violence and the everyday practices of sovereignty by consensus?

A word on episteme and method: most of the research for this book was carried out in a bulletproof vest or within arm's reach of one. In 2009, I began accompanying Civil Police detectives in the city, first in local stations and later in the Homicide Division—Departamento de Homicídios e Proteção á Pessoa. At first the arrangement was informal, hinging on a lucky recommendation and the authorization of a station chief in a good mood. Later, when I moved to the Homicide Division and followed some police as they migrated to new precincts and units, I was encouraged to cover my own ass—and the asses of those I was spending an increasing amount of time with—so to speak. In a system where paperwork is the place where productivity and real police practice goes to die, I thought this was the end. Within a week, however, and to my own surprise, I managed to obtain formal written authorization from the highest echelon of the organization to accompany the police of the Homicide Division.

The bulletproof vest is a helpful way to interpret much of my research. The Civil Police are a "plain clothes" organization. Despite the omnipresence of violence, the bulletproof vest is a rarity for police themselves, even as they each are given one. As such, the marker of a Civil Police detective can be tough to pin down, outside of a dangling badge or a protruding gun—both of which most police avoid showing to the outside world, lest they become a target. Outside of the station, most Civil Police use their plainclothes status to blend in as seamlessly as they can.

As a researcher I, too, was in plainclothes. In an organization where presence among police—and not being in handcuffs, having dark skin or being too young—is an indicator of identity, I was regularly presumed to be a police officer. Both Military and Civil Police presumed that I was a police officer when I met them in the station, as usually did the people that they were dealing with—victims, supposed criminals, witnesses, youth workers, journalists, and the other people police encounter in routine work. Occasionally, the detectives themselves would announce who I was, which often came in a joking fashion. Other times, my identity was revealed when I told police who I was. Almost always, they were surprised. Sometimes they were mildly annoyed for the feeling of having been "duped"—police are, after all, not supposed to be humbled.

I was alongside detectives as they did a huge array of their plainclothes activities—listening to Brahms while writing police killing reports, as they stood and stared at bloodied and dead colleagues, when they told mothers that their sons had been killed by the police officer(s) that just walked by, while they, more than once, watched videos of transsexuals—purportedly Argentines, they always said—having sex, when they talked openly about leaving early to catch the last bus home because bus lines were closing as a result of PCC bus burnings, and when they chided me for not joining them at the *puteiro*—the "whorehouse"—to loosen up.

My off and on use of a bulletproof vest when out of the station is some indication of where I fit in alongside police. I was both an insider and an outsider. The fact that I was never officially given a vest, nor implored to wear one in any official way is—I think—significant. Perhaps those who stamped my authorization papers expected me to stay in the relatively safe confines of the station. Maybe they hoped I would dig deep to talk about how troubled the world of police is. Staying in the station was an impossibility, both for my own curiosity and for the necessity of putting the various pieces of this story together.

In a larger sense, the bulletproof vest is a safety device and an indicator of police identity. To wear it is to identify oneself outwardly as a police officer and to display one of two very different things—weakness or exceptional militarization. The details and imagery of either are obvious, for their complement of accessories, or lack thereof. In my case the vest I used was someone else's. He refused to wear it himself—as most do—and offered it to me to wear not so much as a means of protection but as a way to legitimize the police's willingness to have me along.

Most police that I spent time with let me in. Though, like anywhere, there were variations. Some shared a great deal about their personal circumstances, their frustrations with the system, and their reasons for becoming police. I am grateful to these people, all men, for their earnestness from close to the beginning. Many others warmed up, to a point that I heard about the alcoholism and violence of their fathers that made hitting people—"criminals"—feel good. Police were very curious about me—the novel foreigner with no substantive accent in Portuguese. "Must be a spy," was a statement I heard at least twice (though it was never quite clear who I would spy for). The most common questions were about what police were like in North America. *In Canada, do police get overtime? What about those red uniforms and the horses? I heard it is true that in Texas, anyone who kills a police officer is given the death penalty. That's true, right? I wish it was like that here. . . .* Once, a police officer told a prisoner that I was Canadian, and that I was here to take the *bandidos*—like him—back to feed them to the polar bears. Hearing this filled me with one of the most complex mixes of emotions I've ever encountered.

As I discuss later, my foreign, white, and male status was also a bulletproof vest of sorts. This was true both for me and for detectives. One evening a detective needed some insurance to get a statement from an alleged PCC member against some particularly violent police with whom there was an obvious power asymmetry. He offered to the prisoner to put my name and ID number in the report as a witness as potential safeguard against retribution on the part of the police in question. These police had threatened to kill the man's family if he told a different story than what they said he needed to. I agreed, not really knowing what the alternative would be, and more than a bit unsure that this insurance was all that secure against default—either for the PCC member, for me, or even for the police detective.

Most of the time, though, the real issue was my own curiosity and uncertainty about where I fit among those who rarely wore bulletproof vests. For awhile when I thought I had to use the vest I didn't, and my clumsiness with it was a clear signal. I once got heartily laughed at when we visited a police officer's wife's restaurant, and I stepped out of the car with the vest on. I was told, after everyone stopped laughing, to never wear it in or around the station or in places that police frequent, lest I raise undo questions about the weird guy wearing a vest. If Erving Goffman was to look at this world, he might say that the *backstage* of these police was made accessible by looking as innocuous and invisible as possible within their group—something made more possible because of my gender and appearance.

This research necessarily meant setting aside certain assumptions and looking for the sense in practices that seem utterly senseless to many. In *Flammable*, Auyero and Swistun (2009) make a particularly poignant statement to this end: we rarely see ethnographic texts—larger, social science texts—in which people hesitate, make mistakes, or are plagued by contradictions; subjects who are angry and happy, scared and courageous, violent and violated, subjects who know and don't know. We must better consider why "powerful" subjects don't want anything to do with bulletproof vests because wearing one screams their weaknesses to the world, even if those weaknesses are acute enough to justify the protection a vest offers. In short, ethnographic subjects often come together too neatly, belying the moral complexity of deeply nuanced and contradictory social environments. And if there ever were a group of multifarious (but not necessarily nefarious) characters, it is these police detectives who are so deeply mired in the victim-perpetrator "complex" at the very center of state efforts that supposedly define mortality—and morality in Latin America's largest city.

I hope to relate the ways that police are profoundly imperfect not because I believe they merit our sympathy or our scorn, but because they merit some of both and a lot of something else in the middle that needs some sense-making. Reader beware: there will be loose ends. Even the most exemplary of police and the nicest of people do and say things that are harsh, shocking, and undoubtedly worthy of institutional scrutiny and oversight. But if that oversight departs from a distant moral location, it will do little good. It may do much more harm. These police are ensnared in a deeply unenviable position where they are distrusted by most, hated by many, and wished dead by a great deal more. The things that they say and do cannot be separated from their uniquely paradoxical social position as people entrusted to keep society safe, even as they themselves struggle to defend themselves and their families.

One important note about my own position within this unenviable world: as a deeply trusted colleague once put it simply to me, individuals are not the point of this research. This research seeks to look beyond the violence manifested by one person or another to find the deeper forms of legitimation and the justifications of its "necessity." Though the final choice to use violence or not is still often in the hands of individual police, the chance that a police officer would never use violence are very limited given his (and much less often, her) social context. A system in which a copious amount of violent death occurs on a daily basis, as wielded both by those in public positions and by an organized crime group that has come to represent a more or less defined public, demands an analysis that is attentive to the normative boundaries of such a context. Even where police are thoroughly resistant to violence and support a progressive politics, they cannot escape instances where violence may walk right in to their homes, leaving them virtually forced to shoot and/or kill, or if not, be killed. I will provide examples.

In this book, then, I combine this backstage world of police—the everyday, obscured, and rationalized practices of investigation and survival—with two other complementary ways of knowing. In 2007 and again briefly in 2011, I carried out research in a PCC-controlled community on the east side of São Paulo. Drawing on interviews with residents, community workers, and a PCC member, I bring a more complete understanding of the processes of PCC governance, perceived changes in the lives of residents vis-à-vis violence, and how the PCC regime came about outside of the prison system and on the fringes of this city.[33]

More substantively, I augment this fieldwork in a PCC community with an analysis of a load of documents given to me by an agent in the São Paulo public security system, seized from an arrested PCC member. These documents, I was told, were perhaps safer with me than in the hands of other police—military or civil—likely to use the names, locations, and amounts of drugs and money to either kill or extort. Among the documents were Excel spreadsheets itemizing millions of dollars in weekly sales of cocaine, crack cocaine, and marijuana by area code, as well as photocopies of membership roles including name, nickname, member number (the same as the official prisoner ID), place of residence, last three prisons stops, names of "Godfathers," time and place of "baptism" into the organization, lists of drug distribution and sales by member name and/or nickname, quantity and amount of money owed by individuals, and among other things, inventories of cars and guns. Also included was a document describing a "gun library" of sorts.[34]

These sources of data—two complementary ethnographic perspectives, combined with a related and situated analysis of PCC documents—are three substantial pieces in a larger puzzle about life in urban São Paulo. It is through this amalgam of data that I see the city. They represent concurrent perspectives on everyday life, the efforts to control violence and make life more secure, and the evolving nature of survival—and right and wrong—that shape the way people get by in particularly urban circumstances.

The rest of the book unfolds as follows. Part One, "Surviving," takes the reader through the formats and strategies of survival in São Paulo. In chapter 1, I take the reader on a narrative tour of the city of São Paulo from the perspective of police and chronicle its forms and patterns of violence as they have shifted and continue to shift. Chapter 2 is an overview of the two main sources of violence—the police and the PCC—at the heart of the regulation of life and death in this city. The second part of the book, "Killing," details the everyday configurations, sources, and shared notions of violent death at work. I start with the investigation of "normal" homicides by police detectives in chapter 3 and reflect on what they reveal about PCC governance in urban space. The subject of chapter 4 is the practice and regulation of routine police killings of citizens, known as resistências, by homicide detectives and the reason why detectives often refrain from holding violent police to account. In the following chapter, I examine the ways that the legitimate subject of routine homicides and resistências conforms to similar ideas of deservedness of death. I outline how both practices intermingle as part of a larger moral understanding of who can live and who can die. Chapter 6 is about how that consensual notion of life and death breaks apart, leading to violence. I focus on some of the ways that this happens, the consequences, and how detectives struggle to assert their state-sanctioned regulatory position. Part Three is a departure to ways of thinking and dealing with this violence. The second to last chapter reflects on my effort to add to the public discussion about the crisis at the time, which I did via an Opinion Editorial in the *New York Times*, and some of the responses and repercussions of that decision. Chapter 8 serves to look forward. I ask what the current security-democracy loggerhead means for a certain cohort of states in the world today, and for their police as poorly understood institutions. I suggest that there is good reason to think about a category of states as being defined by a consensual sovereignty. This is not a novel or exceptional mode of governance that will necessarily fade away.

Surviving São Paulo

It's a clear and bright Saturday morning in São Paulo. I ride with the windows down in the back seat of a black-and-white Chevy Blazer from the Civil Police's Homicide Division. In front of me are two plainclothes officers—Brazil's version of the police detective. Unencumbered by work-day traffic, we drive leisurely southbound through the city's expansive sprawl. We are headed to one of the city's southernmost urban districts, a hilly working-class place called Jardim Ângela. As we approach our destination, where I had been once many years prior, I am struck again by how Ângela occupies a distinct place in São Paulo's urban landscape— the urban periphery. Parts of the district are rural and vegetated, dotted with horses, chickens, and fruit trees. Red brick and concrete houses, interspersed with finished and brightly painted homes, flow southward from the city toward the final edge of constructed space. At that edge, sandwiched between empty fields, a fetid urban reservoir that nonetheless nourishes the city, and the expanding brick and mortar of the constructed city, are the new homes. But these homes are in fact nothing new. They are made almost entirely of old bits and pieces: chunks of wood, rusty sheets of aluminum, and jagged bits of broken asbestos roofing tile fastened together by planks of wood—painstaking examples of human agency in a city dramatically and spatially segregated between have and have not.

It is a quiet morning in the city. No one was killed overnight, or if they were, they haven't yet been found. So we've come to have a look

FIGURE 1. Ângela (photo by author).

around. Ângela is where one of these two police, a man I'll call Beto, was raised. It was much different then, when Beto himself grew up and lived in one of these "new" homes. His grandparents who raised him were economic migrants from the northeast region of the country, like hundreds of thousands of others in this and other Brazilian cities through the latter half of the twentieth century. Arriving in Ângela (figure 1) in the late 1970s, Beto's grandfather bought a lot from someone, built a house, and slowly, brick by brick, improved it into a two-story home with suites to rent. The home was a perfectly unexceptional example of the self-built auto-construction that defines urbanization in this city and many other cities in the Global South.[1] Beto could recall it clearly: "I remember as a little boy, a truck showing up with the leftovers from jobs he had worked. They'd take the leftover bricks, wood planks, and bags of cement off the truck and put them in the yard. Then, on his days off, my grandpa would put things together."

Beto went to public school with all the kids in the neighborhood, most of whom likewise came from regional migrant families putting their roots down in this rapidly urbanizing city. After school and on weekends they passed their time playing *futebol* when they could find a reasonably flat and dry campo in this area of steep streets and hillsides. Being a kid wasn't crazy then, Beto explained. The area's residents were full of hope. They had made major sacrifices to come and find a new start in the city, leaving drought and despair behind. While building their homes with their own hands, they were excited about the new world emergent from the demise of Brazil's twenty-year dictatorship. A fresh democracy and a new, decidedly social-justice-oriented federal Constitution in 1988 promised a novel era of inclusion, respect, and prosperity for all. It was about time.

A handful of years later this hopefulness was in shambles. By the early 1990s many of Beto's fellow soccer players and school friends had turned to a new and alluring source of money and status—the drug trade. Ângela erupted into violence. Rival gangs emerged, massacring each other over street corner turf and sending the homicide rate spiraling. Statistics from the Secretariat of Public Security showed that by 1996, 166 per 100,000 residents died in homicides in Ângela. This nearly unbelievable rate of violent death far superseded that of the United States, for example, which was only then emerging from its own crack cocaine epidemic. Ângela's homicide rate was nineteen times higher than the average urban homicide rate of the United States (8.8).[2] Ângela's deadliness, which wasn't different from many other parts of the city, led swiftly to recognition from far and wide—UNESCO tattooed it ignominiously as the "most violent neighborhood on earth."[3]

But it wasn't just drug gangs that fueled the violence. Extermination groups known as *justiceiros*, or *Pés-de-Pato*, composed largely of off-duty or former police, many of whom lived in the area, increasingly took up the moral mantle of removing the "scourge" of marauding drug traffickers by "cleaning" the streets.[4] They killed indiscriminately in their efforts to get rid of criminals, catching and slaying no limit of people—but mostly young men—in the process. Beto himself narrowly escaped on a couple of occasions. He reminded me many times that he would hear the bullets whizzing by his head while sprinting away. As the violence peaked in the late 1990s, many of his former schoolmates lay dead, were arrested, or had just plain disappeared in the chaos and confusion. It didn't much matter who pulled the trigger, whether police, rival gang members, or an extermination group, Beto reflected to me. It was all a blur. There had been shootouts on his street and violence at every corner. Everyone was desensitized. Bodies lay in the streets for days at a time, bloated and waiting for police and the *carro de cadaver* to finally show up. Even to those in the midst of it, the violence seemed unintelligible.

But that was then. Beto no longer lives there. He can't. Not since the dynamic of violence changed so dramatically. Today, there is only one recognized source of order here, an organized crime group known as the Primeiro Comando da Capital, known colloquially as the PCC, 1533, "the party," or just "the family." By 2003, the PCC had emerged from the São Paulo state prison system to establish a "peace among criminals" (*paz entre os ladrões*) and an "ethic of crime" across the urban periphery of São Paulo, uniting those who had been behind much of the violence under one moral banner. Today, in certain parts of the city, homicide is regulated and carried out by the organization—emulating the statelike function of sword and shield. As a public prosecutor once told me, everyone knows that if anyone—a resident, a police officer, or even a PCC member—kills someone without proper justification or PCC authorization, "é bigode no asfalto," it's "moustache to the asphalt" for them.

Paradoxically this centralized control over the streets of Ângela has made it safer for most residents. Under this new system homicides happen only with the explicit authorization of those in charge. They occur much less often as a result. According to the Secretariat for Public Security's own statistics, the numbers of homicides dropped dizzyingly over a few short years.[5] From an apex around the year 2000 the rate fell by 80 percent in some places. Across greater São Paulo—an area of 19.7 million residents spread over 7,951 square kilometers—but particularly in the urban periphery, places like Brasilândia, Sapopemba, Capão Redondo, and Paraisópolis, the story for local residents was much same. The violence that had consumed daily life was receding and residents were feeling more secure. This was well reflected in the fact that upwards of 6000 less people were dying violently each year.

We decide to go for lunch. Beto takes us to one of his old favorites, a bar-cum-country music nightclub with a killer *feijoada* bean stew. We sit down. Beto and Felipe, the other detective with us, turn their chairs to face the doorway. We get a big bottle of Coke to share. Beto and Felipe talk about what is going down these days. Things are in upheaval.

The PCC has been actively seeking out and assassinating police officers, killing them as they leave their houses, shop at the mall, work their second (or third) job, or as they leave for work in the early daylight hours. The count for this year so far is around 85 police dead—an increase of about 115 percent over all of last year. Police these days are visibly and emotionally nervous. For good reason: by the end of the year at least 106 police in São Paulo would be killed.

The reality of police mortality had been laid bare weeks earlier during a particularly troublesome eruption of police assassinations. In the span of three days, eight off-duty police officers were killed. A number of others were wounded or narrowly escaped around the same time, showing up in the Homicide Division not as bodies but as rumor, tale and innuendo—almost more emotionally moving. These events destabilized police even more than usual, exposing unambiguously the insecurity of being a police officer in this city.

When I had arrived at the station on the first night, I ran into Peanut, a detective, still hanging around from the day shift. We sat down to watch some TV in the change room. Other police filed in as they were coming on shift. Peanut started talking: "Something strange is happening," he said. "They're saying that 70 percent of all the police killed last year have been killed just this month. There were two just yesterday." The other police had heard similar things. "What are your friends in the penitentiaries saying?" asked one officer. Peanut shrugged it off, distracted by a commercial on TV.

Later I Googled it on one of the computers in the station: since an incident the Month prior in which a SWAT-styled agency of the patrolling Military Police known as the Rondas Ostensivas Tobias de Aguiar (ROTA) had killed six PCC members in one raid, the PCC had been crying bloody murder. This particularly questionable incident had resulted in four police from that unit being arrested by homicide detectives, and the PCC had stepped up its retaliatory attacks, singling out off-duty cops in particular, for what I would later learn they saw as unjust killings. There had been thirty-three killings of police in just the last six months. One of these had happened just recently on the north side of the city. A cop there was shot thirty-six times, one detective told me.

In the media it was all being disavowed—"they are just corrupt cops," many were intoning. Even the secretary of public security was said to have told the media it was something of a cleansing—a purging of police who were obviously engaged in something fishy and illegal. Layered within that idea the government left little room for interpretation other than that it was okay, perhaps even deserved, that some police were being knocked off. From within the station, the idea of a purging of rotten apples didn't ring true. The two police who had been killed a couple of nights earlier seemed anything but crooked. One had been killed while teaching a class. Three guys came in and shot him up, walking past everyone else on the way in and the way out. The other had been working off-duty doing private security, one of the tens of thousands of police officers who have become accustomed to taking a second job. The detectives in the station understood those fallen police as regular cops just working their moonlight *bico*—as almost all do—in order to get by. And yet from those above—the public face of public security— the tone was obvious, if dismissive: this wave of violence, like many of the killings off-duty police that happen in normal times, was purifying.

Later that night, things were shaken up even more. A message came in over the intranet that there had been a police shooting of a citizen, known as a "resisting arrest followed by death" (*resistência seguida de morte*) in a district on the East Side. A police officer was also dead in the exchange. Yet the preliminary details were sketchy and confusing, giving little clarity about how to classify the incident and the jurisdiction. No one was quite sure how it happened and why both the shooter and the police officer were dead. Was it a homicide? Or did the police officer react to his assailant, a fact that would have made it a resistência?

Over the next two hours the homicide detectives went back and forth over whether the incident was a double homicide or a single resistência. If the officer had been able to respond, by drawing his gun and shooting— but not necessarily killing or even hitting—his attacker, it would be classified as a resistência. But if the police officer had not been able to shoot back, either because he was too surprised to get his gun out or because he wasn't wearing a gun—which would be unlikely—then it would have been a double homicide. To make matters more complex, if the homicide detectives chose to call the incident a homicide, then it would no longer be their jurisdiction. Convoluted rules state that when a homicide suspect is known, the investigation and paperwork falls to the local police precinct to carry out and not to the homicide division.

At first the homicide detectives decided in favor of registering the case as a resistência. The thinking was that the dead assailant had been killed by the police officer, who had reacted to being assaulted by drawing his gun and shooting. Yet within a couple of hours, they changed their mind, deciding that is was indeed a homicide. The reason was this: security footage revealed that the dead police officer had not even pulled out his gun.

He had been checking out his purchases at a pet food store and was too surprised to even have time to reach for anything in self-defense.

This meant that since it was a homicide where the suspect was known, the case should have become the responsibility of the local police precinct—with their absence of specialized homicide detectives and technical resources—to carry out the investigation. But in a startling turn, another key detail came to the fore. Three men had actually been there to kill the police officer. According to security footage and witnesses, one of them had said, "That's him there! Shoot! Shoot! In the head!"

This new revelation left a bizarre fissure in the case. Who had killed the attacker, if it wasn't the dead police officer? And, as it was, it turned out that it was the man who said "Atira!" (Shoot!) that was dead. Not only that, he had been shot from behind. "He was killed by a ghost," a detective told me days later. "No one knows how it happened. It probably was an off-duty police officer working security and [the other police] were protecting him." Protecting him from the homicide detectives. This mysterious third party was indeed a ghost. He or she wasn't visible on camera and didn't even appear in the crime report that was written over the next few hours. As far as the official word and documents went, the person that actually killed the attacker did not exist. There was a phantom shooter.

In the end, the homicide detectives kept the case for their own investigation even though it was technically out of their jurisdiction. This was all especially contorted since the reason for keeping the case, which was that they wanted to keep the identity of the person who shot the assailant quiet, would have made it their jurisdiction anyway.

Not that this seemed to matter all that much. The detectives were more concerned with what was happening these days. One policeman spoke up, "A friend of mine said that a few weeks ago the PCC gave a green light to kill off-duty police." Another responded, "The last few days there have been thousands of calls, you know, from prison to prison."

As one of the homicide teams left to investigate the resistência-cum-homicide scene, the other team was returning to the precinct. It was quiet now, so they had a chance to nap. But at around 2:30 a.m., another call came in. A police station had been attacked in a notorious neighborhood on the south side of the city. One police officer was shot, but saved by his vest. A vehicle pursuit had followed and the police had shot and killed one of the suspects. When the homicide detectives in the station heard the details the mood got tense, and the attention shifted, conjuring memories. Someone mentioned the PCC attacks in May 2006, in which fifty-two police, prison agents, and city law enforcement were killed in three days. The team would have to go to exactly the kind of neighborhood in the city where that violence was most prevalent—and not knowing (but fearing) that another 2006 was crashing down upon them.

It took them a long time to get ready. They kept finding guns. One after the other. Each officer now had multiple guns—some always carried two—and were loading all of them diligently. They loaded their bullets into all manner of handguns, revolvers, and submachine guns. One officer even pulled out an old double-barrel shotgun with a hardwood stock.

I watched as one police detective loaded ammunition clips for his .40 caliber handgun. He had different kinds of bullets, some hollow points, others not, some that splintered differently. To describe them is to describe the intentional boring of live flesh and bone. As he finished he kissed the chamber of one of the guns. When he noticed that I had been watching he smiled shyly. Others were less methodical. One police detective who never wore a bulletproof vest was hassled by his peers to put his on. When he did, it was still in the plastic bag, new. When he lifted it over his head, the hefty Kevlar insert fell clean out of the vest, slapping to the floor. Everyone jeered. He laughed sheepishly. Another police officer stepped in to help out. As he bent over to help pick up the insert, one of his loaded guns fell out of a front jacket pocket onto the floor, clanking heavily. Everyone jeered again, but this time much more nervously, knowing they just escaped a random bullet.

Eventually the team left the station. As they were leaving a group of Military Police came in. Most were in uniform. One wasn't. He was the officer that had been shot during the attack on the police station on the South Side. Among them the talk was all about the PCC. One of them commented, "They're saying that, from here on out, when there are confrontations, we are to kill." Another chimed in, "Because of internal affairs, they say it is better to register things not as *resistências*. It is better [to classify it] as a robbery followed by death [*latrocínio*], that kind of thing." It was as though there was no recognition or little importance given to the fact that they were sitting amongst the very police detectives responsible for investigating police shootings of citizens.

These police weren't just concerned about how to deal with the PCC, however. There was a lot of the talk about the higher-ups, comfortable in their offices and with their armed escorts, moving seamlessly and securely from air-conditioned office to chauffeured car or helicopter and gated home. It was these leaders who had been making public statements that there was no relation between these assassinations of police and the PCC, implying—if not stating outright—that police were ending up that way for good reason. The police in the station knew that the death of a small-time police officer in some distant and poor district of the urban periphery wasn't a big deal for a politician. "They prefer that police die while off duty," said one. "It is easier to hide. Less shocking for the public." Savvy to politics and troublesome security inequities, these police were speaking not just about politicians passing the buck, but also about the importance of urban space and invisibility in questions of urban (and their own) security.

But the police also recognized the pattern of police killings for what it was—a savvy strategy on the part of the PCC that nodded to those very same politics of space and inequality. Eliminating off-duty police was a way to maintain pressure and influence on the bottom rungs of the police—the low hanging and exposed fruit of the public security system. By killing off-duty police in places like Jardim Ângela, the PCC could avoid drawing the attention of the public in the wealthier parts of the city that politicians seemed to care about—the kind of public that, when made to feel insecure, would have demanded a massive police crackdown. The PCC knew this. By staying in the shadows they could force these coercible police back into line, as implicit subjects of the PCC's will, without adversely disrupting their own interests.

Back in Ângela, Beto, Felipe, and I eat our bean stew. "I wouldn't come here at night," says Beto. He feels insecure, but this was still the neighborhood where he grew up and where his family home is. He isn't worried that he doesn't personally know the drug dealers running things like he did so many years ago. Now it was much worse. Just the simple fact that he had grown up there, that everyone knows him and what he does for a living is enough to get him killed. It would just take one person to spread the word to the wrong people that he was hanging out there again, he said. This was why, well before the current crisis, he had to leave the community and work three moonlighting jobs in order to move to a middle-class part of the city. There was just no other way to make sure he and his family could be safe.

We finished our feijoada, paid Beto's friend, and said good-bye. Back in the Blazer, we head north toward Civil Police headquarters downtown. I watched the red brick and asbestos of Ângela slowly fade back to the concrete and wide avenues of the city.

CHAPTER 2

Regulations of Killing

São Paulo is a city in which killing, and the regulation of killing, occurs via parallel and normative logics of violence. These two kinds of killing—homicide and resisting arrest follow by death—are undergirded by a set of urban, spatial, and political conditions under which violent death has become prolific and accepted. On the one hand, the PCC's spatialized regulation over violence and killing is unmistakable. Homicides carry certain "hallmarks" that are presumed, assumed, or implicitly understood to be an outcome of the regulatory structure of the PCC. What we might consider a "normal" homicide in São Paulo is very deeply the product of an authority with its own governance over the conditions of life and death. Inscribed in the work of detectives is an understanding that the PCC is routinely behind the "normal" homicide.

On the other, police kill citizens routinely and in predictable ways. Homicide detectives police the police that kill citizens—in theory at least—arbitrating these killings and making sense of them in the process. According to bureaucratic practice, a police killing is immediately categorized as "resisting arrest followed by death," more colloquially known as "resistências."[1] Under this rubric there is a presumption of guilt for the person shot, and a presumption of innocence for the officer who shot them. Homicide detectives are tasked with investigating these killings and arbitrating whether these presumptions are "appropriate" (figure 2). When not appropriate, homicide detectives must overturn these categories—a resistência becomes a homicide and the offending

FIGURE 2. Investigating a crime scene (photo by author).

police are arrested. Homicide detectives navigate moral and situated notions of deservedness of killing by drawing on signals, queues, and social imaginaries such as the worker (*trabalhador*) and the *bandido*—a differentiated social type, understood as inextricably and holistically criminal, and therefore the legitimate subject of deadly police action.

These two logics collide in the everyday work of homicide detectives. On first glance, they are antagonistic, indicative of a de facto war between the state and organized crime. Empirically, though, they are similar, carrying overlapping notions and a confluence of perceptions of deservedness of death, converging under the same uncontested moral paradigm of legitimate life and death. These logics and their practices of killing nest in an implicit consensus about killing, and are assembled in everyday forms of equilibria between police and the PCC that do not contest the moral paradigm. This is most apparent in who the routine and unexceptional killable subject is: a man, often dark skinned, living and killed in the urban periphery, of a low socioeconomic background, understood to be associated with violence. This subject may be either a perceived criminal or an off-duty police officer, two categories that are often fungible. After death, their identities become mixed. To the outside observer the relative stability of this paradigm of violence mimics a regulatory system in which police are the only body that may kill and arbitrate killing.

Consensus is sustained by the everyday practices of police and the PCC, evident in the coorientation and conversation of gestures that reveal points of agreement and stabilize this equilibrium.[2] In other words, agreement about boundaries and practices is mutually recognized and agreed on, even in the absence of formal communication or concord. But in everyday terms, if some incidents of killing are to be viewed as beyond a boundary recognized by both sides, the force and integrity of that limit shouldn't be analyzed in terms of joint unilateral recognition of it by both sides—not as something that the PCC and police recognize unilaterally and simultaneously in the relative absence of each other—but as something that both "mutually recognize." In other words, it isn't just that the police recognize it and the PCC recognize it, but that police recognize that the PCC recognize it, the PCC recognizes that police recognize it, the police recognize that the PCC recognizes that they recognize it, and so on. It is a shared expectation more or less stable in its existence as a result.[3]

Where it seems like the state has centralized violence, killing and security is actually being regulated in a mutually constituted paradigm— an implicit agreement on a general premise (or set of general premises)— about who can die, where, and under what conditions. Who can die is mutually constructed. But this is a false floor of security. The consensus itself occasionally implodes, rupturing into explosions of violence between these two logics. This helps to explain the oscillations of violence and the chronic struggle for security experienced in cities like São Paulo.

An understanding of police lethality and the place of homicide detectives in its investigation demands some contextual explanation. Police in Brazil could hardly pose a starker contrast to the police that we know so well in the Global North.[4] This is true of both police practice and organizational configurations. In Brazil, state governors control police. This is true even when residents of a city make up the vast majority of a state's population, as in São Paulo or Rio de Janeiro, but where wealthy rural landowners still maintain a disproportionate influence on urban politics. Typically subordinated to a governor-appointed public security secretary, policing functions are split into three different organizations with three distinct but mutually dependent functions (figure 3). The Military Police are a hierarchical and military-trained reserve of the Federal Military responsible for patrolling, receiving emergency calls through the 190 hotline, and responding to those calls. They arrest individuals either in a response to a call, while on patrol, or while checking a person's

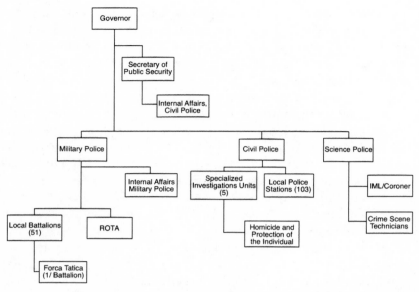

FIGURE 3. Public security system in the city of São Paulo (created by Bill Nelson of Bill Nelson Maps).

identity documents during stop and frisks known as *abordagens*. According to the word of the law, they do not investigate crime. In practice, they often do secretly, such as by surreptitiously tapping phones. Within the Military Police, positions are hierarchical and filled both by advancement and public entry exams. It is not a given that someone who starts at the bottom position—the *soldado*—will reach the next rank, a *cabo*, or the one above it, a *sargento*, over a thirty-year career. In other words, the notion of "entry-level" is meaningless. Lateral entry defines the hierarchy and structure of subordination—one can be a brand new Military Police officer twenty-two years old commanding a battalion of hundreds simply because he or she has a university degree and passed an officer-level exam. It is not uncommon for twenty-five- to thirty-year veterans to be supervised by someone born after they first joined the police. The Military Police are those that any visitor to a Brazilian city will see standing on street corners, walking the beat, or driving around in a squad car. In São Paulo State, home to 41 million people, there are more than ninety-eight thousand Military Police, at least two-thirds of whom are stationed in the metropolitan area.

The Civil Police, by contrast, are a plainclothes investigative police that are much less visible and numerous, with roughly thirty-four thousand members across the state. They are detectives, being responsible for staffing each of the 102 local neighborhood precincts in the city where residents must go to file a police report in person for most crimes.[5] They are then tasked with investigating these reports. These police are not legally excluded from patrolling and making unexpected arrests, though they usually refrain from doing so while on the job. Unlike the Military Police, the Civil Police are divided into different occupations resembling a fordist division of labor. There are *investigadores* (investigators), *papiloscopistas* (fingerprinters), *escrivães* (scribes/report writers), *carceireiros* (prison agents), agents (*agente policial*), *fotógrafos* (crime scene photographers), and telephone attendants (*agente telefónico*). For all of these positions—careers, really—candidates must apply and enter via competitive public service exams. Being successful, they are slotted into task-oriented positions defined by more or less singular functions: to fingerprint, write reports, manage prisoners, take crime scene pictures, investigate leads, or answer the telephone.

Bringing each of these occupations together is a central figure known as the *delegado*—the police chief. The delegado presides over a team of these detectives for a given investigation and is responsible for making the final determination about a given case. He or she—for there are many women delegados—must have a university law degree and is the principal disciple of the law. He or she is the gatekeeper responsible for deciding when and how to act. They are not the only voice or person informing how decisions are made, though it is ultimately their signature that attests to a given decision.

The Science Police (*Polícia Técnico-Científica*) are the third police organization. Within the Science Police there are number of occupations, ranging from medical examiners to crime scene investigators known as *peritos*. It is the peritos that are responsible for technical details of a crime scene, including collecting shell casings, taking fingerprints off of surfaces, taking gunshot residue swabs, seizing and testing drugs, blood, and other fluids. They do these tests at the request of the delegado on a case by case basis. Peritos, and those whom they work with in their labs, also carry out everything from autopsy to ballistics reports for all kinds of crimes such as rapes to home invasions. Across their divisions and labs, these police number in the hundreds and are dramatically underfunded. According to one perito, there are just twenty teams of peritos working the homicide and resistência beat for roughly four thousand cases a year.

With the exception of the delegado and others who also must have a law degree, the police from each of these three organizations make very modest salaries. They also have modest educations, and they come from modest communities. Many struggled mightily to pass exams, finding ways such as by getting up in the wee hours of the night to watch and study via a tutoring program on television. Minimum standards require a middle school education. A healthy number had parents that were police before them. Others grew up at the *fim do barrio*—that space at the end of the urban sprawl defined not just by precarious housing, poverty, and human resilience but also by the emergencies that a dearth of public infrastructure fosters—flash floods, mudslides, waterborne disease, and violence. Ângela is one place among many like this where police come from; a spatial confluence of poverty, state disinvestment, and insecurity—the perfect source of readily expendable and cheap labor. The technocratic design and parameters of stratified police public service exams, which purportedly resist corruption and objectify a meritocracy, all but ensure that many police come from these places.

The formal configuration of the public security system seems a little less than straightforward for many outsiders. More opaque is the functioning of this system, and the practices of the police within it that seemingly defy explanation, especially when it comes to violence. Some of the questions that guided my initial research forays were blunt paradoxes: How can police promote human rights, such as the right to life, if they have little control of over the security of their own life? What is the rule of law when there are, in fact, concurrent rules of law? What is the nature of police accountability to the public when police themselves are often accountable to violent groups like organized crime? What does it mean to be "corrupt" in a system where police must (ab) use their power to make their own lives, and the lives of their immediate families, safer?

The empirics of police practice in the city of São Paulo are often jarring: police—primarily Military Police—kill citizens daily, if not multiple times a day (1.6 on average in 2012); killing is often celebrated socially and within police hierarchies; the Homicide Division is at the bottom of the police's organizational esteem; the most elite and socially celebrated units kill—or are perceived to kill—the most. In other words, the structure and incentives of police here do not aim to limit the number of people being killed—they incite it directly.

The primacy given to killing is subsumed in one kind of police practice, categorically known as "resisting arrest followed by death" (resistência seguida de morte). "Resistências," as I will call them, are police killings of citizens, occurring in the line of duty or off, that are a routine practice of policing today in São Paulo. The regularity of these killings is derived, very liberally, from article 329 of the Brazilian Penal Code that makes it illegal to resist the application of the law. This article makes doing so a "crime against the public administration": "Resistência. . . . Opposing the legal act, with violence or threat, of a functionary competent to execute it or upon one assisting in that execution. Punishment: 2 months to 2 years detention" (Código Penal 1940).

This "law on the books" has come to be practiced not as a crime to be charged against an arrested offender, but as a legal precedent to kill those with certain characteristics who minimally resist the work of police. In an environment where insecurity is the norm and self-defense for police is not a state of exception but a permanent state of being, it is normal for police to shoot and kill. More important, though, resistências have also come to be used in cases where the suspects are believed to have committed a crime recently, regardless of whether they have— yet—resisted arrest. Though the law on the books suggests a punishment of two months to two years in prison, most resistências today conclude with a dead body, if not two.[6]

Resistência is much more than a legal trope delineating the illegality of not bowing down before the law. It is both a type of crime and state of existence, a noun and a verb, and thus a *justification* to kill those who are understood as permanently threatening. In São Paulo these killings are not counted as homicides, nor are they calculated in homicide rates. And yet when they are counted as a statistic of their own, the rate of occurrence per 100,000 is typically higher than the murder rate of countries like the United States.[7]

Nor are those killed in resistências victims. They are in official legal title, a "suspect"—*o averiguado*. The reasoning is circular: criminal in their "decision" to resist arrest, they are presumed guilty in their own death, holding the burden of proving their own innocence—despite the totalized and definitive sentence suffered. The averiguado is thus guilty for his own death, until, or rather, if, proven innocent by homicide detectives. The consequence is indicative of the reason. The subject of the resistência—and thus the official victim—is the police officer who shot and killed a citizen. Threatened or insubordinated in an attempt to apply the law, the police officer is seen as legitimate in responding with force, almost irrespective of the degree of that force. Killing someone for resisting arrest is, thus, a completely legal action in practice. It eliminates an individual, defined and judged criminal by his actions, by answering the question of guilt by its own existence.

Until just recently, the practice of resistências contained an even deeper rotten paradox. After shooting a suspect, police would typically rush (*soccorrer*) the wounded to the hospital in a supposed effort for medical treatment to sustain life. In the process, they could trample all through the crime scene, taking all manner of liberties to purposely or unpurposely alter the evidence—including moving a dead body on the premise that the person was still alive when they did it. This practice obscured a great deal. Among the homicide detectives it was accepted, if usually unspoken, that during the "rush" to the hospital, police might take a slower route in order to make sure that if the bandido wasn't already dead, and had any chance of dying, that they would be by the time they arrived in the emergency room. There are also many instances of individuals being placed in a car with no question of their health but ending up dead on arrival at the hospital. The reason is assumed. In this paradox between the expectation to kill and the rush to secure life, death almost always wins. According to Human Rights Watch, in 2012 police rushed 379 people to the hospital after shooting them. Of those, 360 died.

Clearly, resistências give much more than the benefit of the doubt to police officers. They give police a great deal of discretion in the use of force. As such, many police are involved in multiple resistências over the course of their career—one police officer casually admitted to having been in twelve resistências, some of which included multiple "suspects." There are two police agencies known and celebrated for practicing resistências as a point of organizational and operational identity. The Rondas Ostensivas Tobias de Aguiar (Tobias de Aguiar Patrolling Squad, ROTA), and the Força Tática—the "Tactical Force." Both of these agencies are patrolling police of the State of São Paulo's Military Police who respond to crimes in progress. Though under the control of the state governor, ROTA and the Força Tática are both profoundly urban entities. ROTA's jurisdiction is historically the city of São Paulo, while a unit of the Força Tática exists in each urban battalion, bounded by that same spatial jurisdiction. The ROTA, though, has a long and detailed history that has included military campaigns as well as everyday policing. The degree of their violence or the possibility of it is never in question, and their name has become synonymous with hard-line policing policies. They are routinely involved in massacres, including the killing of 112 at Carandiru Prison complex in 1991—the widely recognized genesis moment of the PCC—and the killing of twelve apparently unarmed prisoners on the highway side in a 2002 incident known as "Operation Castelinho."[8]

Over the years, political leaders have evoked the name of ROTA in public speeches to demarcate a shift toward repressive policing. As Teresa Caldeira has shown vividly in *City of Walls*, such politicians have often been portrayed as *favored by swathes of the population, and espe-cially the poor, because of their use of violence. During a period in the* early 1980s when the postdictatorship role of the ROTA was in question, the agency's chief came out with guns blazing. "We—ROTA—are the only thing that criminals fear," he said, "And as the old saying goes, fear leads to respect, which is transformed into admiration and leads to love" (Bezzera in Caldeira 2000, 171).

Over time, this "love" for ROTA has evolved into a de facto public policy of policing. This is captured in the now-common term "ROTA na rua," *ROTA on the street*—denoting a top-down policy or instance of letting the attack dogs out. When such a policy is in place, residents know what to expect: a high body count with little respect for witnesses, counteropinions, or dissent from the media. And not much has changed over the years. In 2012, the former commander of ROTA, Paulo Telhada, was elected to the state legislature with the most votes of any candidate in the whole state. And when months later, a journalist named Andre Caramante from São Paulo's largest daily newspaper criticized Telhada for promoting the practice of *resistências* on his official Facebook page, Telhada responded by inciting his social media followers to respond. They did so with death threats and other accusations. Caramante was forced to flee Brazil into exile with his family.[9]

Slogans about ROTA that glorify their role as deadly circulate far and wide. One of the most common is regularly repeated among the police themselves: *Deus faz, mae cria, ROTA mata*—God creates, mom raises and ROTA kills. Similarly, their informal anthem entitled "Hot Lead" has been posted by many users on YouTube. With more than 2.3 million hits in one place, it is ripe with refrains about dead fathers, sons, and bandidos who didn't bow down.[10] Though ROTA is by mandate only a patrolling police force, they increasingly play a clandestine investigative role, using public support for their violence to overstep their institutional bounds. Today their de facto work includes collecting intelligence and "anonymous tips"—what many other police recognize as wiretapping.

The Força Tática is a toned-down version of ROTA, carrying less mystique and esteem by those who appreciate a police that kill. Yet because of their similar outlook, many police rise through the ranks of the Força Tática to enter ROTA. The differences between the two, however, are obvious to those in the public security system. Detectives from the Civil Police occasionally refer amongst themselves to the Força Tática as the *Força Trágica*—the "Tragic Force." Though they are often expected to kill like ROTA, the "tragic force" is not specially trained nor well prepared. The result, detectives say, is that they dive headlong into problems and end up causing and killing with abandon. Innocent people die and tragedy tends to follow them around.

Taken together the police from these two agencies vastly outnumber the detectives who are mandated to investigate and resolve both homicides *and* their killings. While the Homicide Division has around 300 detectives across a range of functions and occupations, including hate crimes, kidnapping, and missing persons units, ROTA alone has around 850 police housed in one full *batalião*—a battalion. The Força Tática is not centralized like the ROTA. Rather, each of the 51 police battalions in greater São Paulo has a "company" (*companhia*) of around 110 police assigned to be their Força Tática. By rough count, then, there are roughly 5,610 police in the Força Tática in greater São Paulo. Aggregated with the ROTA endowment, there are no less than 6,460 police in the city of São Paulo who are expected, as a matter of duty and public esteem, to be deadly—twenty-one times the number of homicide detectives.

The work of homicide detectives lies in the midst of this complex and asymmetrical moral topography of violence. Their work is twofold: investigate and solve murders in the city of São Paulo and investigate and clarify the empirical conditions surrounding police killings of citizens in greater São Paulo.[11] Not that it is that simple. To start, there are no less than nine different classifications of potentially violent death—found bones (*ossadas*), found bodies (*corpo achado*), suicide (*suicídio*), suspicious death (*morte suspeita*), death to be clarified (*morte a esclarecer*), robbery followed by death (*roubo seguido de morte*, also known as *latrocínio*), manslaughter (*homicídio culposo*) resisting arrest followed by death (*resistência seguida de morte*), multiple homicide (*chacina*), and last, intentional homicide (*homicídio doloso*). There may even be additional categories. Most become the jurisdiction of homicide detectives only when they are obviously a homicide because of visible signs of violence. This determination is always made first by someone who is not a homicide detective, such as the local precinct chiefs that first visit the scene, or the police officer who pulled the trigger.

Not just that, the work of homicide detectives begins after someone has, to some degree or another, decided about the jurisdiction, motive, and suspect of a given case. This can get exceptionally complicated. More than a few times I witnessed homicide police in long discussions with their own colleagues, with colleagues in local stations, and with others on the phone to figure out who should deal with a case. For example, in a case where someone is shot by police but does not die, the jurisdiction is in limbo. If the person dies, homicide detectives must investigate. If he does not, the Civil Police in the local station must go. The same would technically be true if the person dies days or weeks later. If the police shooting happens outside the city of São Paulo proper, but somehow turns out to be a homicide not really involving police, it is no longer for the Homicide Division to investigate. It might either go to the Homicide Division of the municipality—if it has one—or else just to the local station.

The jurisdiction of "basic" homicides, what detectives call the *homicidio simples*, can similarly be difficult to determine, as the case of the police officer in chapter 1 suggests. Homicides outside the city but within greater São Paulo are not the dominion of homicide detectives. Resistências like this are. In some cases, police go to the scene of a homicide anyway because there is a possibility that they will have to deal with it, or because a police officer was shot in the course of shooting someone, and there is moral disposition to make the situation right. The confusion of jurisdiction is regularly made worse by the impossibility of knowing who shot first and whether, as a result, the incident is a homicide or a resistência. More often than not, homicide detectives avoid investigating if they don't have to, but there are sometimes cases to the contrary.[12] Ultimately, homicide detectives can often find ways to take jurisdiction for a given case if they feel that they need to investigate it further.

The work of the Homicide Division stretches from initial crime scene review to the moment when a completed file is resolved—meaning either archived or passed on to public prosecutors. The process is split into two operational tasks managed by two separate groups—a group of police that go to the crime scene accompanied by the peritos from the Science Police, who take fingerprints, photographs, and take gunshot residue samples from suspected shooters. They catalog the characteristics of the location, using socioeconomic metrics, references to the built environment, ambient weather, and a description of the microlocation where the body (or, commonly, bodies) were found, whether inside, or, much more commonly, outside. Much of this cataloging is subjective. For instance, inquiring about things like "what was the victim doing at the scene?" or about his or her "social profile." Detectives then make decisions about possible suspects and formulate an initial narrative about motives that they incorporate in a report known as a *boletim de occorência*, that they complete with statements from witnesses, surviving victims, police, and any suspects and file on the police intranet. This corresponds with a number that is handwritten into a book that lists the digital case number, date, type of killing, name of victim(s), the team responsible for investigation, and the local precinct number. This report is then passed on to one of the twelve geographically defined homicide investigation teams, or to a team dealing with multiple homicides. Within a span of days these teams then contact witnesses, require them to come to the station for statements, follow leads, ferret out suspects, and gather enough evidence to advance the case for prosecution via the public prosecutor—the *ministerio público*.

Bureaucratic process and manpower numbers are only a tiny part of the story about police work, however. We often think about homicide detectives as being the apex of police skill, achievement, and capacity. In Brazil, however, this assumption is inverted. At best a police career in homicide is denigrated and devalued among police at large. At worst, the Homicide Division is where idealistic but feeble young officers begin and are stripped of their illusions or where tired hands awaiting their pensions go to spend their last days.

Homicide investigation is at the very bottom of the organizational hierarchy. It is a place that police avoid in favor of jobs in local precincts and specialized divisions such as the organized crime (DEIC) and drug investigation (DENARC) divisions where rents from local businesses and residents are expected. In the Homicide Division resources are scarce, rents are largely unavailable, pay is standardly poor, and hugely important pieces of the puzzle, like autopsies, take two months *minimum*. It is also depressing and emotionally exhausting. As a result, detectives themselves are constrained in their ability to do much in the midst of thousands of cases a year.

As a result, though, homicide detectives have a great deal of discretionary space within which to make decisions. How cases proceed, or not, is often the product of police interest and the existence of a defining piece of evidence, in a particular case. Some detectives have had multiple police in multiple cases arrested for fabricating stories to cover up what are arbitrary killings of citizens. Some have never arrested a fellow police officer. Unsurprisingly, their notion of who is a criminal—a bandido—who is deserving of death, and why, are much the same as their fellow police who do the patrolling, and, for the most part, the killing.

They are inclined to believe that, as the saying goes, *bandido bom e ban-dido morto*—"a good criminal is a dead criminal." Yet they do occasionally make integral distinctions between when a bandido can, and cannot, be killed. This informs when they choose to arrest their fellow police, and when they do not. Even from their devalued position vis-à-vis other police officers who are expected to kill, these are the agents of the state responsible for arbitrating the appropriateness and the inappropriateness of killing.

Whether in the decision to arrest a police officer for killing, in their decision to leave work during a period of violence, or their choice to hide from organized crime, police behavior is visible at the scale of the individual. But the repetition of behaviors across individuals reflects much more—a structured social system of within which a range of choices are possible. A police officer can make many decisions from a spectrum of possibilities. But all of these possibilities, and the decision of police to do as their colleagues do, evokes the ways that the behavior of individuals is productive and a product of social relations. In his work on suicide in Cuba, Perez states, "To decide to die was not simply or even principally to respond to a lack of alternatives but rather to choose one alternative among others. It was a choice made for complex personal reasons, but always in a social context and as an enactment of cultural models" (Perez 2005, 8).

In other words, that a police officer may choose to be violent or not in his interactions with organized crime is one thing. That he may be forced to be violent or to kill, as I will discuss in a later case, represents a much more significant structuring of social behavior. That individuals will make decisions is a given. But certain decisions are more or less made for them by widespread violence on the one hand and organized crime on the other.

The PCC is not all that interested in extreme violence, even as it is borne out of it. Most connect the genesis of the PCC with the 1992 Carandiru Prison massacre, in which 111 prisoners were killed systematically.[13] Telling of the horror, a doctor at the prison reported that most of those killed were cowering in their cells and that surviving prisoners were made to carry the dead and to stack the bodies in long rows. Many who resisted were summarily shot by police.[14] The recent trial of 25 police involved in the Carandiru massacre brought many of these images back into the public domain, relating an awe-inspiring the degree of brutality. New testimony from a perito argued that 85 prisoners were shot and killed in their cells where they sat defenseless. Another recalled the horror during his testimony, telling of having the feeling of free-flowing blood washing against his calves as it ran inches deep over the floor.[15]

Directly connected to the massacre or not, months later a group of surviving prisoners at Carandiru drew up a sixteen-point statute outlining a new system of order, justice, and brotherhood for prisoners. The 1993 *estatuto* outlined a vision for unity, identity, and justice among prisoners under the protective banner of a new organization to be known as the Primeiro Comando da Capital. It refers explicitly to the episode: "The massacre will never again be forgotten in the Brazilian conscience," it reads, ". . . because we, the *Comando*, will change the way that prisons are inhumane, full of injustice, oppression, torture, and massacres . . . [members] will respect and hold in solidarity all [other] members . . . any attempt to divide the brotherhood will lead to excommunication and punishment."

Not that violence was at all foreign to these prisoners. As the PCC's imprisoned leader, Marcola, testified during a 2006 parliamentary inquiry, the raison d'être of the PCC makes a great deal of sense in urban violence terms. Prison violence is a sibling of the processes of urban exclusion in Brazilian cities:

> We are all sons of misery, all descendants of violence, from childhood we have been accustomed to live with it, in the misery and the violence. In any favela you'll find a dead body, lying there all day. What I'm saying is that violence is normal for prisoners. This is normal. So, [prisoner groups] come along in an effort to restrain this normal violence. What do they do? They prohibit prisoners from certain behaviors that are otherwise normal, but that in this place infringe on the space of others. (CPI 2006, 25)

The PCC was, in its infancy, a network of prisoners suffering and responding collectively to the violence of the prison system. But it was also a group of men, primarily from lower socioeconomic backgrounds, emergent from the poverty and violence of the urban peripheries of São Paulo—evoking what some are increasingly calling a *carceral geography*.[16]

The PCC's moral system originally enshrined in its first statute was updated in a 2011 version. This new statute builds on the same self-protection sentiment while outlining in more stark terms the nature of punishment surrounding the organization's entrepreneurial push into the drug trade. As the trade has become ever more lucrative, the organization has increasingly cracked down on those seen to be cheating other members. As one public security official explained to me, this same moral system—complete with tribunals, judges, witnesses, a defense, and executioners—is today in place in 135 of 153 prisons in São Paulo State. The remaining handful of prisons house groups outside the scope or distrusted by the organization: the mentally ill, women, sex offenders, former police, and foreigners.

The PCC's self-protection rationale wasn't confined to the prisons for long, however. By 2002, and through a pattern that Loïc Wacquant has called a prison-ghetto "symbiosis," the PCC was making an indelible mark in the historically violent spaces on the margins of the city. As members returned to their home communities they set up new nodes of governance, each under the same moral order and connected via cell phone with leaders in the prison system. "Peace among criminals" agreements were forged between existing gangs that made non-PCC sanctioned violence de facto illegal.[17] Under a new "ethic of crime," guided by a "principle of proportionality" in which retribution was outlawed and responses to violence became measured and governed, the terrain of violence shifted dramatically.

In short order the number of multiple homicides involving three or more people, known as *chacinas*, previously a fixture, plummeted. Within three years, parts of the city like Jardim Ângela, Capão Redondo, Brasilândia, and Sapopemba—each districts of more than 250,000 residents— had their official homicide rates decrease by as much as 80 percent.[18] During interviews in 2006 and again in 2011, I spoke with residents who told of a conflicting environment in which they felt safer than ever to walk on the street and sleep with their doors and windows unlocked. There was some newfound predictability in everyday life. But they were nonetheless burdened under a new system in which they needed to see, hear, and speak no evil of everything coming to pass all around them.[19]

For the most part, the PCC has laid low in terms of the visibility of their violence. As one police officer told me, it is in their security and business interests to be as "muted" as possible in order to avoid public attention. This strategy has paid off in spades, allowing the organization to develop into a sophisticated and expansive organization. According to PCC documents given to me by a public security official, the organization has a top-level leadership (*sintonia final*) and at least eight territorial *sintonias*—divisions—in each of the north, east, south, west, and central regions of São Paulo, as well as one for each of the metropolitan areas surrounding the city (known as the "ABC" after three major satellite cities—Santo André, São Bernardo do Campo, and São Caetano do Sul—another for the port city Santos, as well as for two or three cities in the interior of the state. Each of these sintonias has up to seven subsintonias of its own that divide labor into a number of categories. These include divisions managing social assistance (*Ajuda*); balances of retail drug in/outflows (*Prazo*); activities like robberies and larger-scale drug transfers (*Progresso*); a bi-monthly and member mandatory raffle for houses and cars (*Rifa*); the membership register, including recordings of new members, punishments, and members reincorporated after punishment (*Livro*); and a cohort of lawyers (*Gravatas*). All of these sintonias and subsintonias are coordinated centrally with leaders in the prison system via cell phone. The use of phones is ubiquitous. A 2013 effort to block and register cell phone calls from a prison with two thousand inmates found that in a nine-day span 1,513 cell phone chips were used within the prison.[20] By this measurement it isn't even surprising that a recent parliamentary inquiry revealed that 800 cell phones are seized per month in the prisons of São Paulo state.

The PCC is a highly bureaucratic organization that keeps membership roles as well as Excel spreadsheets of drug sales by area code and region. They also keep track of punishment and have standardized gradations of punishment for certain types or repeat occasions of bad behavior. The need to codify these records is a reflection of the expanse of the organization, made just and legitimate to members because of its absence of personalized and clientelistic relations—in such a format that stands in stark contrast to the leaky and mistrusted bureaucracy of Brazil's formal government.

Even as the organization has flown under the public radar, it has occasionally caused widespread unrest. At least two major episodes of urban strife and crisis have been caused by the PCC. Both of these episodes occurred following incidents where the PCC felt its system of security was at threat and in ways that defied the otherwise normal equilibrium and consensual use of violence with the state.

In May 2006, the PCC coordinated what is now known as the "Mother's Day Violence." Over four days PCC affiliates assassinated more than fifty police officers and prison agents, almost all of whom were off duty at the time. They attacked police stations and banks with bombs and bullets, and burned more than eighty-five buses. For a hundred hours, this global megacity lay almost silent—a modern day ghost town. In response, vigilante death squads, which police themselves acknowledge were made up of off-duty and plainclothes police, killed upwards of 492 people.[21]

Since those attacks, which most police believe were quelled by an agreement between high-level state politicians and leaders of the PCC housed at Presidente Venceslau state prison, there had been no exceptional spikes in violence. For six years, the city benefitted from a relative peace as the PCC stayed underground, attempting to not draw attention to its increasingly lucrative activities with high-profile violence. Until 2012. In one evening in May, the ROTA killed six PCC members while following up on an "anonymous tip" of a meeting underway at a car wash on the east side of the city. In a matter of hours, the PCC retaliated, killings twenty police officers over several days. The Public Security Secretariat declared the killings to be unrelated to each other, dismissing the existence of the PCC while implying that it was a natural process of "debt collection" for corrupt cops. This incident kicked off a new crisis in which the PCC, police, and off-duty police engaged in retaliatory killings and "cleansings." This crisis lasted six months, leaving around a hundred police dead and hundreds of citizens—purportedly PCC members—six feet under.

For the most part, very little has been known about the PCC to date. Until November 2012, at the height of the most recent feud between the PCC and police, public security officials vehemently denied that the organization was anything but a myth. They argued that the PCC name was a "media fabrication" and an enigmatic ploy to drum up readers with drama and violence. That the PCC did not even "exist" until just recently has also been a product of methodological obstacles and epistemological blinders in the academic community. Some researchers have dismissed arguments about PCC governance and regulation of homicide as a "conspiracy theory."[22] These dismissals benefit from a larger discourse at play, in which quantitative inference is a prioritized form of knowledge—and the only way of knowing why homicide has declined. Yet the PCC cannot be easily detected in a body count. It is, in fact, obscured both by the processes of killing and the production and representation of numbers by state authorities. It is the PCC's practices and their systemic affect on public security that are revelatory.

As a result, knowledge about the PCC had been mostly confined to the margins of discussion on public security. But by late 2012 an outburst of international coverage of the violence, from CNN to the *Financial Times*, had put the influence of the PCC on the map. Yet still politicians and police did not openly discuss the PCC in public conversation. Some major media outlets still will not refer to it by name, choosing to only to call it a *facção criminosa*—a criminal faction. This book is likely the first major publication in English to discuss the organization, its pattern of governance, and its broader influence on the public security system in substantive detail.

The PCC has benefitted from being able to be quiet, acting as it does beneath official statistics and on the spatial—but not moral—margins of the city. But this quietness does not mean lack of activity, influence, or an absence of interaction with the state. To the contrary, the PCC is a constant presence across a variety of scales, spaces, moral practices, and in notions of the use and deservedness of violence.

PART TWO

Killing

CHAPTER 3

Homicide

It is Friday evening. The Homicide Division's black-and-white Chevy Blazer screams through the streets, parting already tight lanes of traffic with sirens blaring. Drivers pull their cars over lethargically and not a moment before the Blazer zips by with only inches to spare. For thirty-five kilometers east of downtown this continues, like almost every other time. In this case, the team of four Civil Police is coming back from Cidade Tiradentes, the final municipal district on the extreme eastern flank of São Paulo's urban periphery. There the team left behind what some claim is Latin America's largest public housing complex, a region of 220,000 residents dominated by austere and angular six-story concrete blocks built in the early 1980s. Among these bastions of state-led urban planning is a blanket of self-built homes—one- and two-story terracotta brick and concrete structures that occupy most of the constructible space in between. This decidedly nonpublic blanket augments the 40,000 public housing units with thousands more that flow down into the valleys cutting decisively into the topography of the area (figure 4).

Planned as a dormitory community, Cidade Tiradentes has a lot going against it. The commute to downtown is more than two hours each way on public transport. With a median per capita income of $432 USD a month, and with only two thousand jobs in the district itself, there is little promise for economic security. Services, including public security, were available only sparsely for many decades. On its web site, even the local suboffice of São Paulo's mayor recognizes the challenges: "Even

FIGURE 4. Mixing of planned and unplanned housing in São Paulo (photo by author).

if they came begrudgingly and without any other options, many people came to Cidade Tiradentes dreaming of their own home. The fact that they never found adequate infrastructure and few opportunities for employment has made Cidade Tiradentes a place of transience, a place of passing and not of destination" (Subprefeitura 2013).

These are the conditions of disillusionment. And they have been consequential. In 2000, the district had a homicide rate of 107 per 100,000—more than eighty times the rate in the wealthy areas of the city. Along with periurban districts adjacent to it, as well as many areas in the southern and northern sides of the city, Cidade Tiradentes was synonymous with violence. But gradually, something changed. Homicides in these districts, which once were major contributors to São Paulo's high homicide rate, fell dramatically almost overnight. By 2004, the official homicide rate had dropped by three-quarters in the district. By 2009 it had plummeted by 88 percent. Cidade Tiradentes mirrored the pattern in many other historically violent communities that are now in the foreground of a homicide rate that has declined by 76 percent for the city as a whole over the same period. In this place of unbridled disenchantment, there seemed to be something positive happening, at least in terms of security.

The drama apparent in these statistics is intoxicating, especially in an age of numerical benchmarks and quantitative inference. The hope for positive change—a "bias towards hope"—and violence reduction in cities of the Global South relies too heavily on categorical comparisons and not enough on the practices and power structures behind both the problem in question, and the definition(s) of the categories in question. Homicides, and what we divine from them, are not simply a question of counting—even bodies are no universal measure.[1]

In São Paulo, from the street, there can be no mistaking the lack of congruence between the number of bodies, how they got there, and much later, how they are counted. This was apparent for the group of detectives that had just returned from Cidade Tiradentes, having wrapped up the initial processing of a dead body on the asphalt of a dead-end street tucked into the bottom of one of the steep valleys in the region. Back in the station, they have a story to tell their colleagues: "You could just hear them yelling at us," they told the other police in the station. "Just their voices. But you couldn't see them. 'You're trash. You're going to die,' they kept yelling at us from up on either side. If they had started shooting at us, that would have been it." Now safe in the confines of the precinct, seemingly far from that dead-end street, the police joked loosely (if darkly) with their colleagues about their modicum of escape. "If they had started shooting we would have had to kidnap a little girl and hide behind her to get out of there," one of the police officers half-heartedly kidded. Confronted with that reality, they hurriedly snapped their four or five photos, took fingerprints from the body and hustled back into the SUV. It took them about fifteen minutes, they explained, from car door open to car door closed—at least a few minutes faster than usual.

There can be little doubt that homicide has been a fixture in the urban history of São Paulo. Through different eras, deadly violence has been central to the maintenance or centralization of power. Different dead bodies portray the modes and techniques of power through historical periods, from the slave beaten into submission, to the tortured political dissident, and today, the young man, perforated with gunshots, who lies bleeding on the street somewhere distant from Avenida Paulista.

Quantifying these homicides can be difficult however. From the *Coroneis* of colonial Brazil to shadowy dictatorship police who "disappeared" people as much (or more) as they killed them, to recent assassinations of off-duty police, the production of statistics is deeply intertwined with the troubled exercise of power. In the contemporary period, in which public security is particularly frail, there should be little doubt that the numbers released by public security entities are adjusted, manipulated, subcategorized, or poorly represented to convey rosier images of public security.[2] What the public, scholars, and anyone else who cares to know gets is a body of numbers replete with caveats of the known, not known,

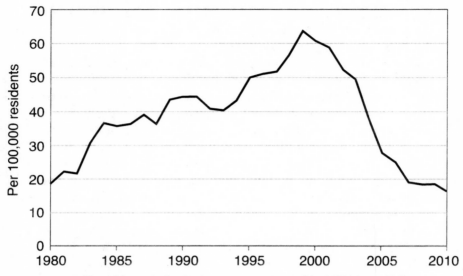

FIGURE 5. Homicide rate in São Paulo, 1980–2010 (created by Bill Nelson of Bill Nelson Maps).

and assumed. Many of these caveats are left out of public discussion, creating illusions of knowledge and power that are treated as fact. The "state of statistics" makes it difficult to discern anything but general trends, or more pessimistically, on the formal discourse of security—what leaders want to portray.

But if we only use general trends as a departure point, some very modest inference is possible. The homicide statistics of the Secretariat of Public Security from the last forty years show two different periods (figure 5). In the first, from 1980 to 1999, the number of homicides in the city of São Paulo rose dramatically, from a low of 18 to a high of 63 per 100,000 residents. In the second, from 2000 to 2010, homicides declined dramatically, around the same amount but over half of the time. The question, then, is: *What changed so severely around the year 2000?*

This dynamic shift suggests that control over violent death has consolidated or strengthened in the years since 2000. Yet amid hopes for a policy success, there remain few answers for the reason(s) why. One way to interrogate the positions and advance our knowledge about the conditions of violent death is to look more deeply at who was being killed and who is surviving, demographically speaking, during these two analytically distinct periods. Who died violently, where, and how in the for-

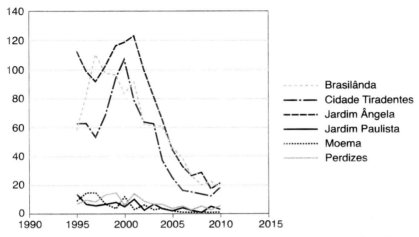

FIGURE 6. Homicide rates (per 100,000) in center versus periphery (created by Bill Nelson of Bill Nelson Maps).

mer period is useful for examining *who is not dying* in the latter. A glance at one constituency in particular—young men—helps to elucidate the nuance of this apex and the apparent decline.

Across the world, young men are often most likely to be homicide victims. This is no different in urban Brazil. Young male involvement in gangs, drug trafficking, and other criminality is a double-edged sword of violence and victimization. Men between the ages of fifteen and twenty-nine die at rates that far exceed other demographics. Imaginaries of violence feed off of this pattern, leading to police profiling of young men such that they become preordained as criminal and meriting of death as a result. One analysis argues that young men in São Paulo during the 1990s were around twenty times more likely to die from homicides than women of the same age.[3]

There is also a distinct spatial component to homicide victimization. A great deal of research has shown that places on the urban periphery, like Jardim Ângela, Cidade Tiradentes, Capão Redondo, and Brasilândia, contributed disproportionally to the number of homicides in the city (figure 6 and map 1). The distinctions are stark: according to state figures, the most violent districts recorded rates of homicide sixty to eighty times higher than those of wealthy districts of the city. Focusing on those areas, and even knowing that the numbers are likely underestimated, Bruno Manso argued in the year 2000 that as many people died in São Paulo in 1999—9,027—as during the Kosovo conflict occurring during the same period.

Locations of districts shown in figure 6 in the city of São Paulo (created by Bill Nelson of Bill Nelson Maps).

If modest quantitative inference into this period is helpful but flawed, qualitative insight is revelatory. In these civil war–like conditions, young men—just like Beto in Jardim Ângela—had to be almost exceptional to (a) not get involved, and (b) not be killed by the violence. In these places so consumed by violence in the 1990s, dead bodies were so routine on the street that they became a nuisance. Colloquially known as "hams" (*presuntos*), the normality of these dead bodies transformed the perceptions of even the most hopeful and strident of people. Manso (2000) recalls a reaction to violent death by a local parish priest in a community on the south side of the city: "Father Dillon went to pull his car out of his garage one morning. When he opened the door, he saw a body spread out right in front of his house. In a hurry to leave, he thought at first: 'why did this guy have to die on the doorstep of my house? The police is going to take hours to get the body out of here and I'll be late.' He surprised himself with his own reaction. He was entirely accustomed to seeing bodies on the street."

If this violence was "normal" for those living in the periphery, so was there also a "common sense" understanding of who killed, who died, and why. Violence was splintered between warring gangs, each of whom fought for control of the small bits of turf increasingly central to the economies of drugs, security and belonging. Rivals of the worst kind, these groups directed their violence at each other and those accompanying them. Multiple homicides (*chacinas*) were abundant and common as killers sought to eliminate witnesses and anyone likely to retaliate. Deeply decentralized, these neighborhood-level battles destabilized all residents, both by opening up space for generalized criminality and by leading to regular and sporadic shoot-outs in public spaces. Streets, parks, and sidewalks weren't safe at any time, day or night.

Not that these killings were devoid of order. The moral borderlines of much of this violence were defined in mostly individual terms, largely as the defense of *honor*, just like the American "code of the street" as detailed by Elijah Anderson in 1999. Ideas of deservedness of death were broad, flexible, and unregulated under this view. Individuals or small groups were able to decide who merited death, culminating in clashes between contrasting ideas about the legitimacy of death—and more killing. Add to the mix roving vigilante groups of off-duty or former police and on-duty police with a propensity to kill and the picture of homicide in urban São Paulo of the 1990s is crowded with a multitude of contradictory and conflictive groups all fighting for moral, economic, and security space.

The consequence of this violence was all consuming. Detectives who grew up in high-homicide areas recalled that virtually all of their school friends and acquaintances who had been wrapped up in the violence were either dead or had been missing for years. Those who escaped the violence—almost surely because they committed it themselves—ended up in the warehouse wasteland that was, and largely continues to be, the Brazilian prison system.

Today, all parties agree that São Paulo is the midst of something exceptional in terms of homicide decline. Young men are dying much less, and the parts of the city that had eroded into civil war–like circumstances have rebounded in remarkable ways. There are two schools of thought on why so many fewer people are being killed violently. One position espoused mostly by analyses hinging on statistical inference points to a number of impactful shifts in state public policy. The other, mainly backed up by qualitative field research, examines the neighborhood-level changes in the places where violence was vertiginous through the 1990s.

In the former camp, studies have found that almost everything is responsible. One such study asserts that, even despite the sharp nature of the change, many factors have contributed. These include demographic changes, unemployment rate, state budget for education and culture, health and sanitation, and the municipal and state budgets for public security, firearms seized, and incarceration rate. All were found to be statistically significant in the reduction of homicides. In this analysis, one of the only variables not found to be significant was the number of police arrests.[4]

Paradoxically, though, a study of descriptive statistics by a former head analyst of the state Secretariat of Public Security argued that improved policing methods were the key factor.[5] This study drew comparisons between the decline in homicides in New York, arguing that, among other changes, "saturation units" were deployed to hot spots, increasing the number of arrests and, by extension, the number of people imprisoned.

International organizations, eager to find positive examples and "best practices" in homicide reduction, have also jumped into the fray. Drawing on the same statistics from the São Paulo Secretariat of Public Security, the United Nations Office on Drugs and Crime (UNODC) praises the decline in a 2011 report, noting its similarities with places like Medellin, Colombia. This high-profile support did not go unnoticed. When criticized, the Secretariat of Public Security publicly cites this study as a defense of its role in the homicide decline. This is in spite of the fact that the UNODC has done nothing to empirically validate the public security policies or to examine the statistical relationships behind the change.[6]

On the other side of the pitch are a cohort of primarily Brazilian anthropologists, sociologists, and urban theorists. Although a minority in terms of following, these researchers posit a much different story, from the ground up. They reveal a world in which the PCC is the principal criminal organization in the city and that has centralized drug trafficking activities. Moreover, it is regulator of crime and violence. If you want to kill someone, you need the authorization of the organization. These researchers have shown in vivid detail that if you feel wronged, you go to the PCC. You'll participate in a tribunal involving everyone but presided over by PCC members that mimics a formal legal trial. This model, they claim, has become the de facto standard of law and order in the urban periphery of São Paulo.[7]

In sum, this group of scholars argues that the PCC, not the state, has the unique ability to define the conditions of life and death in São Paulo's periphery. This "alternative dispute resolution" mechanism is proving deeply consequential. As the data of the Secretariat of Public Security also reflect, homicides are down dramatically in Jardim Ângela, Cidade Tiradentes, Sapopemba, and Brasilandia—among many other urban districts. These are the same places that scholars have found the PCC to play an unmistakable role in terms of social and community relations.[8]

Nothing could be more important than understanding this experience and the changing balance of power in the urban periphery of São Paulo. The PCC is at once a product, a producer, and a regulator of violence. What we know about the PCC, made clear by this vanguard of scholars, provides much-needed insight into the forms of security and governance that are not subsumed by the formal institutions of justice and legality of the state. In these places, so characterized previously by an absence of central authority, the PCC represents a channel of authority that is now more or less uncontested. Relative security, notions of solidarity, and structures of social assistance are pillars of this authority (Dias 2013). Police, forever seen as unreliable, unaccountable, violent, and/or corrupt, have been replaced by a social order complete with its own norms, notions of justice, and modes of punishment.

Some years ago, this was different. When residents did seek out police to deal with local violence, the police would resolve it in a temporary fashion if at all. By contrast, seeking out the authority of those involved with the *tráfico*—drug trafficking—could resolve something permanently, even if in deadly ways. This binary of success and failure in

"justice" created a de facto choice in security provision for residents:
state or nonstate. This choice was formative. When residents found their
insecurity reliably resolved by one authority, they continued to seek it
out at the expense of the other, consolidating, over time, the legitimacy
of that authority.

PCC governance can be understood in terms of social space. Unde-
termined in its boundaries yet firm in its norms, it stretches from the hundreds of prisons in São Paulo (and increasingly beyond), over swathes
of the sprawling *paulistano* periphery with its millions of historically excluded residents, to the day-to-day activities of a major criminal syndi-
cate. Recognized for its relative fairness, it influences everything from
the fairness of lineups on family visitation day at prisons to the rules in
prisons where not a single baptized PCC member is housed. When I did
research in a PCC-controlled community, residents claimed they could
sleep worry free with their doors and windows unlocked. This was something entirely new.

Not just that, PCC power is diffuse and decentered. As one resident
once told me, people in these same communities regularly speak of the
need to be *surdo, mudo, e cego*—deaf, mute, and blind. Shutting the window as we spoke in her kitchen, she elaborated that this is not just because of a fear of members of the PCC, but because the power of the
organization resides in the eyes, ears, and mouths of everyone in the community. Another resident told of a stirring incident in the local health
post. A doctor there had been unkind to patients and was known for
disrespecting the needs of people in the community. Eventually, this broke
a threshold. The PCC forced the hand of someone in charge, and within
days the publicly employed doctor was transferred within the public
health system and replaced with someone more considerate of the needs
of the community.

The PCC's legitimacy is thus deeply woven into social relations. Those
who live under this system engage in a form of self-governance. Even
where the PCC is not explicitly present, its norms are. The PCC notion
of right and wrong is transcendent and diffuse both for those understood
to be within the "familia," meaning not necessarily the *irmaos baptisa-
dos* (baptized brothers), but also for all of those people living under the
PCC's code.

Pervasive in its presence, authority is consolidated in such a way that
dissention is not possible. Those who live in the communities controlled
by the PCC are accountable to the organization and also to their peers

residing under the same terms. In this sense, a structural shift has come to pass in São Paulo. The exercise of violence in the periphery has ceased to be defined by individuals—the "honor" orientation of killing in the 1990s—and is now unquestionably the dominion of a "central" authority.

And there should be little doubt that it is a central authority. In 2012 I got to know a public security analyst who had been working intimately with intelligence and strategic investigations of the PCC. He was struggling to keep his head above water in all of the data they were collecting and, for lack of workers and distrust in many police, were not using. He gave me copies of flash drives seized directly from PCC members. In them were hundreds of documents of all manner of substance.

These detailed almost everything—enough to discover the identities of hundreds of PCC members, their positions within the organization, how much drugs they were usually given to sell and how much of that they had paid back. It seemed enough to dismantle the whole organization with a diligent and coordinated investigation. There were revenue documents, such as Excel spreadsheets detailing the balance of sales of freebase cocaine, marijuana, and crack cocaine by week and month, itemized by region. These same documents included the amount of money spent to pay for family visits to prisons and other purchases on cell phones, vehicle rentals, and laptops, among other things. Other documents itemized the quantity and type of drugs given to hundreds of members for street resale, including any existing debts.

There were membership rolls, with lists of hundreds of names with membership numbers, last prison locations, dates, neighborhood on the outside, role in the organization, names of "godfathers," and punishment, if any, including the names and positions of members involved, and the dates of the judgment. Also included were copies of internal communications, known as *salves*, from the leaders, that highlighted new developments in terms of regulations, discipline, and new benefits—such as the possibility to apply for a loan.

Other documents reported the inventory of resources on hand. This included a list of vehicles, their condition, and under whose care they were in. More important, there were lists of the stock of the "gun libraries" where members could go to get a gun. Within these inventories and other documents were the stipulated conditions for lending. These outlined for what kind of business, whether a simple armed robbery or a bank heist, a weapon could be borrowed—"no one shall be given a machine gun for a car-jacking," one point relates. Not only do these documents show a means of organization, they relate a centralized control over the use of violence. Not only is ownership of guns centralized but diffuse, it comes with a set of regulations about the conditions under which those guns may be used. The PCC has, in other words, its own system of gun control.[9]

Perhaps most telling, these records related in thick detail the different modes and gradations of penalty employed by the organization. Punishment is not arbitrary, nor trivial. This is ensured by one of the divisions of labor within the organization. *Disciplinas*—disciplinarians—are baptized PCC members responsible for upholding the norms of the system.[10] Their work is twofold. On the one hand, they are responsible for regulating the moral economy of the organization—following up on lost money, drugs, missed membership payments, delinquent debts, improper violence on the part of members, and any other number of contraventions to the PCC statute. On the other hand, they are also empowered as judges, both of contraventions of the rules by members, as well as by those living in the community under the system of the "family."

Rarely, if ever, does a single individual decide punishment. And certainly not in severe cases. Especially in crimes of moderate or high importance, a number of *disciplinas* take part in deciding on the verdict of the crime—guilty or not—and in deciding the mode of punishment. The system of punishment is different for members than for unbaptized members. In both cases their punishment ranges proportionally to the supposed crime. There are at least three differentiations in the severity of "crimes" committed and the punishments vary accordingly. For small crimes—what we might call "small claims"—only local members preside. For moderate issues, regional PCC members are brought in by cell phone. For the most the important crimes—unsanctioned murder, theft from the "family," rape, pedophilia, becoming involved with the girlfriend of a PCC member, a complete tribunal will take place, involving a telephone conference call that webs together PCC members in various prisons throughout the state. These more complex cases can take many hours of intricate deliberation. One case, captured by a police wire tap, took more than twenty-four hours of deliberation—with breaks in between not counted in the deliberation time.

For members of the PCC there is a graduated system of sanctions, with specific forms of punishment for first, second, and third infractions. Demonstrative of centralized, bureaucrat and impersonal management, one document related this in precise and codified detail, as though instructing future record keepers:

> For members, first suspension [*prazo*] is 15 days. If they pay they're back, if they don't pay they're out of the comando.

> 2nd suspension
> 90 days automatically
> and 15 more days to pay.
> If they don't pay
> they're out.

> 3rd suspension
> Automatically out.
> And are entered into a period of twenty days as a *companheiro* [nonpaying sympathizer].

> Noted:
> Whatever is arranged between the
> debtor and the system [*sintonia*] after
> the suspension expires.
> Whatever negotiation
> takes place between the two parties
> is to be told in detail.

> For recording suspensions,
> the following details are needed.

> Name
> Member number
> Aliases
> Neighborhood
> Date of baptism
> Place of baptism
> Aliases of Godfather and neighborhood of Godfather
> Last three prisons
> If they have been punished by the family.
> If so, the place and date and reason why
> Last three positions in the organization
> Day out of prison
> Red telephone number
> Names of members present [in punishment]
>   Regional leader
>   Local leader
>   Neighborhood leader
>   Which book it is registered
> The date of suspension

Expiry or if indeterminate
Those baptized[11]

The detail of this bookkeeping, both here in terms of "human resources" and in other documents in terms of revenue, guns, and cars,
reflect a fledgling but covert bureaucracy. They relate a sophisticated system of authority and hierarchy in the PCC. The organization utilizes many
forms of punishment before relying on physical violence. Members that
have not paid debts, who are in delinquent in their membership payments,
who fail to satisfy any number of other membership obligations, or whom
commit a violent crime—such as a murder—that was not previously au-
thorized but is understood postfact to have been "reasonable," are subject
to a series of nonviolent punishments. Graded temporary suspensions
are part of this. Complete expulsion is at the end of that continuum. Kick-
ing out a member of the PCC—temporarily or permanently—carries
with it many real world consequences. No access to a highly lucrative
drug economy, less physical protection from violence, and if the person is
sent to prison, no access to any of the supplies and comforts guaranteed
by the organization. This almost certainly pushes such "marginalized"
individuals into risky and low-margin crimes, either to recoup money
for outstanding debts or to try to make ends meet after being completely
expelled.[12] Being expelled from the organization makes someone nothing
less than a common criminal, still subjected to the laws of the PCC but
without any of the benefits of membership. As one police detective saw it,
being expelled was second to death in terms of punishment. In a community context where everyone knows everything, this is a perfect humiliation that revokes social status, eliminates a lucrative source of income,
removes access to guns, and excludes from a circle of belonging. It is like
a tradespersons being stripped of their occupational certification.

There are of course many other violent forms of punishment. Killing,
as a punishment, is reserved for crimes of the highest order, and only
after there is consensus of the guilt of the person in question. An array
of violent punishments are utilized for other crimes against the PCC
order. These range from creating the maximum amount of pain without
death—like a beating only from the neck down, as a public prosecutor
explained to me—to pain plus moral suffering—a beating and being
placed unconscious on a bus to a remote region of the country with a
formal warning to never return—to the maximum amount of pain plus
death—having armed and legs broken and eyes gouged out—as in the
case of a pedophile.[13] When someone is found "guilty" of the most se-

vere of crimes the punishment is carried out immediately—and not necessarily by a member of the PCC. The person sanctioned to carry out
the sentence is often someone seeking restitution in the case. These forms
of punishment that culminate in killing constitute the apex of an unmistakable authority over life and death exercised over members and over
communities as a whole. This alternative system of authority is well
acknowledged by those who should have authority. Who the PCC kills
has moral parameters that do not necessarily clash with those empowered to investigate homicide on the part of the state.

Homicide detectives understand death according to a set of taken-for-
granted moral and pragmatic parameters about deservedness, which informs how much they engage their discretionary space to ensure that
those who should not die, do not in the future. Homicide police are the
dull edge of a floundering public security system tossed asunder by a number of social and structural forces focused much more on meting out
violent death than on finding out who kills.

Even with their underprivileged position within the public security
system, there is something much more complex at play. A much more
formidable force than their fellow police undermines the work of homicide police. The PCC's regulation of death is the single most predominant factor in the control over life and death in São Paulo. Even without the load of having to investigate resistências, the Homicide Division
would certainly struggle to overcome or disarticulate the PCC's concurrent system of governance.

The relationship between the work of the homicide police and the PCC
ranges broadly. At times, this relationship teeters on the edge of violent
confrontation, as when the detectives visited Cidade Tiradentes. Other
times, the influence of the PCC is implicit. It need not be talked about
openly; it is assumed by police detectives that certain forces are evident
in the background of their cases.

This doesn't mean that the two groups are antagonistic. They do not
exist in isolation of each other. Much to the contrary. The PCC system
is known to use the formal system of justice as a form of punishment
for certain circumstances. PCC members are not "untouchable," nor does
the PCC's decision to have someone killed mean that police will never
find or arrest the killers. In fact they do, thanks to resources at their disposal like fingerprints, security camera footage, and anonymous tips.[14]

Thus the PCC's system of justice is not impenetrable by the formal
system. Instead they are deeply interlinked. I argue here that they are, in

fact, siblings that depend on each other. The PCC system depends on the centralized state power that maintains the prisons—where all PCC activity originates and is centrally regulated. PCC leaders housed in the prison system are in many ways protected and sheltered by the same walls that were intended to remove its "criminality" from the street in the first place. When it comes to homicide, those who are arrested by detectives for killing someone are only briefly exposed to the routines of the formal legal system. Arriving in jail they are once again left to live under a set of norms determined by the PCC. To be arrested by police for murder is to enter a system in which the costs of your imprisonment are paid for by the membership dues of PCC "brothers" outside. Your survival in the prison is made possible not because of a state justice system that is capable, just, or even moral, but rather, by the rules, regulations, and social support provided by a criminal organization. As such, making killers accountable for their actions and forcing them to serve time in prison, as homicide convictions intend, takes on a whole new significance. But beyond this sibling relationship within the prison system, the state and the PCC logics of killing are deeply linked in the "normal homicide." Or so I will argue.

The vast majority of homicides in São Paulo occur in places far from downtown. Police know these kinds of places by their precinct numbers—Thirty-seventh, Seventy-second, Forty-sixth, Sixty-ninth, Twenty-fourth, and Fifty-fourth—that disguise the names of places well known in the lore of São Paulo's urban violence: Campo Limpo, Cidade Dutra, Perus, Sapopemba, São Miguel Paulista, and Cidade Tiradentes. These places are on the margins of the city, both geographically and metaphorically—as are their victims of homicide. These victims are drug users, drug dealers, young men of marginal origin—or understood by detectives to be something similar. This real or perceived social position of victims constitutes the *padrão*—the pattern—of homicides in this city. And "não tem muitos que fogem do padrão" (Not many defy the pattern), as Beto once put it.

The normal homicide mirrors the concept advanced by Sudnow (1965) and Garfinkel (1949), who argue that the "normalcy" of some crimes shapes the routine operation and decision-making processes of accompanying those cases within the system. "Normal crimes" are those that meet a certain level of "typicality" of pattern and persons involved. As Sudnow (1965) puts it of the criminal justice worker, "He learns to speak knowledgeably of 'burglars,' 'petty thieves,' 'drunks,' 'rapists,' 'narcos,' etc. and to attribute to them personal biographies, modes of usual criminal activity, criminal histories, psychological characteristics, and social backgrounds" (259).

The normal crime is one in which the normal characteristics of both perpetrator and victim—gender, space, race, and social status—contain an element of redundancy. The predictability of these crimes gives way to a set of socially embedded and taken-for-granted "unstated recipes" that constitute a status quo of practice. Where enough people die violently, a "normal" homicide is possible. The racial and spatial components of homicides in particular, presumed similar and lacking a deeper engagement with the origin of the crime, come to determine repertoires of treatment for given victim-offender relationships. With every "normal" victim comes a presumed offender, and vice versa, justifying a regular form of action.

That there are enough homicides in Sao Paulo—despite the recent decline—to still have a normal homicide, is a remarkable fact. Routine killing of a certain category of people on a daily basis might constitute genocide or ethnic cleansing in other places. But in São Paulo it has been this way for decades—if not centuries. One respected academic recently argued that there have been more than 1 million homicides in Brazil since the 1980s—with cities like São Paulo taking the ignominious lead.[15] The regularity of certain subjects of homicide and a concordant police practice is more or less easy to decipher, even as the moral structure behind routine killing has changed since the year 2000.

A "normal" homicide—*um homicídio simples*—in São Paulo goes something like this:

> It is 10:30 p.m. and I have just arrived for another night shift at the homicide department. A message arrives via the intranet to detectives waiting in the station. The body of a young man has been found in the area of the 101st precinct. He's been shot multiple times, at least a few times in the head. Witnesses are few, and won't say much—though just one good one would do. Military Police arrived at the scene at around 7:30 p.m. after an anonymous call to the emergency line 190. They arrived to find the man, apparently dead for some time. They are guarding the scene for the arrival for homicide detectives. The homicide detectives get their things together. One of them calls in a request for crime scene analysts from the Science Police—*peritos da Polícia Técnico-Científica*. They'll meet them at the scene. They grab their camera, the fingerprinting kit, and load their guns. The team is composed of five police—one delegado [chief], one investigador [investigator], one papiloscopista [fingerprinter], a carcereiro [prison guard], a fotógrafo [photographer], and me. Of the five, one or two put on a bulletproof vest. From the arrival of the message to the time we are out the door is about forty-five minutes. The message often arrives at the station hours after the body is first found.

We arrive at the scene in about an hour's drive. The perito crime scene analysts aren't here yet. The chief detective shares a word with the Military Police about what they know. They don't know much, other than that the neighbors in the area say they didn't hear anything weird. Which is funny, because the body appeared right as many people came home from work. One person said that the dead man is known around there and that he was involved with drugs. He doesn't want to be an official witness. The chief asks the investigator and the prison guard to look for security cameras and to acquire any relevant footage. Meanwhile, the fingerprinter and the photographer are struggling to open one of the man's hands. It takes the two of them to pry it open. Someone else helps to hold it in place while the fingerprinter applies black ink on all the fingers before rolling them, one by one, on to a paper fingerprint form. The two analysts have now arrived. One walks around to look for capsules. She asks the Military Police if they saw any or marked where they were. They didn't see any, not that it is their job—strictly speaking—to look anyway. The other steps in alongside the fingerprinter to cut the man's clothes off. It takes a couple of them to roll the body over. The photographer takes about seven pictures, mostly of the wounds, the head and face, one or two of the surrounding area and one each of the tattoos on the man's shoulder and forearm. The analyst also takes pictures, which will be part of the report they will file through their own channels. It will join the case file at a much later date. Back from looking for video camera coverage, the investigator now fills out the standard three- to four-page standard crime scene checklist. This form assesses many details in a multiple-choice format. It includes categories for everything from characteristics of the body (age, sex, race), initial indications of cause of death (blunt trauma, gunshots, knife wounds, etc.), ambient environment (wet, dry, humid), and physical location of the body, whether inside, outside, on a public street, among houses, shacks, gated homes, or other domicile possibilities.

In the meantime, the chief stands back and observes, trying to piece together an understanding of how and why this body ended up bloody and lifeless on this quiet suburban street, with him looking at it. Half an hour later or so, everyone is done. We all jump in the car. Someone's cell phone rings. It is the station. Another *morto*. This one at a precinct on the North Side. The other team suggests that our group process the scene, since we're already out on the street. The chief accepts. The prison guard is driving. He turns on the sirens and accelerates as the Blazer turns onto a larger thoroughfare.

The routine homicide in São Paulo is not a crime of passion, the result of a domestic row, or a plight of missing sex workers, though each of these occur in great frequency and need also be of substantive concern. The routine homicide is a violent death with unavoidable markings, some spatial, some gendered, some physical, of a deep and thorough underpinning. For police on the ground the logic behind the hundreds of dead young men is obvious, if taken for granted. There is something calculated, controlled, and managed about many of these deaths, evident not just in the unwillingness of obvious witnesses to talk but also in their repetitiveness. The places where bodies are found and the states in which they are found—seemingly tossed aside—indicate a certain kind of disregard to the abilities of homicide investigators. Nobody is taking much time for cover-ups here. There is something particularly brazen, time consuming, and public about the way that these people end up. From all around, there are suggestions of a public secret. Detectives are often left standing on the outside looking in at something that audaciously confronts their ability to control violence. Everyone knows what is in play, even if it isn't often said. That is, until December 2012, when the Secretariat of Public Security finally went public and finally agreed that the "PCC is responsible for a large part of the homicides in the city" (Estado de São Paulo 2012b).

The tacit but unavoidable nature of this reality is evident throughout my fieldnotes, which relate the way that violent death, though routine, reflects a high degree of organization, planning, and ostentaciousness. Whether this degree of structure is assumed or disregarded by detectives doesn't much matter.

Even where there is outward evidence of the involvement of organized crime, the response of detectives tends toward apathy. One particular case reflects the barren approach to the routine homicide. I recall:

It had been a long day in the car. One homicide scene and two police killings, plus stops at two public hospital morgues so far. We've put about 170 kilometers behind us in a zigzag pattern across the city since this morning. By now it is getting late. We're on our way to the other side of the city for (hopefully only) one more homicide scene. The place we're going is past the sprawl and into the forest. Or so I'm told.

You could smell it when we drove past. Samuel, a police detective, stops the Blazer. There is a truck there from the coroner's office that will take the body after we're done. We get out and chat with the detectives from the other Blazer that has accompanied us all day. There are also some Military Police there who have been guarding the scene. It isn't clear who they would be guarding it from though. The last few houses were a couple of kilometers back. There is no traffic on this dirt road. So little, in fact, that anyone who drives by would probably be noticeable.

Walking down the road a little bit, we come to a clearing in the trees and the smell. A wet embankment slopes off the side of the road. It is strewn with bits of garbage, metal refuse, mud, and who knows what else. At the bottom is a burned out but relatively new model car resting in a small creek bed. Trees with long vines tower over it. Somewhere down there is a decomposing body. For all of the smell, no one can see it. Someone strings up a rope to help get down. Of the ten police from the Homicide Division, plus myself, only two of us decide to go down. Someone passes me some rubber gloves. I grab the rope and step down the wet slope.

We were basically on top of them when we realized it. Not one but two burnt bodies, covered in beetles and in an advanced state of decomposition. Up close you could make out much more. Covering them, particularly around their head and upper bodies, were what looked like wires—rusted and frayed as they were. "A man and a woman," the police officer beside me said. [Pointing] "The torso on this one is much smaller." It didn't seem so obvious to me. The bodies kind of blended into the mud, their dark earthy tones made similar over time. Somehow, the smell wasn't as bad this close to the actual bodies. But in the absence of the smell, the sight of the two damp, partly burnt, and decomposing bodies was a shocking enough replacement.

The car was down the hill a bit further. It was empty. No seats, no engine, no tail-lights nor a windshield. The police up above surmised about what went over the hill first, the bodies or the car. Without a motor, the car would have had no way to get to this remote place without a rig towing it. If the motor and everything else were removed after the fact, it would have been a heck of a job to get it up the hill. If the car had come after the bodies, it would have run right over them, likely spreading the remains all over the place. It must have been there before, they figured, since people dump stuff like this all the time. They concluded that the car, though burnt and not identifiable outside of brand and model, was unrelated to the bodies. Not that any one of them even went near the car to look for a serial number on the dash or anywhere else.

For the police, the bodies and the scene gave few immediate clues. Plus it stank. There was an air of resignation and impatience, like the bodies had been there for so long that nothing obvious would come of this. The detectives in the regional squad would pick this up and be better suited to deal with it once the autopsy report comes back in two months time.

But from up closer, you could see a lot. The wires were virtually all parallel and uniform, curving slightly and running under and over both of the bodies. It was tire belting. The rubber had burned away entirely, leaving only hoops of now-rusting tire belting behind. Those tires would have burned hot for hours—if not days—with thick black smoke. The presence of tires was more than a curiosity. These two people were killed by what is known as *micro-ondas*—the "microwave." These two were likely killed after someone forced two or three tires over their shoulders, doused them with some kind of accelerant and set them on fire. They would have been burned alive while standing. This is a form of particularly horrific killing that is used both as a way to create a horrible amount of pain for those suffering it but also to emotionally shock anyone witnessing or picturing it in their mind's eye. Less well known but not unheard of for the PCC in São Paulo, "micro-ondas" are much more commonly used by drug trafficking groups in Rio de Janeiro. It seemed to me, in this case, and despite my obvious naiveté, to be a big loose end.

The police up above, who by some strange effect were getting a much stronger smell, started prodding us to go. Someone tossed down two body bags. One of the men from the coroner's office came down. I grabbed the rope and scrambled up. Someone reached down to help me take the final step up. I took off the gloves. "They're falling apart," moaned one of the coroner workers as he tried to pick up part of the body. They laid out one bag. With the body language of revulsion, he grasped one of the bodies by the spine, picked it up and tossed it on the bag. The arm, head and the all the rest from the first body came flying in soon after.

The conditions of bodies are inseparable from their victimization. Stinking, dismembered, decaying, or burnt, these bodies would disincline almost anyone from seeing them everyday, multiple times a day. But the condition of bodies also implies their physical location, both in the city, and on the ground where they lie—putrid, foul, and visceral in inhuman detail. Found immersed in muck, in fetid streams of sewage, or surrounded by gazing eyes in the midst of a known PCC hot spot, these bodies become the best reason for a get-in-get-out investigation. Beyond a detectives' own notions of disposable lives, the condition of the "normal" victim is often a perfect excuse to leave as quickly as possible. The two or three emissaries that took the four or five pictures often suffice as a description for the state of the body, filling out the running narrative as to the "typicality" of the circumstance.

Within this typicality is the taken-for-granted role of the PCC. That there is some deeper form of organization and rationale behind the deaths does not force police to take extra measures. Quite to the contrary, they may even approach these kinds of cases with less diligence. As for these victims, who are the subject of murder under the hefty and violent moral system of the PCC, they can be located, at least in imagination, as bandidos of the worst order. The PCC, most understand, kill people who did something to deserve it.

This doesn't mean that further investigation of the two bodies in this case won't result in the identification of a suspect or an eventual arrest. The coroners will eventually do a deeper analysis to try to identify the bodies and the cause of death. If identified, a host of other investigative doors will be opened up, both in terms of who the victims are (where they lived, how old they were, their gender) but also in terms of what they were (good or bad people, with criminal records of some variety, or not). But this kind of case, onerous and difficult to investigate as it is, is just one of thousands that come to pass each year.

Though it may seem like the onus is on homicide detectives to stem the bloodshed in this city, it is, in large part, out of their control. Their body language and approach to their job mirrors this reality. They may solve many homicides and arrest those who are responsible for killing.

But resolving individual homicides is not the issue at play. Individual res-
olutions do little to dismantle the system of governance and security that
validates and legitimates them.

There is a somewhat lighter, if nonetheless troubling, side to routine
homicides in São Paulo. As effective governors of death, the PCC and
its influence can also be discerned in the numbers of people that are not
dying. As may not have been so easy in the past, avoiding violent death
in spite of "reprehensible" behavior has been made possible. The scales
of PCC punishment and the different moral thresholds serve as both a
deterrent and justification for punishing repeated transgressors increasingly more severely. To escape death does not mean you just walk away
with your life. In exchange for life, people that are punished by the PCC
can face other excruciatingly damning forms of physical and emotional
suffering. Both Dias (2013) and Feltran (2010) discuss in great detail the
"judicial" processes through which life and death hinges, and when it
falls in favor of life over death.

Feltran tells the story of one young man, whom he calls Jorge. As an
eighteen-year-old, Jorge was involved with the local drug trade in a community on the east side of the city. In 2006, Jorge was sent to a tribunal
for his involvement in a robbery of guns and merchandise that went sour.
Different versions of the story spread, and he was accused of taking money
from the "family." In what would previously have certainly meant sum-
mary execution, Jorge was invited to defend himself from the accusations.
If Jorge was found guilty he would have been forced to pay everything
back, have been beaten extensively, kicked out of the *favela*, or killed.
From someone at the tribunal:

> They had a debate about whether they would kill Jorge . . . we all went there,
> and when we arrived, we saw the guys accusing him, we could see him being
> very brave right in the middle of everything. They decided that they weren't
> going to kill him, but that they were going to give him a correction. . . . He
> got pelted. Man they tore him up. He got totally depressed about the world
> of crime, there was no way to go back. Then a guy came by, and I knew that
> he was the leader of all the traffickers. . . . When I saw him I said: "Jeez, things
> are really bad." This guy was really easy going though, and he knew that they
> wouldn't kill Jorge, he wouldn't let them. (Feltran 2010, 65)

They ended up absolving Jorge of the original accusation of treason.
This wasn't the first time that Jorge had been punished though. He'd
already been suspended for thirty days from working. Because he was
involved in another problem, they beat him up and kicked him out of
the drug trafficking business, something particularly demoralizing in the

view of the community. He could no longer deal drugs and had no more access to the source of income that he'd had since he was twelve years old. Still, he saw it as a chance to keep his life.

In São Paulo understanding the practice of homicide is as important as understanding the product. Why people die, and who allows for it to happen, tells us much more than the numbers of bodies that pile up. The PCC is a system of governance and moral order in the urban spaces that have struggled with homicide, police repression, and extermination groups historically. In many of these places the rationale of homicide was once connected to notions of personal or small group honor. Today control over this violence is much more centralized and vested in an authority that is well identified and heeded by residents. Beyond the fact that police are widely distrusted and citizens in these places choose to avoid them, reporting violence and crime to police is seen as a betrayal by those in charge locally.

For detectives, and particularly in terms of homicide, this makes resolving cases particularly difficult. Little faith in the justice system—a problem that transcends the role of police—and a lack of trust results in few witnesses stepping forward. Cases depend instead on other types of incontrovertible evidence like security camera footage. Stuck on the outside and looking in on a complex system of social relations, homicide detectives are engaged in an uphill battle to assert their authority over the conditions of life and death.

Not only that, processes of governance—codified in formalities of the drug trafficking business and in social convention—deter violence and limit the need to kill as the primary mode of punishment. As such, behind most dead bodies is a deep and nuanced history of punishment, moral regulation, and an idea of deservedness of death. For homicide detectives who appear only once a body ends up on the street, that history is obscured and difficult to access—even if known. Though they see many glimpses of this, and though some police are exposed to the reality of this kind of governance in their own neighborhoods, their capacity to reconstruct the course of events of a homicide, with all of its social workings and scaffoldings of power, is massively obstructed. This, of course, generates all manners of behavior, such as resignation to the likelihood of a negative outcome and anger and violence directed at those who, even police believe, escape from justice—the bandido.

CHAPTER 4

Resistências

On an afternoon in early 2012, Miguel was roused from his sleep by a noise outside his window. On the other side of the wall he heard a woman and a man in a rushed conversation. "Let go of your purse," the man said. Miguel grabbed his gun from his bedside table and got up to look out the window. Not fifteen feet away but lower down than he was he saw a man taking the woman's purse. He shouted for the thief to put his hands up. Then, he shot.

Miguel was an active but off-duty Military Police officer, resting from a graveyard shift the night before. As he told his story to the detective at the Homicide Division, it raised a few questions. Did he identify himself as a police officer before he shot? Why did he shoot if it wasn't clear that the now-dead man had a gun? Was his life, or the life of the woman, in imminent enough danger to merit pulling the trigger?

But for police detectives investigating the case these questions were all rather peripheral. Their answers were highly unlikely to reveal a bigger story or any ulterior motive. This was a rather open and shut case—a lucky case, really—in which a police officer was able to immediately foil a robbery in progress. There was no reason to doubt that the thief was in fact a thief. In fact, it was unlike a recent case involving a group of Military Police in which it was discovered by homicide detectives that the group had altered the crime scene, threatened witnesses, and concocted a dramatically different story. This case looked to be, by almost all intents, a more or less normal resistência. For the homicide detectives

FIGURE 7. Collecting evidence in the midst of crisis (photo by author).

this was nothing out of the ordinary. It would end up just as 546 cases did in 2012 alone—with at least one bandido dead and a policeman seen to be doing his job.[1]

As Brazil approaches thirty years since the end of the dictatorship, police seem no less lethal than in that much darker chapter of the past. Outside of institutional and path dependency suppositions about police violence, we continue to know little about why police kill so much and why. And despite major efforts to reform the status quo death at the hands of police continues to be mundane. I point toward two intertwined and prominent questions: How are resistências investigated? And, why, despite the Homicide Division's new mandate to investigate all these cases, has there been little substantive change in the practice of deadly policing?

Homicide detectives are wedged between these two sources of violence—police that kill citizens and the PCC. They are charged with investigating and regulating the killings of both groups—killings that occur everyday and usually multiple times a day (figure 7). Their practices, observations, and moral outlooks about the decentralized mode of violence in the city inform the decisions that they make about when life needs to be defended and when it does not. Though police, they are no more secure than anyone else. Their own sense of insecurity as residents of precisely the same subaltern spaces that lacked adequate policing—in fact any beneficent state presence—for so long is what made them good candidates for low paying jobs in the police bureaucracy. Now, mandated to make the city a safer place, their notions about the (il)legitimacy of some lives, embedded as they are in larger notions of good and evil, constitute the moral ground on which they survey when it is wrong and when it is right for police to kill. Their actions are both substantive and acute: their decisions convey the street-level practice of when the state believes it can kill and when it cannot.

The bandido—bandit, gangster, robber, drug trafficker, thug, criminal, thief—is a fixture in society, research, and life in urban Brazil. Studies of democracy, public participation, violence, marginality, space, clientelism, police reform, and social movements all point to the centrality of this individual in urban social relations.[2] Representations of the bandido are often crude and one-dimensional, deploying sweeping and dichotomizing notions of criminality, violence, and morality. But *he* is no primitive rebel or rural raider in the mold of Hobsbawm.[3] The bandido is a complex social formation that connects many realms of social relations. Wrapped up in this concept are productive processes of bodies, space, place, urban marginality, a built environment, illicit economies, and governance. The term *bandido* is deployed in a multitude of forms, each of which holds a key association with crime. The concept reveals an individual (*o bandido*), a social unit (*os bandidos*), an activity (*bandidagem*), a form of governance (*bandido social*), a form of belonging (*somos bandidos*), and a physical and typically racialized face (*cara de bandido*). Building on the work of Garcia (2009) and Misse (1999), I define the bandido as a differentiated social type, understood as inextricably and holistically criminal, being incapable of moral retrieval, and therefore as understood by many as the legitimate target of deadly violence on the part of the state.

Though the bandido is a plastic social category, it is often held to be static by police. It becomes, as a result, the basis of action and a moral justification for certain behaviors. For police—both those who kill citizens and the homicide detectives that investigate them—the bandido is an assumed category on which notions of innocence and deservedness of violent death hinge. Not only does this notion factor into who police kill, it underpins how homicide detectives mediate the identities and the deservedness of those who have been killed. Considerations of whether someone has the trademarks of a bandido help to shape whether police decide killings are legitimate or not, and whether they choose to pursue an investigation with extra diligence, to let certain doubts or holes in the story go unaddressed, or to take the more forceful step of arresting the police involved for homicide.

In their investigations homicide detectives typically assemble a narrative about the course of events that lead up to the moment in which the resistência occurred. They gather information from witnesses, the crime scene, criminal history (if any), kinds of weapons used or seized (if any) and other definitive personal features, such as tattoos. Each of these sources of information can contribute to a better understanding of the person killed. This is often contrasted with how the killing occurred—during a shootout with police or with evidence of execution—and other people involved, if seen to be innocent or not. Each of the categories of information can yield evidence, however subjective, about how to locate an individual vis-à-vis the bandido imaginary.

Police judgments about "bandidohood" are also rooted deeply in a dichotomy of good versus bad. This is operationalized in two different binaries: police versus bandido and *trabalhador* (worker) versus bandido. Police routinely justify—usually successfully—that their killing was "good" because it took one more bandido off the streets. As the trope goes: "Bandido bom e bandido morto"—a good bandido is a dead bandido. And when the going gets tough, as when the city is in the throes of violent crisis, some police simplify the equation: if you have a criminal record, you can be killed.

One police officer, who I'll call Diego, told me how this worked in the 2006 Mother's Day Attacks. After the PCC launched a series of assaults, killing 52 police in a three-day span, police went on a retaliatory spree. Research found that over the next three weeks 564 people ended up in the morgue with gunshot wounds.[4] Some of these killings were carried out by on-duty police. Other times marauding extermination groups were operating behind the scenes. Sometimes it was a more direct partnership between the two. At checkpoints throughout the city, armed and uniformed officers would stop residents to check their papers. Via radio, they would have colleagues run their name, *RG* (National Identification), and other documents like *Carteira de Motorista* (driver's license). Finding nothing, they would let the person go. When they found a criminal record, they would also let them go. In the process they would call ahead to off-duty police waiting around the corner. In assembly-line fashion, these police would eliminate the men as they came by.

Reports of the same kind of behavior also surfaced in the midst of the 2012 violence. The chief of the Civil Police summarized the ongoing dynamic: "In a number of past homicide crimes, we detected that the victims, before they died, had their criminal records checked by the police. This is very emblematic, but we've had some difficulty to figure out who it was that pulled the record for that victim. . . . but we checked this out and verified that this is exactly what happened" (*Folha de São Paulo* 2012a).

This linear connection between "evil" and "criminal" is what undergirds the notion of the bandido. Killing is often understood as a form of *limpeza* (cleansing) that eradicates the otherwise intractable and destabilizing problem of criminality and disorder. For the bandido, redemption is impossible; there is no *re* in *cidivism*. Evil is preordained. This binary divides society in unhelpfully stark and antagonistic ways.

In the work of police, and in broader social discourse, the bandido is also routinely defined in opposition to another socially constructed category—the trabalhador (worker). These two discursive imaginaries are the dominant public platforms for making sense of violence, particularly in the high-violence spaces in the *periferia* of this city. In public discourse, the trabalhador is gainfully employed, a positive contributor to society who, in spite of the hardship of finding and keeping a job, is morally opposed to taking short cuts through criminality. The worker respects the rights of others and has the "right to his rights" as a result (Feltran 2011, 24). Her life is valued, demanding protection from the arbitrariness of police violence that occasionally strays from its deserving subject. As a productive member of society, the worker may mobilize through democratically productive channels to make her claims, such as through NGOs, social movements, or union affiliations.

The bandido is much the opposite. As police explained on a number of occasions, he seeks the easy way to wealth and power that comes at the expense of others. He detracts from productive society by leeching from "good citizens" and "workers" by robbing and killing with no regard for life itself. He is indiscriminate, defying rules and relying on profits that devalue—if not kill—others. His reliance on violence is not understood as a mode of claim making but as a superficial search for status rooted in vices like sex, drugs, and violence.

This dichotomy is a useful tool for police. Both categories contain dualizing metrics enabling measurements and evaluations of their subjects. People who are gainfully employed, holding a *carteira de trabalho* (formal employment booklet), can be shown to be in the former category. They'll have a history of employment in the formal sector, a routine income with a bank account and no criminal record. The bandido has much the contrary—a criminal record, large amounts of cash, and no record of formal employment. Moreover, for police, only bandidos leave the house without their national ID card (*RG*) or any other identification. If you're arrested without documents, police take it as a signal of your intentions.

There is a sense that violent death is the destiny of a bandido. Police act on this notion. Mothers fear for their sons who choose to become criminals.[5] The media shows only a passing interest in reporting the deaths of those fitting the bandido mold—and only then to make the argument, usually implicitly, that a particular incident has removed two or three bad people from the earth. Much of what the idea of the bandido means, and how it is acted on, was captured one night while I was in the station:

> It is the dark of night, around 2:00 a.m. Police detectives are busy putting together the paperwork of a case that has just gone down. Some hours prior Military Police had shot and killed a young man. A call had come in: stolen car, last seen near the intersection of two streets in an eastern district of the city. Squad cars departed, canvassing the area. Within a short period, they found it rushing down a major road. They gave chase, forcing the car to spin out and blow a tire. Three youths jumped out. They shot one dead, hitting him six times—four times in the upper body and twice in the scrotum. The two others tried to flee, but were caught and arrested. They were then shepherded into a squad car and brought to the Homicide Division downtown.
>
> Now, they are handcuffed and standing against a wall. Their heads are downcast and their eyes mostly shut. They are around seventeen and eighteen years old. One has a red, orange, and black tattoo of a menacing carp spanning the length of his forearm. The other is wearing a hoodie, which is dried red with blood from an unknown wound on him or someone else. His leg is slightly malformed, probably from having a brush with polio as a child. They have been standing in this position for around four hours now, foreheads centimeters from the wall. In the same main room, detectives mull and sit at desks, taking statements from the Military Police—who likewise loiter carefree. All the police are unconcerned, taking the incident in stride. Some are bothered that this case will take so long since it involves people being arrested.[6] Usually these kinds of cases are easier. It is much simpler, and much more common when there aren't prisoners to process because there aren't any survivors. One police detective opines as much to me: "It should have been the opposite: two dead, one alive."
>
> Of course, they still need to visit the scene with crime scene analysts to take pictures, find the relevant bullet casings, and write a description of the scene. But when there are no surviving suspects they don't need to remand them into custody, to take fingerprints, statements, and in this case, to call their family to advise them their underaged sons have been arrested. Instead,

they would have just needed to apprehend the guns and important personal effects of the dead suspects, to take the guns of the police who shot, have gunshot residue swabs done and take statements for the report for filing in the intranet system.

Occasionally one of the suspects stretches, turns his head or coughs. Though they can hear everything, they know not to look up. Earlier in the evening one of them did, setting off a near riot that ended up with a wooden clipboard landing repeatedly and decisively on each of their heads. One police officer became totally incensed when one of the youths hollered to have them stop. He had an ear condition, he said, and the hitting would make it worse. This officer tore into him in a red-faced rage—how dare he use that as an excuse, he shouted to everyone and no one at the same time. "Don't tell me that," he bellowed, "you rob and kill. I have the same problem, but I don't rob and kill." "Yeah," chimed in another officer, "but maybe we should just call you the retard gang [*quadrilha dos deficientes*]—you two and your friend who has no balls left." "Next time that will be you," says another detective sitting at a desk and typing up a report at the back of the room.

Some time later a detective pulls me aside to ask if I know what the carp tattoo means. "It is associated with the PCC," he says. "Have you heard of them? Everyone knows they exist, but the state won't say it. They're involved in all sorts of things, like bus companies and samba schools. These young kids, who look so meek now, aren't just that simple. Outside they have no respect for anyone, marauding with guns to steal cars and rob women at gun point." "Se bobear, ta morto," with these kind of people, he says—if you hesitate with them, you're dead.

I move to stand near a detective who is taking a statement from one of the officers involved in the shooting. The case seems pretty clear cut to him. The way he sees it, the youth who was killed had exited the car and started to shoot. One of the others had a gun but didn't shoot. He dropped it after getting out the car. So he was alive. Police were right to shoot the now-dead youth, he claimed. He had resisted arrest, meriting a decisive response.

"I have to ask this," says the detective to one of the police officers involved in the shooting, "for them (pointing upstairs) and the records. How many killings [resistências] have you been involved in?" The officer responds with a whim: nine. At a desk adjacent, the other team of homicide detectives is now working on a different police killing. I'm told it has something to do with one bandido dead and two that got away.

The paperwork is dragging on. It is going on four hours of work, with at least two remaining. Military Police play musical chairs, filing in and sitting to give their statements before getting up to stand and talk with colleagues across the room, down the hall, or out by the elevators. Someone comes in to ask when the report will be ready. The family needs it to take to the Coroner (Instituto Médico Legal) to have the body released for the funeral. A police detective named Francisco, gets up to talk with them. As he walks down the hallway, I follow him, passing by one of the police officers who had shot the youth.

Outside the doorway to the division are three or four chairs. Three mothers sit in them surrounded by one or two other family members each. Across from them are a group of the police who were involved in the shooting. They stop talking amongst themselves to listen in. I notice that today there aren't any witnesses loitering in the group while waiting to give their statement as well. Francisco approaches the mothers. "Who is the mother of Andre?" he asks. One woman raises her hand. She has dry eyes and a look of resignation. "Do you know each other?" he asks the mothers. They shake their heads. "Did you know Andre, Ricardo, and Felipe to be friends?" he asks each of them. They shake their heads again. No. The other police look on, severe in their dark blue-grey uniforms and berets. Francisco says nothing. He later tells me they were obviously lying.

The report is still hours from being finished, Francisco tells them. You can wait if you want, he says, but it might just be better to come back in the morning. It needs to be picked up by an immediate family member but not necessarily by you. The family decides to wait for the report. There is no public transport home at this hour and there will be heavy traffic coming back this way in the morning rush.

As we step away to move back inside, a group of other detectives file out with the two young men in handcuffs. They're headed to the elevators. They are all on their way to Fundação Casa, the juvenile detention system. Upon seeing her son, one of the mothers begins to sob. Porque?! She shouts at him. Why!? To my own shock, I realize she is shouting at her son. It wasn't that she wasn't mad at the police, but rather, it seemed to me that she could see her son's future in the fate of the young man he had been with.

In the eyes of the police, and of the detectives that investigate them, these two surviving young men were prototypical of the bandido. They were caught in the midst of a crime, had guns and fit well within age, gender, racial, and spatial lines of *bandidismo*. One had even already been through the juvenile detention system for armed robbery. The tattoo on the other was a dead giveaway, or so they chose to believe.

All of these markers meant that they were easily slotted into the metaimaginary of those who destabilize the city. Cast as being responsible for the vulnerability of good citizens and police themselves, these two were sitting ducks to scorn. Given the chance to reestablish some authority over "evil," police took it by degrading, hitting, and threatening those they perceived as the emissaries of their own vulnerability.

Police are violent, at least in part, because they feel violated and insecure. In their jobs they fail dramatically to overcome crime. And then at home, in the lower-income and spatial margins of the city, they must often find ways to coexist with those same forces being stronger than they are. In this city, most low-level police live in or alongside the kinds of spaces controlled by the PCC. Many grew up in places like Ângela as Beto did, having found their way into careers as police officers after surviving the violence of their youth. With some light at the end of the tunnel, they studied like mad to pass public entry exams.

This didn't necessarily get them out of the violent spaces, however. The salary of entry-level police in São Paulo puts them in the fourth of five socioeconomic classes (five being the lowest), as defined by the national statistics institute, IBGE. Entry-level police detectives make between $1,050 and $1,300 USD a month. Upward career mobility is not possible without retaking public exams, and the difference between the salary of year one and year thirty at end of career for an *investigador* is $320.[7] Police note that, for a family, it is very difficult to get by—their salary pushes them into (or holds them in) the types of urban spaces that all too often are under the regime of the PCC.

Life in these circumstances is complicated. The rules of the PCC stipulate that interaction with police is not allowed and collusion is punishable by severe beating or death. For ordinary residents, reporting crimes to police is also heavily frowned on, carrying consequences of potential violence and distrust in the community. Not only that, residents are highly suspicious of police because of memorable incidents of extrajudicial killings and ongoing patterns of extortion. For residents, police have always been unpredictable. You never know if they will beat you up, extort you, threaten to kill you, or show up later on a motorbike, wielding a gun and wearing a black balaclava.

These sentiments and perceptions about who all police are also make it difficult for police themselves. To avoid suspicion and unwanted attention in their home communities, they often pretend they are not a police officer. Many either conceal their identities or use their second or third jobs to suggest they are something other than police—a taxi driver, a dentist, an engineer, a furniture upholsterer, or a private security guard.[8] In order to survive, police must avoid tipping the everyday balance between the PCC and police that allows for relative nonviolence and predictability to prevail. To speak out, to act violently, or to attempt to repress the activities of the PCC is to isolate yourself and to draw a Palm Sunday–like crosshair on your own forehead. And so, many police find solutions by compromising.

One solution is to try to become invisible, forgotten, or overlooked. For some police, making this kind of sacrifice is just part of the job description. As a detective named Fernando told me once, it takes a deep personal dedication to get and maintain a stable state salary in a place torn apart with violence: "As young guys, we used to go hang out on the street and drink beers with our friends and relax. You know, at night.

We'd be there, no worries at all. But when you're a police, you can't do that. You need eyes on the back of your head [*ficar esperto*]. You never know when someone is going to come after you because of who you are. You always have to be alert. And you can't do that just hanging out on the street."

And yet, there is more to police insecurity than just trying your best to avoid public spaces and coping with the idea that people will want to do you wrong. It isn't always possible to stay inside or to hide from targeted violence. When there are long histories of acquaintance, respect, or kinship, because people have grown up together or even become family, it is impossible to be invisible and forgotten.

Public life and camaraderie is a key aspect of belonging that often precedes and rides underneath police identities. Setting aside deadly differences can be part and parcel of getting along in tricky circumstances. This requires a more active sort of negotiation in which two otherwise repelling forces choose to find peace beneath the storm clouds of violence. One police officer portrayed these everyday circumstances:

> Here we don't live in favelas. We live near them, but we don't live in them. Still you see the *traficante* [drug trafficker] at the corner bar. You know, he's there, you're here [pointing]. You'll have a beer together, hug each other [*abraçar*], and exchange small talk. It doesn't much matter that down the street you are Mr. X and he is Mr. Y. It is a cold war. A cold war. You know who each other are but you're from the same place. You take off your uniform before you come home and you know that if he goes over the top [*vai pra cima*], you will too.

If police can manage their own insecurity by negotiating directly with those that may target them, they have more difficulty protecting themselves from the ambient criminality in the city. This threat is much more diffuse and invasive. There is no safety even in the home, the only place outside of the station where police sometimes feel secure. This experience of insecurity is fed by the circulation of stories among the police about police homes being invaded. These stories carry compelling undertones of vulnerability that resonate widely. One police officer related, "The other day one of my family members, who is a police officer and so is his wife, had his house broken into. When the criminals saw one of his police shirts, they went crazy. Beat them all up. The only reason they didn't kill them, they said, is because the kids were there." He continued, "I have nothing in my house, no items or vestiges that show that I'm a police. It has to be that way. I've gotten rid of everything. The only thing that is there is my gun and my badge, but I keep them hidden.

Because when they break in and see that I'm police I know it is over. I've even told my son that if someone breaks in when we are there, that he should tell them that I teach history in the public school. He understands that he can't say I'm a police . . . and it confuses him, but what can you do?"

Not that this is an extreme reaction. The possibility of violence motivates police to adapt their routines profoundly. Not only that, police sometimes willingly set aside their role as a state-adorned authority figure because doing so actually makes them more secure. Being passive in the face of criminality, to turn a blind eye—*ficar de olho grosso*—is one way to avoid being singled out. Given the structural paradigm of violence, resignation to the consequences and individual pragmatism often prevails.

But pragmatism isn't just an everyday solution either. It also dominates during periods of acute crisis, when the public security system is systemically failing. Even then, police often decide to make sure that they and their loved ones are safe, above all else. Speaking about the PCC attacks in May 2006, one detective who worked at the Homicide Division at the time had this to say, "They told us to stay at the office . . . that we needed to be there. It was safer. But I was like, 'Fuck that. My mother is home alone. I need to get back to make sure she is okay at my house.' I didn't know if they were going to break in there and shoot the place up. Once I got home and saw she was okay, we locked up the house and barricaded ourselves inside. I came back to work the next day."

When the failure of the system is exposed, police are often the first to flee from its supposedly protective umbrella. In these moments the fallacy of the "public good" behind public security system is most starkly shown. When the system fails for police, livelihood and survival become the primary rationale.

It should come as little surprise that while some police choose to be more passive in the face of violence, others react differently. Some police use violence to stare down their insecurity, and even, as a bonus, to make some money on the side. Extermination groups have clear self-protection rationales, particularly when composed of police in a spatial constituency. Areas of work or residence, or both, often help define these constituencies. Not that space is the only defining characteristic. Any combination of factors can serve as a modus for organization against bandidos. Similar training, a common class background, collective histories of coping with violence, a moral outlook gained from a state-enshrined mandate of authority, the modes of masculinity that are associated with this authority, shared notions of risk—both on the job and off—access to guns, the allure of a security economy, and taking the hope for a more peaceful society into their own hands can all serve as platforms for police rallying in violent ways. Yet working out of the shadows these groups often employ a "cleansing" (*limpeza*) modus operandi aimed at eliminating bandidos—their professional and personal nemesis of insecurity.

The linkage between police experiences of insecurity and the killing of bandidos isn't always this clear however. Structural conditions often push police from nonviolent to violent realms of action. Police who prefer nonviolence are often placed in circumstances where they have little choice but to shoot and kill. The regularity of killing contributes to it being understood not as a practice to be avoided, but rather, as a more or less inevitable practice that is part and parcel of controlling the bandidos who threaten the city, its "good" citizens, and the police.

The inevitability of killing citizens pulls in police who envision other solutions. Police who may seek to avoid killing citizens, either because they disagree with the simplicity of the crime-equals-evil equation, because they are inexperienced, or because they simply don't aspire to engage with this notion of successful policing, are likely to get dragged into the reality of resistência as "solution." Much in contrast to other contexts, there is almost no way out of killing citizens. Resistências are validated, expected, and institutionally ordained as normal, becoming in a crude way, a whether-you-like-it-or-not rite of passage. Killing is as much a moral outlook as it is part and parcel of surviving as a police officer. This dynamic was well illustrated in one case involving a police officer that I call Rafael:

> Rafael came into the homicide department on account of a resistência that had happened earlier that night. It was late and he had been closing up his sister's store—a very modest shop in a very modest community where they sold candy and other sweets at a cottage scale. The retractable metal door was partly pulled down and Rafael was tallying the money earned from the day. It was night and, being off duty, he was in plainclothes. Gun in hand, a young man burst in through the door. Confusion ensued and Rafael was at a loss to explain what came next. In the aftermath, the young man lay dead on the ground, shot nine times.
>
> Rafael lived down the street, in what a detective described to me as "one of the worst parts of São Paulo." This community, which I call Villa Andre, was "horrible," he said, almost certainly among the most awful places in the city. And yet, this community was also less than a couple of kilometers away from some of the most expensive gated communities in all of Brazil—where personal helicopter traffic buzzes from morning and night. I asked Rafael if there were other police that lived in this neighborhood. "Many," he said,

"I was born there, and so I see it differently than most people see it." Poor it was, he implied, but it was still the place where he grew up, had family, friends, and now that he was a police officer, police colleagues. Was it unsafe? Yes. He put it in a rather self-incriminating binary: "There are basically two choices for police that live in Villa Andre. Become a criminal or leave the community—except it is too hard to get out, and so you make do. All the police that live in the community grew up there. None moved there after the fact."

Later in my conversation with the head homicide detective, he explained that in Rafael's shooting of the man, he saw someone "making do." Rafael was a young police officer. This was his first resistência. He was nervous and so he just kept on shooting, even after the man was on the ground. Was this an *abuso* [an abuse of force]? Maybe, if strictly speaking.

The detective told me about a recent case of a police officer being killed after a home invasion. He had been shot just because the suspect had seen his police uniform they said. This kind of thing was bad for police, who end up feeling scared and sometimes reacting rashly to violence. He segued the discussion to another case he had worked like Rafael's. There was some doubt about whether in a particular resistência, the officer had gone too far in killing an assailant. As he debated with other detectives whether the police officer should have done what he did, the phone rang. It was a notification of another case, just like the other one, but where the police officer was dead and the assailant long gone.

The detective continued on with his interpretation of Rafael's case: he was worried about the number of shots. Nine was a lot to come from one police officer. It was a bit excessive. But he seemed to trust Rafael. "He was nervous," he told me. Shooting someone is a big deal, and it is hard to control yourself—especially when it happens in your own place. "He did go too far, but he will learn how to defend himself properly." When all the paperwork was done, he went to have a word with Rafael about what was going to happen next. "You're aware the prosecutor is going to notice how many shots you fired," he said, "You need to practice." Just tell the prosecutor the truth; that this is your first resistência. You were nervous because it was your first time. Next time don't shoot as many times, and just aim for the middle.

Another group of police filed in to the room, related to another resistência that had recently occurred. Having heard about Rafael's case, these other police had questions to ask. "Quem matou o bandido? [Who killed the bandido?]" asked one. Rafael stood up to acknowledge. "It was you? Congratulations, my man!" beamed the incoming officers.

Killing is routine, institutionally appreciated, and as many police understand it, it serves an important function—to make them all more secure. The inexperience of Rafael is made to seem temporary. The next time he has to kill—which he almost certainly will—he'll be much more effective. He'll kill in such a way that it reflects the need of police to have a feeling of control over their security situation while at the same time not raising the ire of those concerned about police killings.

But in empirical terms, killing is a reflection of the real or perceived failure of the public security system. This system is itself a vicious circle for police that wraps together paradoxical kinds of police action. Conflicting police practices—killing, on the one hand, and the need to hide or defer to drug traffickers, on the other—is at the heart of Rafael's story.

For so long, Rafael was squarely in one category of police behavior: trying to just get by in the face of violence. As so many other police, he was confined to one of "the worst places in São Paulo," yielding to the real and imagined threats of the bandidos governing his community. Just as other police described their own lives to me, he was one of countless others who needed to "dry his uniform behind the fridge"—far from public view. With this shooting, in a situation in which he had determined that he had little other choice but to shoot, Rafael "matured" into a police officer of a different order: one who kills.

The question, then, is not why police officers kill so much. Rather, it illuminates a set of conditions that allow—and perhaps even necessitate—this kind of violence. The ability of police to respond with nonviolence, or to seek proactive and peaceful solutions, is dampened when the structural conditions of violence come walking in the front door. Rafael's experience is a study in contrast, not just between two predominant kinds of police behavior, but also of the greater social context. In a world where police need to hide, and to kill, a yawning gap exists between democratic expectations of them and the capacity of police to respond to the hopefulness of a better world.

When it comes to police killings of citizens, detectives must balance the blunt and bloody reality of police insecurity. They often understand this world via a kill-or-be-killed binary, rooted in their own notions of justice. Though police killings may appear to outsiders to run unchecked, there are modes of accountability and contrasting notions of the "appropriateness" of death. Police can kill illegitimately, and it is the role of the homicide detective—backed by the underwhelming power of internal affairs, prosecutors. and his peers, as well as middling methods of evidence collection—to draw the line between an appropriate and an inappropriate resistência. This process of adjudication is deeply informed by the imaginary of the bandido. Resistência investigations are underpinned by these two conditions—the insecurity of police themselves, which is perceived to come from bandidos—and whether the person killed by police can be located in either the bandido or trabalhador category.

The strength of these categories can shift the outcomes of cases, even in spite of the initial hunches and evidence available to detectives. Even where there are strong indications that a police killing may have happened in problematic ways, the imagery of a man lying dead with the hallmarks of the bandidismo can push detectives toward the status quo. As one case suggested:

I was traveling with the homicide detectives to a part of town knowing that in the recent weeks there had been a number of bus burnings and a handful of assassination attempts on police. In the midst of the most recent PCC-police violence, this place had made the news a bunch of times. Today though, there was only one resistência here. One man was dead, shot by a bunch of police after he apparently attempted to break in to a house. But within a few minutes of arriving at the scene, things didn't quite seem like they had been reported in the official message. The homicide detective in charge caught on to a hole in the story that differentiated starkly from that we had heard from police. When the call about the incident first came, not to the Homicide Division but to a local police, it was because local residents reported someone trying to break in to a house. Residents of the area had caught the man, who they knew, and beat him to try to teach him a lesson. He was a crack addict, they said, and was known to be involved in low-level crime from time to time. They didn't like him much, but they weren't scared of him either.

The actual crime scene where the man was killed by police was on a different street, further down a different road. It was there that this man had apparently exchanged gunshots with police, ending up dead after being shot eleven times. His body, as nearly all others killed in resistências, had been rushed to the hospital where he was pronounced dead. For the detective, the story didn't jive for a couple of reasons. If this was the same man who was beaten by residents just minutes before his death, where did he get his gun from? There was no report that he was armed and, certainly, residents wouldn't have beaten him if he had a gun. Not only that, there was no evidence of his gun being shot at the scene where he died. If he had shot at the police, which they claimed he did, he had missed everything—walls, houses, and police. "Even if he didn't have a gun," said the detective, in a hushed voice but less than twenty feet from the police from the same unit that was guarding the scene, "the police will say he did. Which is the sad thing, because one of these cops will probably end up in jail."

The homicide detectives walked past the police who were involved, always courteous but tight lipped about what they observed. I could feel an air of suspicion, on both parts, even as friendly banter was exchanged. At one point, one of the police started talking to me about some attacks on police that had happened a day earlier on the other side of the city. It was deeply unnerving. Within a half an hour of arriving at the scene we were back in the Blazer, scene scoured, photos taken, and on our way to the hospital.

Our next stop was at the morgue. An attendant came down to the back door to let us in. The room smelled like cleanser. Beside a granite table was a trolley with a body bag on it. One of the detectives stepped over and unzipped the bag. Peeling it back revealed a man around thirty years old, perforated and bloody with bullet holes. His lean brown body looked weathered from scarcity, drug use, and/or prison. His hair was short. On his shoulders, hands and legs he had a number of tattoos: a black and white ying-yang, a scraggly spider's web, and another illegible and hastily done image on his shoulder. On his feet he had a series of barely legible letters—of the quality done by hand with pins and pen ink in prison, one detective pointed out. Each of these was symbolic. The ying-yang was the giveaway—an unmistakable trademark as spray painted on the walls of favelas, during prison riots, and headlining PCC Facebook and YouTube pages.

The tone shifted as the police took pictures of the body. "Those police probably wanted him dead," the detective told me later as we ate lunch. "When we pull his record, we'll find he's wanted for something, maybe even killing a cop." The lucidity with which he had earlier seen and interrogated the holes in this case had given way to disinterest. The imagery of this man and the power of the symbols that adorned his body—prison, crime, drugs, dead police—destabilized the momentum towards finding the pith of the issue. The people involved in beating this guy were already at the station giving their statements, so that story would come out. There was no need now to push the issue. He'd let this case fall to another detective further down the line. They could decide about the guilt of the police involved. For now, he had decided that this situation—this man—wasn't worth proactively ending a police person's [or persons'] career over—not with what could be deduced about the dead man from his own appearance.

Make no mistake, homicide detectives are sympathetic to the challenges faced by police that kill. They are inclined to understand the rationale of these police much more than they are likely to appreciate and align with pressures for nonviolence. For detectives there is a fine line between locating the actions of police as immoral and thus worthy of punishment and viewing a resistência as appropriate because it occurred in reaction to a threat to the life—very broadly defined—of police. Responsibility for arresting police means distinguishing between the omnipresent threat to the lives of police, and police who kill with a nefarious motive other than that which is in the interest of the security of police.

This has been heightened by some new factors, such as access to technology. The regularity of police killings of citizens, and PCC killings of police, combined with a decentralized security environment in which private security cameras grab much of the urban world, has meant a proliferation of videos of violent death. On demand, anyone can watch a police officer or a PCC member being executed.[9] These videos lay bare the vulnerability and cruelty of both of these groups while also lending a degree of humanity to victimhood.

One evening in the station I noticed Beto watching a two-tone video on YouTube. The video was ripped from a security camera in a hotel in downtown São Paulo. As we watched, the video showed a hooded young man walk up the stairs into the reception area. Not recognizing the threat at first, the attendant approaches the man, who pulls a gun. For a few minutes, they appear to talk as the receptionist pulls the money from behind the counter. Some time later, the man walks down the stairs, cash in his pockets. Seconds later, though, he comes back up. This time, followed by a police officer, gun in hand. The man tries to take the receptionist hostage by standing behind him, but the receptionist keeps him from pulling up his gun. They tussle, and the police officer manages to get a clear shot. He shoots, then shoots again. The hostage flees and the man falls behind the counter. The police officer reaches over the desk and keeps shooting, his hands visibly trembling. The man slowly stops moving and dies while lying on the floor behind the counter. The video flashes to a news anchorwoman. She concludes the story: "The man, 29 years old, had a criminal record. The case was registered as an attempted robbery and resisting arrest followed by death."[10] Beto says to me, "I heard this police officer was arrested. But it looks like a good resistência to me. He was scared. You can see his hand shaking when he is about to shoot." It was unclear to me what Beto took away from watching the video, except perhaps a heightened sensation of vulnerability to both violence and the internal affairs division.

The uncertainty of violence is unnerving to these detectives, who feel persecuted on two sides. On the one hand, there is a loud and raucous population pushing for a police that respects human rights, are more accountable, and much less violent. On the other hand, there is a vocal sector of society that sees police killings as the only means of ridding the city of criminality. And yet both of these groups overlook the very personal impact of violence on police officers. Once a police officer leaves the station he or she can't leave the images and experience of violence behind. Outside the station and off duty, the reality of that violence is much more acute, and their actions in response are often deeply scrutinized.

Though some police avoid violence by leaving all vestiges of police identity in the station, others choose to carry their gun with them at all times. This is their way of feeling safer. When a police officer uses a gun off duty, because they are held up or stumble across a crime in progress, it is rarely scrutinized in detail—even if there is evidence of excessive force. It is assumed that if a criminal confronts a police officer, he can respond by killing the assailant—just as in the case of Rafael. These kinds of cases are routine, even mundane.

> One evening in the homicide department, a call came in about two resistências. Two teenage boys had robbed an off-duty police detective as he sat in his parked car on the street where a family member lived. The two boys had told him it was a robbery and shouted for him to get out of the car. In the process, though, they saw his gun wedged between his leg and the seat. One of the boys fired a shot, but it missed. The detective responded. He shot five times, hitting one of the boys in the head and killing him instantly. The other boy was found dead down the street and around the corner, shot four times. The investigation barely went that far. Homicide detectives took his statement. Because there were no witnesses, he was the only one with a story, augmented only by five photos, a gunshot residue swab on the detective and the teenagers, and the statements given by the police who responded after the shooting. There was no way to know—nor much interest in—the details. There was no need to ask questions. This was straightforward.

Sometimes detectives make the decision to arrest police for killing citizens inappropriately. When police arrest their peers, it is typically a product of weighing the circumstances and surveying the evidence at hand. It does not necessarily mean that police have killed a trabalhador or someone other than a "deserving" bandido. They occasionally arrest police for killing bandidos, too. At the heart of the matter is the amount of discretion and freedom to decide that homicide detectives have. Detectives operate with a large discretionary space. They can choose to investigate diligently, or not. Analysis of blood spatter patterns or different blood types at the scene is rarely, if ever, undertaken. They can, however, call for blood, drug, brain matter, subfingernail, and other exams at their discretion. Only one of these exams is mandatory—gunshot residue for police involved in a resistência. They can choose to sympathize with their fellow police, or to disagree with them and dig deeper for more evidence. It is their decision to search for witnesses and contradictory statements, or to only use the word of the police involved. They make all of these decisions based on their own understanding of the story—or stories— that presents itself to them. The more they appear to make sense, conveying a logical sequence of events, the less likely the detectives are to seek alternative hypotheses. In many cases, it doesn't much matter what the outcomes are, because either the person is dead—a subject of a resistência—or he is one of the thousands of homicides that go "uncleared" in the city every year. Oversight of police detectives, in other words, ranges from weak and undemanding to nonexistent.[11] The single most important resource for a homicide detective is his moral compass.

The puzzle, then, is why police will occasionally make decisions to subvert the status quo, to support people that conform to dominant notions of the bandido and to arrest their fellow police for something that they do routinely otherwise. The large discretionary space and the lack of dependence on evidence means that police make their decisions by drawing heavily on their own moral position. It rests on the shoulders of individual detectives to determine whether they agree or disagree with a particular case, and whether the actions of police merit arresting them for homicide. For this reason, not all homicide detectives choose to arrest police. Many do, however, finding ways to hold up a different moral standard in the face of divergent pressures, most notably from other police, the PCC, and even more, civil society and new public accountability agencies.

To get the outcome that he or she wants, homicide detectives often need to cobble together solutions for gaps that become prominent because of a lack of evidence, the unwillingness of someone to talk, or resistance from a group of police that shelter their colleagues. Since these detectives are almost always set up to fail, they need to be highly proactive to find success. An imbalance in power between influential police agencies like ROTA and the Tactical Force, whose role is understood as killing bandidos, overshadows the mandate of homicide detectives. The regular need to question the activity of these deadly agencies means that detectives must have a compelling and outstanding case in order to take the step of arresting police from these places. Failing that, they may need to find alternative channels to satisfy their notion of justice. This puts them in an unenviable David versus Goliath position, where the inclination is to agree with Goliath rather than to throw stones. Overturning the dominant notion of deservedness of death, taking a gatekeeper or two with it, is no small task—but it does occur.

Homicide detectives do take pride in their job—even if that job is nearly impossible to do. Occasionally they are held up as examples of moral righteousness and diligence for solving certain cases or choosing to stand up to police that kill citizens. One police officer told me about the challenges of being placed in a position that exposes you as a relative enemy to the two different groups. Months earlier a detective had arrested a number of police for a so-called resistência in which the police claimed they were defending themselves from a viable threat. More recently, he had been at the heart of a major case in which police from another high profile SWAT-like unit had been arrested for executing a member of the PCC. These police had ferreted out the PCC member, bringing him into the street. In the process, one of the police decided to end it all right there. He raised his gun and shot the PCC member in the head. He failed to kill him however, and an amateur video taken at the time shows him running away down the street, only to eventually end up dead at a local hospital labeled as a "john doe."

The higher-ups in the system wanted someone to take credit for the arrest of the group. "The secretary for public security wanted me to do a press conference. There's no way I want to be recognized for that," the detective told me. Instead of being propped up as positive example of antiviolence, it was much safer to stay in the shadows. In situations like this, where police have been so violent, and there is evidence to show that they overstepped their powers, it is a challenging situation. On the one hand, the detective can decide to overlook some evidence or other factors—but be left to reconcile with his own conscience. On the other, he can arrest police for killing someone that he may agree is deserving of death—something that might even make him feel just a little bit safer. He summed up the predicament pithily, "I'm screwed if I do it, and I'm screwed if I don't" (*se faço, me ferro, se não faço, me ferro*). In a world that pits two relative evils against each other, these detectives go looking for the lesser. This isn't because they are pawns that bow in the face of pressures. Rather, they find ways to uphold their hunches—be that in letting hundreds of bandidos die a year, or as they occasionally choose, to find video that allows them to rid the streets of the "corrupt cops that make it hard for the rest of us."

Arrests of police that kill citizens are neither routine nor exceptional. They do not evoke a new era of police accountability. The overriding considerations are too great and too widely shared among police. Not only that, the Homicide Division has gained a reputation among all police. Alongside the internal affairs division, they are seen less as colleagues with whom to share information or to joke around with and more as adversaries to keep at arms length. The Homicide Division's ugly stepchild position within the public security system is nothing less than a reflection of the value the system gives to life in general. As long as the Homicide Division is the place where police careers are born and go to die in relative infamy—an inversion of what theories of sovereignty might suggest—their capacity to regulate the killings of both police and the PCC will be muted.

Resistências continue to be used as a vital tool of policing because they are believed to be the only way to manage a population of bandidos that are understood to be beyond moral retrieval. The alternative,

to lock them up indeterminately in prison, is to feed the cycle of violence emergent from the depths of prison injustice that started the mess
in the first place. Moreover, police believe that this population is responsible for insecurity, both as experienced by all citizens in the city and in
their own vivid everyday individual police struggles for safety. The bandido is at the center of a complex imaginary of urban violence. It is *the*
hegemonic lens through which criminality is framed in broader society
and by police in particular. The imaginary of the bandido structures police practice as though sifting through the population to separate which
citizens can and cannot be killed.

CHAPTER 5

The Killing Consensus

In March 2012, a leaked report from the Intelligence Division of the Civil Police surfaced on prime time television. News anchors from one of the largest television networks laid out the report's findings: organized crime and the elite unit of the Military Police, ROTA, were in league. Seeking to avoid scrutiny, the PCC was paying members of the ROTA to kill those whom they wanted dead. The ROTA was carrying out these killings under the guise of resistências. The report outlined a scenario in which a number of recent ROTA resistências were hired killings being paid for by the PCC. Disguised as routine police activity, and less methodically investigated as a result, these killings benefitted both parties. Police were paid handsomely, while the PCC could maintain its power and stay out of the limelight. Not just that, the PCC could simultaneously curry favor with a police agency that, quite paradoxically, had been vociferous and widely celebrated in its violent role fighting organized crime.

This leaked report is one suggestion of the ways that the killing of the PCC and ROTA coincide. But this collusion is rarely as public or overt as what was concluded in the Civil Police report—if true. For the most part, this dynamic is more obscured, playing out implicitly at the everyday level of resistências, homicides, and assassinated police. Between the PCC's regulation of death and the police's killing of bandidos, it is evident that the state does not uniquely preside over the regulation of killing. Rather, that "right" is exercised first and foremost by the PCC, but nested within the normative apparatus of the state. In other words, those who are formally mandated to limit violent death, homicide detectives, benefit from, and in many senses depend on, the PCC's regulation of death as a means to limit how many people are dying in homicides in the city. If the PCC was not such a strong regulator, the Homicide Division would be at the center of a highly visible public security crisis.

The governance of killing has a deeply normative and moral foundation. The killing practice of both of these groups envisions a similar and expendable subject. As long as the PCC's killing does not step outside a set of normative bounds, their control over the conditions and regulations of life and death in many parts of the city are implied. That is, their influence is more or less accepted, presumed, and taken for granted by homicide detectives and the state apparatus more widely.

The idea of a bounded and expendable or marginal group that is defined by their right to be killed without consequence—and the ways that sovereign power is reflected in the ability to define what killing is exceptional in that regard—has been thoroughly and widely theorized. Yet most accepted theorizations are premised on an assumption of centralized power and control by a sovereign of the territory in question. The margins are seen as passive. They rarely grapple with the possibility of a second group, emergent from the margins that *also* governs the margins. Much less does theory come to grips with that second group becoming an integral part of the larger structure of violence and social control. Put differently, if the focus of much scholarship has been on structural, institutionalized, or symbolic violence, with the state implicitly or explicitly at the core of such assertions, the PCC represents a new—but also complementary—structure of violence in and of marginality.

In São Paulo, the expendable subject is a product of such a dual—but not indistinct—system. These two powers are not "naturally" antagonistic as they may seem at first glance. Rather, they are morally and practically nested, operating in mutually beneficial and symbiotic ways. Under this configuration, who can live and who may die, and the relative stability of this outlook as "normal," hinges on the moral overlap between (a) those charged with regulating death within the state—either through investigation of violent death or the act of killing—and (b) the moral system of the PCC. Parallel notions of legitimate killing agglomerate in such a way as to define and create a de facto and pseudostate dominion over the right to kill.

That who can live and who may die is decided in a de facto partnership between the state and an organized crime group should raise eyebrows.

That the PCC has become the mechanism regulating how many people can die—having, as it were, contributed to a *massive* and internationally recognized decline in homicides in the city—is problematic for more than just the thinking on the definitions and governance of the conditions of life and death. It also sets in motion a cyclical pattern of calm and crisis, where explosions of violence occur as the consensus is ruptured and periods of relative calm and predictability resume when it recouples.

This nested configuration of the formal state and the PCC can be separated into two dynamics in particular. First, these two distinct logics of killing operate in conjuncture. Under this configuration, there is a preference for a *predictability* of killing in which one can exercise a degree of control over a more complete or monopolized security on one hand, or the total instability or unpredictability of violence on the other. This arrangement is subsumed in long periods of *relative peace.* Second, this consensus can be "killed"—breaking apart with, and into, violence. In these circumstances, the two prominent sources of killing in the city, the PCC and police, turn their attention away from the forms of equilibria, to attack each other directly. This sends both the number of homicides and the toll of assassinated police through the roof. These moments of large-scale upheaval—May 2006 and the latter half of 2012—result in waves of retribution killings, playing out in PCC affiliates killing police, police killing suspected PCC members in resistências, and shadowy extermination groups, made up of off-duty police, engaging in multiple-homicide cleansings. In these moments, each group struggles to reestablish some semblance of control through violence, as the predictability of consensus killing and the expendable subject is shattered.

If the normal is relative peace and the exception is crisis, the normal is often visible in the exceptional. Exceptional moments of upheaval can be highly localized, not destabilizing the city—and beyond—as occurred in 2006 and 2012. Such a case occurred in 2010:

> Word spread quickly in the community sandwiched between a rail line and a swamp. They said that the man had sexually abused his daughter and three other children. People were in an uproar. Lynching was a real possibility, before the PCC guys came and took the man away to a remote location. There they organized a tribunal and discussed punishment. The mothers of the children and the children themselves participated. The conclusion was predictable for this kind of crime—he was briefly tortured before being killed, likely by having his head cut off from his body. Not that his body was anywhere to be found at first. Normally, this kind of treatment for a sex offender would be rather unexceptional. According to the PCC's moral rubric,

the punishment must be proportional to the crime—in this case a shocking and painful crime deserved a shocking and painful response. This kind of response was normal and accepted, if not applauded, by a constituency for which sexual crime involving children were among the worst crimes that can be committed.

But unlike other incidents with the same result for the same crime, this incident became far from normal. This was for one reason: the man that the PCC judged and subsequently killed was the brother of a Military Police officer. There was discord about who should be in charge, and the Military Police were hot under the collar. For two weeks the brother and his colleagues sowed terror in the community as they searched for the body. At first, it was humiliation, punches, kicks, and the like directed not just at young men, but at women, the elderly, and children for their supposed unwillingness to share information about the body. According to some media accounts, a head was found with eyes removed, serving both as a response to police demands and an unmistakable provocation.

The pressure grew. After sixteen days of *sofrimento*—"suffering," as one resident put it—there was a decisive response. Late one evening, two motorcycles carrying two men each cornered a Military Policeman in his car. With automatic machine guns they shot and killed him in the driver's seat—at least ten bullets hitting his body. The situation exploded. The night later five people were assassinated in the poor neighborhood where the alleged child abuser had been taken from. Days later, five more. Schools closed for the rest of the week. In total, some twenty-three people would be killed in feudlike fashion that masked—but only in an ultra thin veil—the actions of the two parties. The violence would only cease when arrests were made—not of anyone involved in the initial tribunal or the police killing—but of a group of police that responded. Eighteen military police officers were carted to prison, de facto strengthening the PCC's system of governance and authority.

This case never destabilized an entire city. But in its exceptionality it does reveal a great deal about what things are *usually* like. There is, for the most part, very little that is done to question PCC authority. Rather, the status quo is more or less obvious: the PCC resolves problems in ways that police cannot or do not, making them a much more legitimate actor in the communities they have thus come to control. More than that, though, when there are responses from the public security system to feuding and violence between police and the PCC, it tends to be the police who are more tightly regulated. After all, it is the police who are expected to serve and protect according to a democratic system of rules and accountability.

In normal times, though, not much of this is even visible. When violence is not about *law making*, it tends to be quiet, presumed. The everyday and normal relative peace allows for certain people to die as part and parcel of a specific moral alignment of appropriate death. Child molesters may—in fact, should—die. That the police cannot follow through on such a position, but the PCC will without apology, shows a nested relationship in which the larger moral system legitimates the killing of such a subject, which is then carried out by another body within it—in this case the PCC.   *judget no courts used*

This is because both logics of violence have strong moral frameworks by which they judge the deservedness of death. These logics are convergent. While police who kill often do so with an understanding that the subject is a bandido, the subject of a PCC killing is imagined as an individual who does not even follow the bandido's rules of the game. Herein is the crux: those who formally regulate death position those killed by the PCC, implicitly, if not explicitly, as worse than a bandido. The subject of PCC killing is by operational definition "hyper" undeserving of life. He has failed the moral tests of both worlds—those governed by police and those governed by the much more severe regulations of the PCC. Twice judged, the bodies of these young men—for they are almost always young men—constitute many of the numbers of those who die violently in this city. In killing those deemed exceptionally unredeemable by the state, the definitive role of the PCC goes largely uncontested by the state. While individual homicides committed by the PCC might be solved, those arrested by the police are quickly returned to the regulatory space of the PCC as it exists within the prison system. The moral system of the PCC is thus rarely substantively disputed.

This is at least partly because the PCC's regulation of death has come to fill a distinct void in state's provision of public security. The PCC provides a service for the state, and in doing so has nested itself in the moral and institutional infrastructure of the state. As a product of violence, the PCC gained its privileged position because the state failed to secure the city and prisons through the late 1980s and 1990s. This was largely because of a twisted amalgam of incapacity and disinterest that opened space for the PCC's emergence as a self-security organization.[1] Today, though, this has morphed into a difficult paradox. Independent of incapacity or disinterest, police are obstructed from making more complete investigations because of the regime of the PCC, under which communication with police—by members, residents, witnesses—is largely forbidden. The state now finds itself in a much more troublesome conundrum—it is both obstructed by the PCC in its investigation of violent death *and* beholden to its single-sourced dominion over killing, to which the monumental decline in homicides can be attributed.

But the PCC also depends on the state. If it is clear that the PCC has a dominant regulatory regime over death, it may be less clear how that system—and its related drug trafficking economy—is also deeply part of the formal system of justice, albeit in obscured ways. This occurs in ways both apparent—the control of the PCC over the inside of nearly every prison in São Paulo state—and concealed—fewer people die because the PCC says so. More notably, the day-to-day interactions between these two systems is visible in police work. One such way is when the PCC chooses to punish residents by utilizing the formal system in order to avoid the investigative scrutiny of police. Rather than having someone killed, and potentially get arrested for it—which would be a waste—it is just more pragmatic to coerce the accused person into the indignities of the formal system. This has benefits for the formal system as well. The police get their man, the statistic is theirs, and they find a resolution to a case that might otherwise have stayed open for the long haul.

One such case occurred early in 2012. One afternoon a call came in to the Homicide Division. The body of a young woman, who I'll call Gabriella, had been found dead on the north side of the city.[2] She was visibly pregnant and was found naked in the bushes off of a road at the very edge of the urban sprawl. There was an ID, and some description about her last known whereabouts. Residents had reported that she was addicted to crack cocaine. Her boyfriend had also been recently arrested. Detectives threw out many possibilities: her boyfriend was out for a holiday break and had killed her.[3] The boyfriend had arranged for her to be killed. A sexual predator was at loose in the community, as evidenced by a handful of reported rapes. Considering the nature of the violence and the difficult imagery that accompanied a death like this, there was some concern that it might get a great deal of media attention. All the stops were pulled out. The chief detectives ordered all manner of exams to be done on the body, from cavity exams for semen, to subcutaneous exams for skin and blood, blood tests, and drug and alcohol exams. The other detectives were using all of the databases—motor vehicle, criminal record, national identity, among others—for more details about the husband, his known accomplices, and for more about this potential sexual predator. It was late in the shift, and this was early in my research when I was still new to the division. This time the chief didn't feel comfortable taking me to the scene. We parted ways as the team walked out the door to get in the Blazer and go to the scene. After departing I went to a local corner bar and wrote up my field notes, indicating to myself to follow up about this case, both in the media and with this same team the next time I saw them.

Days later I saw the chief again and asked what had come of the case. Arriving at the scene, he explained, they had tried desperately to solve the crime, canvassing the area, talking with residents, seeking out known sex offenders and digging into recent sexual crimes in the area. Their efforts had been fruitless, and none of the possible theories had panned out. With few leads and even fewer witnesses the case was passed on to secondary investigators. Thankfully, though, the media hadn't picked up on the case. Or, if they had, they were likely turned off by the fact that Gabriella was using crack while pregnant.

And yet out of the dearth of answers came a conclusion. The offender walked right into the station and turned himself in. The chief told me the story: the offender claimed that Gabriella's death wasn't a rape, but, rather that she had died when a consensual sex-for-crack exchange went bad. They had gone to the bushes to make the "deal." After the sex, she had collapsed and became irresponsive. Scared about what to do, he fled, leaving her to die naked and alone in the brush by the side of the road. He hadn't been around when the detectives came looking for answers but he had heard all about it.

That wasn't the problem. People in the community were talking about him and what he had done. There was hearsay that he had raped Gabriella. No one tolerates a rapist—most especially those in charge in these places. A formal discussion took place with *os caras de lá*—"the guys"— from there, meaning the leading PCC affiliates in the neighborhood. No one in the community disputed that the man turning himself in was involved, or that there was intercourse and ejaculation. Her death wasn't the problem. The case hinged on one difficult to discern but highly moral turning point: for "the guys" the most important piece of information was whether the sex had been consensual or not.

The problem was, no one there could say for sure. To the PCC affiliates in charge there wasn't clear evidence that he had been violent, taking advantage of her on a dark street. Nor was there evidence that she had consented because she wanted crack—despite her habit and reputation as a user. The sex-for-crack exchange was interrupted and never fully came to pass. After a great deal of deliberation but no unanimity about who was at fault, they came to a resolution about how to settle the problem. The local PCC affiliates decided to give him a choice: walk himself in to the police station and take responsibility for Gabriella's death, or be killed. According to the man who turned himself in, if he could have proved that the incident wasn't a rape, but instead that the whole mess was just about a girl—who happened to be pregnant—that was willing to pay for crack with sex, then they would have let him go. Failing to do so, he took the only real option open to him—turn himself in and keep on living.

The irony, of course, is that this man would only leave the PCC's moral space for days, if not hours. After writing up the report, giving his statement and completing other formalities in the police station, he would go straight into a prison system controlled almost in its entirety by the PCC's moral regime. There he would be governed by the same system—now much more obviously embedded within the state—that forced him to surrender to it in the first place. In many ways, it seemed like the PCC had decided that the suspect deserved jail time, not capital punishment, and used the detectives at the police station to move him into what is essentially their own regime. Read this way, police detectives seem like little more than bureaucratic cogs in the PCC machinery.

More nuanced still though is the fact that this man was likely judged, at least in part, from inside the formal system. Tribunals occur when PCC members responsible for punishment—known as a *disciplina*—connect from inside prison via cell phone with local PCC members to judge a specific case. On the one hand, this moral regime is contingent on the relative safety and protective confines of those in the prison system. On the other, it hinges on those outside of the prison system being subordinated to a leadership distant from the location of the "crime." But the subordination of those on the outside is made possible by the near inevitability that they will find themselves inside the prison system, where they will be in need of the structure of rules and the goods provided to incarcerated PCC members from the fees collected from the membership on the outside.

A case like this is also indicative of the ways that the PCC is easily made invisible by the front stage of the system. This is particularly true in terms of the production of statistics. This man was entirely a product of PCC governance. And yet, he became a vital thing for a formal system so auspicious in its inability to ascertain one single meaningful piece of information or evidence—not a single person willing to go on the record—about the case on its own. And yet it solved the case. This man was now the ultravaluable representation of good police work in the contemporary times: a statistic of a closed murder case. More valuable even was the near certainty that the man would be found guilty—despite the fact that there was no evidence—and it was only because he himself said so. Above all, he was also one less dead person.

The integration of PCC moralities within the criminal justice system ensures that those believed to be on the wrong side of the PCC's law will rarely—if ever—go unpunished. This was put on brutal public display in 2012, following a particularly heinous crime that shocked the city—and police. During a home robbery in a poor community on the west side of the city, five men assaulted a Bolivian family for not giving them enough money. In the tumult a young boy named Brayan started to cry, begging the men not to hurt his mother. In short order one of the men shot Brayan point blank, killing him beside his parents. Taking what money had been given to them by the family the five men then fled.

For weeks the case captured public attention. The Bolivian ambassador spoke out, Bolivians and Brazilians held rallies calling for justice and an end to impunity, and television personalities hosted hours-long diatribes railing against the failure of public security in the city. The sense of disgust was so thick, that even police themselves were wrapped up in it. Sometime after the event I spoke with some of the homicide detectives. Pressure from upstairs was heavy to resolve the case, they said, not that the detectives themselves felt any less desire to make sure the five men got their due.

Their worry was not so much that the five men would get away with murder. Instead, everyone that I spoke with understood that the resolution to this case would come. There was little doubt. But it would come after a foot race. At hand was who would find the men first—the PCC or police. A standing order was issued to the Homicide Division to notify higher-ups about any bodies found in or around the district where the robbery took place. It was no secret that a killing like this contravened both the law on the books and the law of the PCC. Yet in the midst of PCC-police violence, I wondered whether it was also possible that this case was evidence of a breakdown in the PCC control over crime. The detectives didn't entertain that idea. Credit for the resolution would go either to police or to the law of the PCC—or both. Either way, many detectives said, the five men would get what was coming to them.

The first two were found less than ten days later—but neither could be identified until fingerprint results came back more than a month later. Both had been shot in the head multiple times, their bodies found separately but near each other on the outskirts of the city and not far from the international airport. As police awaited word on the identity of these two bodies, they found two of the other men alive. Broadcast live, and incessantly afterward, both were mobbed and nearly lynched during their arrival at the precinct. They were arrested, charged, and eventually forwarded to the pretrial detention center.

Within hours both were dead. According to police, they had been forced to drink a lethal cocktail of cocaine, creatine, water and Viagra, known as "Gatorade." The *Folha de São Paulo* newspaper reported that when the two bodies were removed from the jail the prison staff were told they didn't need to look for the other two any longer. Both had been dealt with. A short time later, the fingerprint results for the first two came back positive.

Multiple newspaper reports related that the fifth, a minor, was being held in a juvenile detention center. He would apparently survive. In the aftermath of the four dead bodies ultimately paying the price for the death of Brayan, hundreds of subsequent media broadcasts celebrated the resolution as just and merited. There seemed exceptionally little debate about the "good" of the resolution.

The race between police and the PCC to find the five men was essentially a tie. Even so, the message of the PCC came across much more clearly. Newspapers posted "infographics" of the timelines of the killings, liking them directly to the PCC. Not only that, it was later leaked that the PCC leadership at Presidente Venceslau prison had sent out a *salve geral* to all members just three days after Brayan's death. The message made it unequivocally clear how the organization would treat killings of children (figure 8). Found by authorities in at least three prisons, the message read:

> The leadership [sintonia final] informs everyone that from this day on, no violence against children will be tolerated. Anyone who commits or is involved in such violence will be found and eliminated. We are, above all, human beings. We have family and we know our feelings for those around us. We cannot respect someone who commits this type of crime, which is totally contrary to the basic principles of any honorable criminal. The ends of these actions do not justify the means. We leave this in the hands of each regional leadership. Observation: Via this note, it is decided that there will be zero tolerance for committing this crime. It is worth remembering. The comando is the voice of crime, and we will not allow it. Thanks to all. Signed, Sintonia Final.

From a distant prison thousands of kilometers away, the leadership of the organization mobilized its members in a massive manhunt for the young men involved. In a city of 20 million, they found them in short order. More savvy, flexible, and smarter that the criminal justice system—

02/07/2013 - SALVE GERAL DO SISTEMA E RUA

"A sintonia final do Comando deixa a todos cientes que a partir desta data (2/7), não será tolerado nem um tipo de violência contra criança aquele que vier a cometer e cair nessa será avaliado e cobrado. Somos, antes de tudo, seres humanos, temos família e sabemos como nos sentimos em relação a ela. Não dá para ter respeito com quem comete este tipo de crime, que contraria totalmente os princípios *bázico* de todo criminoso que tem honra. Os meios destes estados não justifica o crime. caberá a sintonia respectiva resumo. Obs: *cendo* assim fica decidido tolerância zero sendo quem cometeu tal. Vale lembrar. O comando é a voz do crime e não admitiremos isso. Agradecemos a todos. Assinado. Sintonia Final"

FIGURE 8. PCC salve to members: zero tolerance for violence against children.

and certainly more violent—the message was unambiguous: if you do not follow the rules and morality of the organization—formally affiliated or not—you will not escape punishment.

As in the case of Gabriella, the viability of the PCC's structure of justice thus depends on the regular flow of people to the formal system and back again. To separate the inside from the outside and the informal from the formal would disarticulate a highly centralized system of moral governance—made possible by a lucrative drug trade with many envious and violent onlookers. The nesting of the PCC's right to kill, which is at once distinct and indistinct from the punitiveness of the state, has been made possible because of the paradoxical relationship between urban social exclusion. The violence that was allowed to run unchecked through the 1990s and the state's attempt to manage that violence by transplanting those perceived responsible into an equally violent and marginal place (now within the state) resulted in two systems of moral governance, deeply intertwined.

As long as the state has no authority, I'm going to take care of my own.
—Homicide detective

Police and the PCC meet and mesh on the street, in the prisons, and in the police stations of the city of São Paulo. According to most of the literature on policing, and to conventional notions of who police should be and what they should do, this "deviance" from the rules constitutes corruption.[4] Rarely, though, is the threat or reality of formidable violence considered. And when it is, we often fall into a popular, if snappy, binary: *plata ou plomo*. Silver or lead. Wealth or death. You choose, public servant.[5]

This binary is much the same as Rafael described his situation living in the "worst neighbourhood in São Paulo." But it is unhelpful. Much more fine grained are the everyday ways that police get by in the face of violence. These are *forms of equilibria*. Forms of equilibria are two things. First, they are a pattern of adaptive actions, used to avoid violence, that prioritize personal security over other demands. Second, they invoke a kind of mutually beneficial relationship, real or implicit, that produces predictability and a semblance of security. That predictability is balanced on shared notions of who can live and who can die. In this sense, police both defer and are deferred to, but not for the reasons that we may suppose.[6] Problematic as they may be, forms of equilibria between police and PCC members keeps both more secure, if only temporarily. Nobody benefits when the police and PCC are at each other's throats. Deference is necessary because violence, disorder, and unpredictability are always a possibility. Violence between these two seemingly antagonistic parties is not common because compromise on both parts is routine. Deference among the lowest street-level actors is so common that it has become the glue that sustains sovereignty by consensus.

Police who live in or near PCC communities must conceal their identities at all costs. Patrolling police must contend with a devalued position in society and a chronic inability to manage criminal activity. Homicide detectives suffer from a lack of resources and capacity to solve killings by police, the PCC, or others in between. Affiliates of the PCC accept routine extortion and beatings from police, who need to feign control over criminality and the drug trade.[7] In prison, the PCC is left much to its own devices, which suits the needs of both the prison guards who are tasked with hundreds of prisoners per staffer and political power holders, who are happy with containment and quiet. On the other side of the coin, handfuls of off-duty police die without upheaval, police routinely kill PCC affiliates in shootouts, and the PCC can kill its own members and residents of its communities with little decisive threat to the organization. In other words, each group has its own understandings of who can be killed (and how) without destabilization and crisis.

The PCC, for its part, outlines for its own members what kind of violence is routine and acceptable and what is not. PCC members can and will die in the course of what they do. They are, according to the PCC itself, criminals in a criminal organization working for the betterment of crime. That these armed criminals will come into conflict with police is a given. It is the rules of this engagement that matter. According to the PCC statute, "cowardice" and "injustice" on the part of police, where liberties are taken in order to assassinate or execute a member, are not tolerated. Other PCC documents speak similarly of being killed in the course of duty and the normal loss of colleagues to "confrontations" with police. Being killed appears to be seen as somewhat of an occupational hazard that is part and parcel of having a criminal identity. It is in instances of cowardice and injustice defined by the organization and typically not at the scale of the individual—one person is never enough to decide if violence is right or wrong—that the PCC has sought revenge.

These forms of deference are mutually recognized gestures that inform mutually observed notions of who can die. The ways that both parties cede space, property, or authority in exchange for some semblance of predictability and security means that generalized insecurity prevails.

On the part of police, this deference occurs to fill the gap in personal security. Most police understand this simply as having to take security matters into your own hands. This is a complex issue since there is a widespread and diffuse sensation of vulnerability. As one police detective related: "We are walking targets. It is impossible to hide that the community doesn't know who the police are. Especially when you were raised there." The decentralized nature of violence in the city is a powerful motivating force in which police routinely forfeit their authority in favor of the relative security of anonymity. Rather than heeding the mantra that "no police officer is ever off duty," police often decide to "deviate" from what we might assume they should do in order to make themselves feel safer. Another detective put it this way about his everyday commute: "I don't even take anything with me when I leave the station. No gun, no badge. It isn't worth risking it. I have an expensive motorbike, but I'd much rather them just take that than be dead over it. It is just not worth it. Just take the bike."

This dynamic is even more acute for police who live in or around areas controlled by the PCC. The influence of the organization transcends boundaries, having a chilling effect of the ability of police to be recognized as anything so authoritative. With the alternative being violence and/or death, there can be little option but to lay low. One police detective I got to know lived in the same area where I had studied the moral order of the PCC during previous research. Knowing the empirical trappings of the place, I was surprised that this was at all viable for a police officer. Picture what this place is like:

> A ridge runs like a spine through this community, upon which a main avenue is superimposed. Along that main avenue are all manner of public services—the Civil Police station, gas stations, a fire hall, a health post, and the like. There are also many private establishments, like small supermarkets, bakeries, and

other local shops. There is no bank around here, though you can find one further down a connecting avenue, not so far from a McDonald's.

Falling down from this central spine is a mix of landscapes. Close to the top are pockets of public housing units, four- or five-story blocks that are bland shades of taupe. On the one side, they are around thirty years old. On the other, they are almost new, though not much in their design will allow most observers to know the difference once the fresh paint fades. One difference, residents tell me is that one was wholly publicly funded, while the other is a public-private partnership, reflecting different eras of state policy. Originally, the publicly funded units physically replaced multiple blocks of self-built housing under a rubric of risk and safety. But around them the pattern continues apace. Along the main roads some of these self-built houses look almost upscale. They are properly faced with concrete, some are nicely painted, and others are even on lots large enough to have gated driveways—but barely. With at least two generations of investments in these homes, things have improved substantially. Further down away from the spine, and in corners sandwiched behind more central roads, is much more precarious housing. On the one side the valley falls away sharply, coming to a flattish area covered nearly entirely with this type of housing. Further down the valley converges entirely, spitting out only a black and fetid stream a few feet wide. One-room shacks of wood and other things surrounded it.

All of this area—the main avenue, public housing, generational self-built housing, and precarious housing—is part of what is known and referred to as the periphery. Much of it existed historically very much in spite of the state. Today all of it is the domain of a PCC control that transcends different urban spaces and built environments. It is a control that is premised on recognition and belonging. As we walked through the entire area, my friend told me of the different named gangs that had controlled different spaces and had historically been at war with each other. It was the revenge spirals of these groups that fed the homicide rate, they said. Each of these still existed but were now subordinated to the PCC's rule of *peace among criminals*. Nor did it matter much that this control hovered around, beside, and seemingly over the police station and other public services, either. No one would ever think of going to the police to solve their problems, both because they felt like they'd more likely be extorted than helped but also because the PCC wouldn't approve of anything like that.

What mattered, though, were spaces within these spaces—particularly in precarious areas—that are the hubs of PCC control where drugs were collected, stored, and sold. Although on-duty police freely patrolled the spine, ate at restaurants there, and got gas, these spaces were largely off-limits to anyone not in the company of a local. The week before I entered one such space, a representative of the local electric utility had been escorted out at the barrel of a gun. When I spoke with a PCC member in the community very briefly, he was rather frank about those spaces: *a polícia não entra*—the police do not enter. But these are not the only places where drugs are sold. Other places are spaces of negotiation where police regularly show up and take money, drugs, or someone.

The difference between these spaces is not lost on police themselves—especially for the police that grew up there. So I asked this detective how he managed navigating this difficult moral and geographical terrain:

> I grew up in that community. I was there way before them, so I guess they must respect that or something. But really, I just don't mess with them, and they don't mess with me. Don't worry, if they did, I know where to find guns. It is like that saying, "I'd rather be judged by seven of my peers than carried in a coffin by eight." If it ever went to trial, I know how it would work out. They aren't going to bury me.

Leaving them alone suggests a spatial and pragmatic strategy, even as it is unavoidable to see, hear, and be witness to a system of control that should be alien to the one that he represents. One individual confronting such a system does not make a great deal of sense. When confrontation is necessary, he suggested that there is already a well-established and historical logic of response in place and ready to go.

The idea that violence may one day be necessary is a common theme among police. But for most, outward violence against the PCC is understood to be a last resort with clear consequences for them and their families. To be associated with that violence would mean having to relocate to another part of the city, forcing them to leave behind a strong sense of belonging. Not only that, it would require working two or three extra jobs in order to keep up with the cost of living in a place where anonymity can be afforded.

In the eastern part of São Paulo, residents spoke about a tacit "no shots fired" agreement, in which police regularly raid PCC drug sales points in order to pocket money or drugs. Failing drugs and money, residents said, they would take prisoners.[8] Any kind of capital would do. This echoes a larger dynamic known to be at play in which police seek to extract value from the organization while leaving with a sensation that they are still fighting crime to the best of their ability given the structural nature of the beast and the organizational weakness of public security to respond in a coherent way. Police in the Homicide Division spoke about this dynamic as well, referring to the *pedágio*, "tolls," that are collected and redistributed at the station level—making neighborhood precincts attractive places to be stationed.

But these forms of equilibria are not necessarily so organized. Sometimes they function in small and flexible groups of police who meet while off duty. One police officer told me that it was part and parcel of a choice that a police officer must make. In a world when police must work one or two extra jobs to sustain themselves and their families they may choose between two options, neither of which are particularly safe. Most decide to moonlight as security guards, armed escorts, or covering shifts for colleagues. Some choose the unsafe but easier and more lucrative option, to join a group of colleagues hitting up fair game drug spots. On the day that I spoke with him, the detective was covering a shift, having turned down the latter option for today.

This type of work is certainly not for all police—though the allure of easy money is powerful. Still, many recognize the inherent trade-offs are not worth it, both for personal security and for the security of their families. One detective put it succinctly one evening over beers after work: "I'm not going to dirty myself with that shit. Only if it is a loooottt of money. If not, my family will be stuck with no salary, and I'll be in jail, without a pension and making no money at all. It has to be a hell of a lot of money."

There are plenty of good reasons to avoid making money by extorting drug dealers. But whether police choose to lay low and avoid organized crime, or to engage with it as a way to make a buck, they are deferring. They both dull the power of the state and cede space to organized crime, while also serving a purpose for those on the frontlines who are taking advantage of a depleted system and trying to save face given the failure of the system in which they are primary representatives. These kinds of everyday negotiations evoke the empirical nature of relations that crisscross the blurry threshold between the state and organized crime. "Dirty togetherness" or not, these practices are systemic, conveying not institutionalized corruption but instead a fractured and failing system in which individuals must struggle mightily, in one way or another, to get by. It is the ways that they get by, woven through with compromise, which allow some predictability to exist under a moral rubric and mutual understanding about the appropriateness of violence.

CHAPTER 6

A Consensus Killed

Just as a consensus can be sustained, it can be torn apart. São Paulo's periods of relative peace have been blown apart by dramatic urban-scale instances of violence. Even as they last years, those periods of relative peace and stability rest on a false floor that occasionally gives way when the buttresses supporting it crumble. This occurs when one of the two key parties—the state or the PCC—makes a move that is deemed exceptional by the other. Such a move is exceptional when it breaks with the mutually acknowledged boundaries and behaviors that delineate the forms of everyday survival of either party and the larger moral status quo.

On May 12, 2006, a Friday evening at the beginning of the Mother's Day weekend, a police officer named Marcus was at a bar with friends. As they sat at a table on the sidewalk in a community on the north side of São Paulo, two teenagers broke through the crowd. Without giving the officer much time to react, the assailants shot him repeatedly before walking away calmly. This was no ordinary incident. It was the first of many in an eruption of violence in which fifty-two police, prison guards, and their family members were assassinated in a span of four days. Marcus's death rocked police to their core and sent shockwaves of panic and disarray through the workplace. According to one detective, "I remember it clearly. It was like, we'd get a call of one [police] getting shot, but before we'd really gotten started there would be three more up on the board. Police just getting gunned down. . . . There isn't much information in the [crime] reports—there was no time to get to scenes or anything like that. No one knew what the hell was going on."

The situation was made more intense because this was the first time that this kind of acute attack had happened. At the time there was no real narrative of who was doing this or why. It came almost out of nowhere. Since then, the Mother's Day attacks by members of the PCC have become one of the most infamous periods in São Paulo's recent history. They are inscribed in the imagination of police. In what police describe as a state of utter "chaos" and "terror," policemen and women were tracked down and assassinated outside their homes, in their cars, and on public streets. Buses were burned and banks were also hit with home-made bombs. For days the city streets were nearly deserted, with police roadblocks—as fear inspiring to many residents as anything—among the only presence on the roads.

For police themselves, this was an uncertain time in which all bets were off, especially in places I've described. The same detective who once told me how he survived there during normal times, also told me how he managed the disorienting effect of those attacks: "Well, I went to work on my motorbike with a machine gun on my back. There was no one on the street. Totally deserted. I told my wife to close and lock the door and not to let anyone in. And that I would call her when I was about to get home so she could come down and open the door to let me in and close it again immediately. I told her that if anyone else came by she shouldn't even go downstairs."

If police were rightfully confused about what was happening, the rationale was clear from the other side of the fence. During a statement much later to a Federal Inquiry Committee investigating the events, the PCC's supposed leader, William Herbas Marcos de Camacho, known simply as Marcola, gave his version of the reasons why PCC affiliates carried out the attacks: an administrator in the penitentiary system had made a rash and very consequential decision to transfer a number of PCC leaders from open confinement to a supermaximum arrangement, replete with restrictions and mistreatment in the process.[1] In front of seven federal congressmen during an inquiry Marcola related:

> At 6:00 a.m. we had been taken from our respective penitentiaries, where things were normal, open confinement, because there was no reason for us to be in super-maximum or solitary.[2] They put us in the trailers, which are actually trucks, and we made the painful trip of seven or eight hours to get to Presidente Venceslau II. We arrived dead tired because those trucks are horrible. We arrived dead tired, hungry, thirsty, needing to use the toilet, and

they left us inside the trucks for another seven hours, breathing in exhaust fumes. When they put us in the cells, we had nothing. No clothes. Just shoes, a T-shirt, and flip-flops. No sweater, nothing. Nothing at all. They gave us no food. When we got there, inside the hall, which was maximum security, there were still cell phones in the adjacent halls, there from the last riot. The other prisoners simply went, took these phones out of their hiding places, and in the moment of anger amongst all the prisoners—this was something for all of us now—in that moment of anger, a bunch of prisoners called out to their places, to their friends, to other people to ask for relief. So, that is why this whole situation happened, becoming so excessive as it was. (CPI 2006, 11)

And so it was. Young men on the outside attacked police as a form of retribution on behalf of their people on the inside. Many of them gave their lives in the name of solidarity. The confusion of those three days of assassinations eventually gave way to a massive wave of retribution on the part of police. By that point some sense had been made about who was doing this, and how they could be targeted. But the response by police was telling—it came largely through "informal" channels: off-duty, plainclothes, and disguised police lashed out indiscriminately. Over a three-week period more than 440 citizens were killed, many in small groups, and shot multiple times at close range.[3] Though most of these killings remain mysterious and unsolved, it is clear among both police and civil society groups that what transpired was a wave of retribution and extermination, pure and simple.

Yet, there remains no publicly stated explanation for why the violence stopped, as it did, almost overnight. One predominant conviction—accepted by police detectives—is that the crisis came to a close after secret negotiations between PCC and government leaders took place at one of the most high-security prisons in the country. Rumors of government appointees flying via helicopter with bags of cash are rife. Most believe a treaty was struck between the secretary for penitentiary administration and the leaders of the PCC. The secretary himself at the time has admitted that there were discussions. Almost immediately, homicide statistics returned to the same levels, even declining further below the six-year trend. And for the next six years, with some minor ebb and flow, São Paulo returned to its normal state of relative peace.

The event has never left the imagination of police, however. In 2009, in my early days spending hour after hour in neighborhood stations, the events would sometimes be talked about as a means to explain something that didn't make sense. In one station late one night a detective came back inside hurriedly from standing outside for a break. A van with tinted windows had rolled by the station twice, slowly. By itself on an otherwise quiet night, this was out of place. She decided that for the rest of the night she would stay inside the station—made mostly of concrete pillars—in case this was the beginning of a similar attack involving the same kinds of weapons, grenades, automatic machine guns, and bombs. Other times, small outbreaks of violence garnered particular worry and uncertainty from police. There was a precedent for mass assassination and explosive violence. This was certainly particularly true for detectives when investigating a spate of unexplained killings of their colleagues, particularly if there were some hallmarks or chatter of PCC involvement. If 2006 had seen more than fifty police assassinated in a three-day span, what would the next attack be like? No one knew, but they could imagine.

Even as the event continued to destabilize the police, the PCC appeared to most to have gone fallow. "Quanto mais mudo, melhor" ("the more muted the better"), a detective told me of the PCC rationale one afternoon. Outside of the routine shootings of off-duty police, who most assumed had it coming anyway, nothing serious had happened since May 2006. This was an astute move on the part of an organization concerned more with its own security than with a revolutionary cause. Unlike Rio de Janeiro, which has historically suffered from a more routine pattern of urban-scale crises, São Paulo's relative stability has been the stuff of envy—as has its homicide decline. The PCC has been cautious to not draw undue attention to its activities, a tactic that has seen them expand deeply into money laundering, particularly in cash-heavy businesses like gas stations, used car sales, and if one prosecutor I interviewed has it right, into the privately owned but publicly subsidized urban transportation system of buses and minibuses.

But even this desire for security, stability, and slow growth can be ruptured by a sense of injustice. On May 29, 2012, things changed. On this evening, the ROTA received an "anonymous tip"—believed by detectives to have come from an illicit wiretap—about a potential gathering of PCC members. The tipster provided information that these PCC members were gathered at a car wash in the east side of the city and preparing to bust a fellow member out of a nearby prison. Twenty-four ROTA police arrived at the scene in six Toyota Hilux SUVs with guns blazing. According to the police report, what occurred was harrowing. Five alleged PCC members lay dead in short order, supposedly after a shootout. Two people, a woman and a man, were arrested alive with a sundry of drugs, cash, a number of handguns, and a 7.62 machine gun stamped with the words *Ejercito Argentino*—Argentine Military—with its serial number scratched away. The ROTA police sustained no injuries, no damage to cars and no otherwise noteworthy signs of having taken shelter from gunshots.

But that wasn't the end of the story. Homicide detectives soon discovered that one man had been taken from the scene alive. The man had been put in a ROTA vehicle bound for the homicide department. But as it turned out, the man was wanted as a suspect for the assassination of a police officer in greater São Paulo two months prior. Of all of the people at the car wash, this man was particularly known and wanted by police. GPS records would later show that the ROTA car deviated kilometers from a reasonable route to the Homicide Division, where the case was registered. In the process, it stopped on the side of a major highway. There the man was apparently tortured and interrogated, in what the ROTA police almost certainly thought would be just another dead police-killing PCC member.

It was not to be. A highway traffic camera caught the event. In addition, a local resident saw the event and narrated what she saw live by telephone. The ROTA police removed the alive but bloodied man from the car and shot him multiple times on the side of the highway. They then did what was routine when police shoot someone who has resisted arrest. Under the auspice that the man was still alive and with a fighting chance to live, they picked up the body, put it back in the car and drove to a hospital (figure 9). He never made it to the Homicide Division. He was dead on arrival at the hospital.

At first, the detective police report made little mention of this man. As detectives told me later, word of the incident only made it to the station some time later. The evidence of the killing arrived soon after. The chief detective had an obvious course of action. In partnership with the Internal Affairs Division of the Military Police—used often to defuse tensions between the two police forces—the four ROTA police involved were arrested. Some also advocated for the rest of the ROTA police involved in the car wash raid to be arrested as well, on the grounds of obstructing justice and related charges. Nonetheless, they never were. As those suffering from someone resisting arrest, they remained listed as *vítimas*—victims—on the police report. This event capped a month in which ROTA *alone* killed 17 people in resistências in greater São Paulo.[4]

The case sent shock waves in many directions, including back into the world of the PCC. Arrested PCC members later told of regional meetings in which the order was given to target police. An eye for an eye.

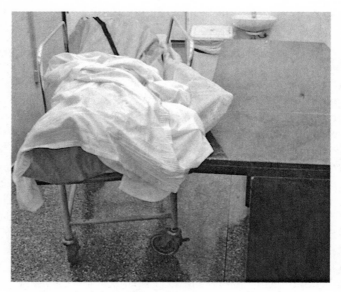

FIGURE 9. A body brought by police to a morgue (photo by author).

But the word was that the PCC leadership was also incentivizing members with debts to the organization to clear their slate by assassinating a police officer. Within days, affiliates of the organization were targeting off-duty police in their neighborhoods, while they were driving to work, paying for groceries, and while moonlighting. Over the course of the month of June twelve police were killed, all while off duty. Countless more had been shot and injured.

Police retaliated in kind. According to official statistics, the number of resistências shot up by 40 percent over the year prior, denoting a deadly shift among on-duty police. Not that these official statistics are the only measure of the police response by any stretch. It is well understood among police that resistências are more scrutinized than other modes of killing and retribution. The possibility of being captive to formal investigation drives adaptive patterns of killing. In my conversations with Military Police, they spoke of higher-ups suggesting categorizing their killings differently, such as *roubo seguida de morte* (robbery followed by death), which would garner less attention.

There were also more "self-help" forms of violence that emerged. As in May 2006, police vigilante groups sprung up in areas where police had been killed or targeted. A pattern of multiple homicides in parts of the periphery near shootings of police emerged. Savvy about how to kill without leaving evidence, most of these homicides were carried out by hooded men on motorcycles without license plates who arrived, shot and killed three, four or five young men before calmly picking up their shell casings and driving away.

For the next six months, the city devolved into a blood feud between the PCC and police along these same lines. Police killed with extra abandon. After a couple of lulls in assassinations of police officers, the PCC came back with a vengeance following a spectacular massacre of nine people by ROTA on the far eastern periphery of the city. Buses were being burned regularly enough that the police first began providing armed escorts, before deciding to put plainclothes police officers on buses at random to deter more attacks. The multiple homicides continued with abandon, particularly in the south side of the city and in places like Guarulhos where the international airport is located and many police also make their home. Police even surmised that they were seeing a rise in reactionary homicides, like crimes of passion, because the PCC's control over the circumstances of killing was being destabilized.

All of this killing was running the homicide detectives off their feet. I had returned back to the United States and Canada for a short period, but followed the violence from afar as it escalated. The homicide department that I came back to was almost unrecognizable. "Welcome to Pandora's box," one detective said. "We're standing in it." It was clear that things had changed for the worse. Some police were leaving work early in order to get back on the last bus because bus schedules had been curtailed for fear of more burnings. "No more naps," said Pedro to me with a typical Brazilian side hug to welcome me back. They were now routinely visiting four to six different scenes a day, as compared to the one or two that were normal. The detectives had arrested a number of police for homicide because their resistências were out of line. By the end of the year, the number of arrested police would reach twenty-eight.

Unmistakably, the homicide detectives are the ones expected to contain the violence. But this is a very complex task in the midst of serious power asymmetries that become even more acute during moments of crisis. That police should be arresting police in the midst of violence targeting all of them is an irony not lost on many. And yet it manages to happen, as I recall from my fieldnotes:

> In the midst of this new surge in violence, I'd been trying to keep on top of the news. Every day there were reports of police being killed. It was hard to keep up, and the media never even managed all that well. Before going to the precinct for a shift I'd read through the latest stories by Googling "dead police

São Paulo." There were new hits everyday. And those were just the dead police that made the news, not the injured or other ones.

On this particular night the news reports were talking about more buses being burned, more multiple homicides in the last few days, and a marked spike in homicides overall. Nine homicides, including the chacina yesterday they said. Police authorities are now saying that they recognize there is a connection between police killings and the PCC. They have some evidence, gleaned from wiretaps of PCC members that they'll *sentar o pau*—"will make them feel the pain"—a phrase apparently coming from the mouth of a PCC leader in a well known PCC district. As I walk to the homicide department I can't avoid the feeling that I am about as close to the middle of this as anyone.

Three blocks from the station three or four new Toyota SUVs fly by on the street, with lights flashing and sirens blaring.[5] Something big was probably happening, I thought. Arriving at the station, I saw a couple of police from a notorious unit standing sentry, gruff as they are with stern statures and dark hats. The Civil Police officer at the reception gave me a tough time about giving me my pass. I didn't know him, which was abnormal by now. He was resistant to me being there, maybe because he didn't know me, the city was full of unanswered questions and probably because the place was crawling with these guys. Eventually I convinced him to call upstairs to ask if I had permission to go up. He did, and they said yes. He passed me my swipe card, begrudgingly.

I walked up the four flights of stairs that wind up through the inside of this old station. As I stepped out of the stairwell there was a cloud of troops— probably between twelve and fifteen. Among them was a man in handcuffs. One troop was holding two long and slender bricks of some kind of drug— that I later learned was 1.5 kilos of marijuana. I said good evening to all and walked past into the office. A mix of people were there, most still getting off of the day shift. One or two had arrived for the night shift. Two detectives were waiting for more information on a case that had happened earlier in the day. The rest of their team was still in the field, dealing with the shooting of a police officer from a specialized unit that went down at a shopping mall. The official line was that it was an attempted robbery that occurred following an ATM withdrawal [*saidinha de banco*]. Not according to some of the police in the station, though. "It was totally an execution," said one. "He got shot in the face. They took no money. And have you ever heard of someone going around robbing people with a bullet proof car [*carro blindado*]?"

That a member of an elite unit, this time from the Civil Police, had been attacked was precedent setting. "Now they'll put those guys on the street. Just to kill," said one detective. "They don't care. When there is a hostage situation, they just send in a sniper. One shot, it's done. . . ."

This incident hit close to home for these police. This fellow worked down the hall and many new him by nickname. "It sounds like he's going to die. It hit his lungs. They were trying to stabilize so they can operate. But its complicated. His chance of living, on a scale from zero to ten, he was a five."

It was confusing to me why the homicide department was dealing with the case, since, strictly speaking, no one had died, and the victim was rushed to emergency. Not until it becomes a homicide are these police supposed to investigate, a procedure that tends to marginalize the importance of evidence at the crime scene. And, in any case, this shooting happened outside the jurisdiction of the metropolitan Homicide Division, having occurred in greater São Paulo. There may have been special orders.

Regardless, the troops were heating up outside the door and attention was turning that way. No one yet knew why there was a cloud of police outside the door. No message had arrived on the intranet about anything involving this unit and there was no word of a *resistência*—which was almost always why they showed up. "They're deciding what they're going to say," said one detective. "How they are going to walk through the case."

The reason became clear soon enough. Word arrived from upstairs that these troops had been told to bring a case to homicide—even through there was no one dead. Someone important didn't want them taking this case to the organized crime or drug units, both of which, police always say, are thoroughly crooked. Homicide had a reputation for being more reliable and by the book. They had arrested cops from this unit before, after all.

As the troops came in with a suspect, many of the detectives started jumping all over him, interrogating him about what happened. One or two were particularly forceful, screaming in his face "I'm going to fuck you. I'm going to hang you up.[6] I'm going to fuck your wife, and then your mom, if you don't tell me the truth." But after awhile, these same police realized that the story they'd been told by the guys from the unit actually wasn't that clear. One of the detectives went to his superior to tell him that there were big gaps in the story. And it was too perfect. It just didn't make sense. The troops said that the prisoner was a PCC member and that he knew all sorts of things about what had gone down in recent months. They had stumbled across him while patrolling. After stopping him on the street, they found drugs. He then confessed to being a PCC member and to knowing about a meeting when a "salve"—a message to all PCC affiliates—was made that called for police to be assassinated.

The suspect, however, had a very different story. He was picked up by plainclothes police, whom he thought were Civil Police detectives. These police approached him about a debt he owed to the PCC for two machine guns that he'd lost. They asked him about being *cobrado* [charged] with his life for having lost the guns by a PCC member named "Duque." He told them he knew nothing of the story, that he was now living under a different alias and hadn't had a single interaction with the organization since he had fled prison in 2008. Initially, he'd had trouble with a powerful PCC member whose girlfriend he had messed around with. These first police had told him that they would "throw him to the unit to kill" unless he could give some information. They'd told him, "You'll take these bricks (of marijuana), say they are yours, and you'll take the charge so you don't make us look bad." If you change your story, they had said, we'll kill your wife and daughter.

The yawning gap between these two stories—one simple and logical, the other complex and nuanced—raised doubt and suspicion among the police detectives. At least one of them very significant: what was the suspect's motive to rat on the PCC, especially knowing that he would be back in their midst in the prison in a matter of days? But he was much less worried about the PCC than he was about this police unit. He didn't want to say everything on paper, or to be recorded. The police unit would be able to read everything, and he didn't trust that a videotaped statement wouldn't end up in their hands either. Detectives had already prepared the video camera but he steadfastly refused. But the detective found a novel way to get the suspect's story out. The suspect had mentioned knowing about a particular group of murders of women that this unit had carried out years prior. And the suspect knew exactly which police officer had pulled the trigger.

So the detective convinced him to put down most of his version of the story with a novel tool: me. The detective wanted to use me as a witness of his statement. This "Canadian sociologist" would verify and serve as a guarantee against any retaliation. He could feel good about this because I was there, formally, and the guys from the unit would also know that. The man agreed to write his statement of the night's events without details that undermined the unit's story. He would approve it, and he would not be prosecuted for everything that the unit was charging he did, but he could stay the night in the station's jail, where he would be safe. In exchange he would give up everything he knew about the other incident. In that testimony he could also share everything about what happened that night. This statement would not be available to the unit, particularly if he chose to give that statement as a confidential witness.

After the statement was finished and the other detectives took the man away, I asked the detective about the circumstances. Was he a PCC member, after all? Where the drugs his? He's definitely a PCC member, he told me. "He is PCC. Maybe he isn't all that involved anymore, but he is. The smart ones don't carry guns." The drugs were harder to know. "It's difficult," he said, "But I think so." He wasn't worried too much about whether the troops were fucking with this guy. But he was interested in how this case could help solve the other incident. He spoke about the need to be serious about not letting anyone—police or PCC—"kill innocent people," as they did in that incident two years prior. Another detective told me more:

"In this report the statement is just basic. They'll have access to this report. Tomorrow at a different investigation unit they'll take everything that he said here and everything else that he knows about the killings years ago."

A bit later, the police from the unit came in to talk about how things progressed with the suspect. A conversation ensued about the violent feud between the PCC and police, and the degree of instability pervading the city as a whole—but for police in particular. "When he told us about the *salve* where they decided to kill police, I wanted to wring his neck," said an officer from the unit.

In the Homicide Division they had been investigating all of the police killings since they started to come in big numbers. More than anyone they were seeing firsthand the ways that police had been picked off. The detective recalled one of these in a conversation with a police officer from the unit. "It is all on film. The security camera shows the police guy getting shot, twice. You can see everything. Him stumbling [holds his arms out and wavering]. The bandido walks up, holds his head and . . . [feigns holding both a head and a gun, pulls the trigger repeatedly]."

"For me, a police officer is a police officer," said an officer from the unit, lamentingly. "From top to bottom. If one dies we all have to back him up. If not, they will eat us alive."

And yet both the detective and I knew something that the officer did not. Weeks prior a detective from this homicide group had a group of these officers arrested for killing a member of the PCC. I was surprised when the detective brought it up later in a conversation with the officers. "My close friend was the one that had your co-workers arrested. But he kept a few of them out. There were a whole bunch that stayed behind at the crime scene. Internal affairs wanted all of them. He argued that they weren't involved." The ROTA officer stood and listened, not showing obvious reaction, almost as though he already knew how and why that case went down the way it did.

Just then the phone rang. A police detective typing a report on a desktop computer picked it up. Another resistência, he said. Police killed a bandido on the South Side. "One less," said the detective. "While on the job?" asked the unit officer. "*Boooooooaaaa.*" Goooood.

Doubt and suspicion was almost everywhere. This was simply not normal times. The difference was stark, especially for the detectives doing their routine tasks in the midst of it all. Where they otherwise might have been more lenient to the violence of the Tactical Squad or ROTA, homicide detectives were politically enabled by someone up above. There were expectations, earned from past performance, that they would stand their investigative ground. And yet the structural power asymmetry was real. If a violent police officer wanted to settle a score, he could use this moment to conceal it. It might not even have gone all that well noticed since so much was in disarray.

Things were also very different for those running around and doing the investigations of the crazy amount of people dying. I chatted with a crime scene analyst one day at a scene. She had a moment while waiting for investigators to pull the dead man's hands out of rigor mortis and into a position that they could take prints on their form. His hands kept springing back violently, almost as though slapping the investigators away. The perito told me that she had blown the mind of a friend who had the same job as hers in Europe. Over the phone she had explained to him that things were especially crazy these days because of the crisis. Usually she would attend to two or three multiple homicide cases a month. This month she had been to twelve. In their conversation her friend misunderstood. "Wow, twelve in a year is a lot," he'd said. "No," she'd corrected him, emphatically gesturing at the phone her hand had become. The twelve had been just this month *so far*. There were still a few days still to go. And in terms of body count, that was outside of any resistências or single or double murders she would investigate.

She did a rough calculation for me of how nuts things really were. There are twenty perito crews working the homicide circuit in the city of São Paulo. If each crew had an average case-load around the same size as hers, with a minimum of three dead in each multiple homicide (as per the definition), then around 800 people were dead just in multiple homicide cases. She said it to me slowly, "This. Month. Alone."

Multiple homicides are not typical of PCC governance or of normal times of stability. In fact, the PCC regime has tended to decrease the number of chacinas. This is because, historically, multiple homicides are a hallmark of moments of retribution and vengeance, the kind of rash and unmeasured violence the PCC abhors. Multiple homicides are a kind of violence connected with the violation of "respect." Multiple homicides are often about sending a notice and eliminating, indiscriminately, people of a certain adversarial group. They are rarely that well targeted but instead reflect who may be in a given place—like a drug sales point—in given times. There are strong parallels between the drive-by shootings of gangland spaces in the United States—except that in crisis-ridden São Paulo, it is not a rival gang doing the shooting. It is off-duty police. And unlike in the United States, these drive-by shootings are also as much about social cleansing as they are about retribution.

If this was a new pattern of violence that suggested how police were trying to deal with targeted assassinations, there was also evidence of increases in seemingly unconnected crimes. One afternoon we tore southward through the traffic, squeezing between narrow lanes in order to get to a scene. The police didn't have much evidence yet, except that the dead person was a man found early in the morning on a road leading into a rural area out of a periurban neighborhood. It didn't take us too long, but the ride was never boring. Along the way, some alarm bells went off when detectives noticed that a car was following them in the wake of cars inching over to either side. It was a weird situation, and at first none of them knew what to make of it. They could see just one person in the car, which inched closer to the SUV we were in. Things got tense, and the detectives snapped ideas about it back and forth. Someone suggested drawing their guns and stopping to confront the situation head on. Another said not to, that they could get in trouble if it didn't turn

into anything. A third thought the person was probably just nuts—
louco—and that they could scare him well enough without drawing their
guns. We stopped at a light, and our driver waved up the car. It crept
forward slowly.

It quickly became apparent that it was a regular old fool, who just
wanted to get ahead of everyone else, at any cost. They yelled at him,
called him an *idiota*, an asshole (*babaca*), and a *filho da puta* (a son of
a whore) who they would have taken in to the station if they weren't
going somewhere important. The man looked somewhere between un-
perturbed and pleased, as though he couldn't have cared less about the
scolding but managed to get a rise out of the police. It was really only
the detectives who took this seriously.

It started to rain heavily as we came off the main avenue and weaved
our way through a couple of streets. It was always a mystery as to where
exactly the body would be found. Usually the most obvious indicator
was where the Military Police car was, though not always. Often times
it was a walk from the road, into a field or a gully. We came to the end
of the paved road and started into the muck of a road running downhill
that had become more of a stream. Not far down we saw the Military
Police car. It looked like the body was right behind it. Eternally confused
by São Paulo's weather, I was wearing just a short sleeve button-up shirt.
Others pulled out the raincoats that they often had with them. I resolved
to get wet. The body was on the road and covered in a fitted white bed
sheet, by now almost transparent from the rain and laying on a down-
ward slant. There was a single round bloodstain where the head seemed to
be, and a trickle of blood coming from underneath it was being washed
away into the mud. It was about ten in the morning. Bystanders and a
couple of relatives were there. Relatives said that the man had left for
work in the morning, having probably come to this point by five-thirty as
he usually did on his way to work. He had been interrupted on his walk.

Someone pulled off the bedsheet. There was a single gunshot wound
to the man's forehead, and a tear on the knee of his jeans. The detective
called it almost right away. "Crime of passion"—*crime passional*—he
said. Already, this case did not fit with the normal homicide. The man was
a *trabalhador* with a job. Someone knew his route and the time he went
to work, having chosen to meet him along the way. Because it was a reasonably busy road—lots of people trying to get to the closest bus stop at
that time of the morning—the person would have done it quickly. Add to
that the cause of death—a single shot to the head from the top down-
wards, likely taken after the man had been forced to kneel. Someone

wanted him to feel subordinated. We found out sometime soon after, from a relative—who was there and speaking to police (again abnormal)—that the man *may have* been seeing a married woman. The logic fit. "Esse crime tá resolvido," said the chief detective ("this case is solved").

But this case was not quite that straightforward. "It is possible that this happened because of the situation," one detective told me. The violence between police and the PCC had left the moral system and its "bureaucrats" distracted. Normally, a crime like this would be forbidden. If the wronged man had taken the situation to the PCC, there would have been a tribunal involving everyone. In all likelihood the now dead man would have been punished—the process of punishment often delegated from the PCC to the person wronged. The punishment would not be death, though. It seemed that the killer had risked being held accountable by the system, in spite of the severity of the potential punishment for killing someone without prior authorization—death itself.

The difference from the normal was also unmistakable in the amount of attention that was now being directed at the police nearly every day (and every night). There were satellite-equipped vans from the major television stations parked outside the homicide station. Press conferences now seemed routine, and we would watch the presenters standing outside pre-recording their segments, sometimes over and over and over, until they got it perfect. It was often surprising how many times it took to get a two-minute segment right. More than a few times the reporters would be wearing a suit on the top but shabby and untucked jeans on the bottom while talking about extrajudicial killings and bloody multiple homicides.

Just as things had changed in terms of media coverage and the amount of work for homicide detectives, it had also shifted the conditions on the ground for police in and around their homes. I dedicated a portion of my research time to reading the homicide reports of police that had been killed. Some of these told of distinct histories and longstanding, but nonetheless precarious, relationships between police and the PCC. In one case, a police officer who I call Matheus was known and well liked in the community were he both lived and worked. He was recognized by many for being diligent in making drug seizures and confronting the organization with regular arrests, taking an obvious toll on their day-to-day activities. But it was clear that there were underlying antagonisms. He had survived threats during the violence of May 2006 and had been involved in arresting high-profile local leaders in recent years. And yet the PCC did nothing until the right moment. Early one morning, as

Matheus drank coffee at a food stand, two men approached him. They stepped past other bystanders and the man serving the coffee and shot Matheus over and over and over again, before grabbing his gun and running off.

Matheus had been receiving threats for weeks. His colleagues told of cars waiting ominously outside of their houses off and on since the beginning of the violence. Sometimes they would have to be late for work—hours late—because they didn't want to leave the house until the car was gone. Some police had chosen to go on leave, fearing that they or their families would be imminently assassinated. They wanted to wait out the storm. Locals told of a system of power in Matheus's neighborhood in which no one could rob, let alone kill, without the authorization of a specific PCC leader. The conclusion was clear: Matheus's killing was a much longed for conclusion that only came to pass when the moment was right. This might have been a killing about settling a score. But it was not the kind of score that some—including the governor—had suggested was behind many off-duty police deaths. By all indications, Matheus was killed by the PCC because he was a thorn in their side, not because of some dirty togetherness.

The details of endless cases like this repeated themselves and echoed in the changes in the behavior of the detectives that I was hanging out with. Most were very cautious about when they would go home—if they would—and how they would manage things once there. Like my visit with Beto to Jardim Ângela, police wanted to control their situation as much as possible. They traveled less at night, always sat facing the door in public places, and chose to come to work on their motorcycle if they had one—as opposed to by car or bus, where they were sitting ducks in traffic. Always keep moving, they said. The predictability of normal times was gone and safety was impossible now. The trap door in the false floor was wide open.

There was so much uncertainty in the air among police, partly because the situation was largely out of their hands, fed and fueled by a cohort of violent police actively engaged in trying to eradicate the PCC and incentivized by political leaders. And while a handful of police were engaged in that all-out *guerra particular*—this "private war"—most police just wanted to lay low and let the violence blow over, even if only for their own deeply personal reasons.

On many night shifts I would arrive at 9:00 p.m. or so. And when it was cold, we would often walk down the street to the last place open within walking distance. This was a fairly upscale place, even if it was surrounded by cheap boarding houses, sex workers, and was a block or two away from the crackland (*cracolândia*)—a mass of hundreds of sad-looking homeless men, women, and children living in and around what look like bombed-out old buildings. This *barzinho* (little bar) served a great *sopa* that would warm things up a little and make the cold and unheated station a little warmer when the temperature would dip to the single digits. The detectives rarely talked at any length about important police concerns while out. And though there were many issues of substance to discuss, the conversation inevitably surrounded how much a particular *futebol* team sucked this year and—egging on those who supported them—how imminent relegation and a sullied reputation of that storied team was.

The streets of this part of São Paulo are deserted at night. When the iron covers of storefronts close they bring the graffiti, dust, and dirt down with them, as though purposely creating a new social and temporal environment. I never found it all that comforting. The walk back in groups of two or three was always quiet, save for the occasional crack cocaine addict rummaging through piles of garbage and cardboard. It always struck me that anything could happen here, if someone really wanted it to—though this part of town was far from where it would typically occur. And, besides, since the office where the Homicide Division is had been bombed during the 2006 attacks, they had taken a few measures. Security cameras covered the block. On the street in front of the station they had installed a speed camera that would capture any wise guy that thought it a good idea to speed by and lob a grenade or two out the passenger side window.

The memory of 2006 was looming large in the ways that police surmised how this crisis would end. It had ended so abruptly the last time. From one moment to the next, a question of hours, it went from utter bloodshed to ominous silence, with normalcy creeping back in. After a bowl of hot soup on this cool night we chatted in the gray room of the division. After months of killing and unpredictability, the discussion among police was starting to shift. The protracted nature of this iteration of crisis left many detectives looking for answers as to how, exactly, it would end. One detective was all over it. "Houve acordo," he said. There's been an agreement. Things had been quiet for a day, which was something new. When it gets this quiet this fast, something had happened. He was sure of it.

These police understood that the issue at hand was not whether the war against the PCC—from the few, but affecting the many—could be won. There was unity among the detectives that the assassination of real or perceived PCC members, whether carried out by off-duty or on-duty via resistências, was not productive. As one police officer put it, to kill PCC members and their families in cold blood was to stoop to the level of the bandido. "A state can't be reactive like that," he said, summarizing the point neatly, "we're sinking to their standards." It was circular and there was no stability. The state was not rising above or regulating the violence, it was inciting it. And no one was going to become safer with more violence.

A detective named Robson placed it in a binary. He explained that it could be resolved in one of two ways: either the state cracks down entirely, drawing all of the public security system together into a coordinated war, with an expectation and acceptance among all that the effect would be an all-out and bloody campaign of multiple years at least. Think Mexico, circa 2007, except that this situation was perhaps much larger in terms of the membership of both parties involved.

If not, the alternative was some politician gets in a helicopter and flies to the prison to meet the PCC leadership, just like last time. They'd banter and reach some accord, backed up by money, guarantees, and who knows what. Relative peace would come again overnight, and day-by-day, bit-by-bit, things would become predictable and return, more or less, to "normal." The former option was virtually impossible given the federal government, the strength of civil society, and the hesitance among many police themselves to risk everything for something so uncertain and untrustworthy. It was deeply in question whether the resources of the system could even feasibly allow for such a scenario. This is not to mention what it would do to the city, surely turning it into a graveyard many scales greater than Tijuana, Ciudad Juárez, or Monterrey—where the violence of crisis pales even to São Paulo's normal. The coordination between investigation and repression—between the worlds of the Military and Civil Police, in other words—was also just not there to support a strategy like this. Between the two there was way too much suspicion and doubt about sharing intelligence, much less a mutual trust of the capacity or interests of the other. A partnership like this would doubtless aggravate even further the street-level assassinations of police living in and around the PCC. But more important, it was obvious that an all-out attack on the PCC was something no politician would take on. Detectives themselves referenced the policy shift in Mexico to crack down on cartels that led to a very public and explosive war. The lesson, it seemed, was: don't mess with the status quo. But underscoring the unlikelihood of some kind of orchestrated crackdown or policy shift was the idea that too many people near the top were benefitting directly or indirectly from either or both of the PCC's lucrative control over the drug trade or its effect on homicide and sensations of security in the city during "normal" times.

The only logical course of action was the latter. An agreement like the last time—2006—would reestablish some calm and set the minds of most police at ease. In the absence of violence, it would remove the issue that had recently consumed the local, national, and international media. It would also avoid the type of destabilizing public discussion that had already toppled the secretary for public security and the chiefs of both the Military and Civil Police. Not that the detective felt that public discussion was counterproductive. It was good to have their struggles better understood. But everyone seemed to agree: this solution was deeply flawed, amounting to an effort to sweep a three-ton elephant under a rug with a corn broom.

Not just that, this kind of reaction—to reestablish a pact—would further embed a trajectory of cyclical crisis. Pushing the PCC back underground, as per the pattern over the last decade, would allow it to continue to expand its ligatures and influence in surreptitious and uninhibited ways. This course of action would ultimately prioritize periods of calm over the dramatic spike of all-consuming violence. To the detectives, it also seemed a universally better solution than an all-out war between the state and the PCC.

If one other thing was clear from the detectives' reflections on the troublesome dualism of potential solutions, it was that such a pact and subsequent consensus cannot be reestablished by police on the street. The scale of the problem—urban and beyond—was much too big for local groups or individuals to mend in one neighborhood or another. Only a top-down solution, affected in a systematic way and acknowledged by both parties, could reset some kind of common foundation for relative peace to reemerge. What people needed was some indication that the rules were back in place. The incentive to follow those rules was never in short supply.

This months-long crisis was lasting much longer than that which occurred in a matter of days and weeks in May of 2006. The ebb and flow of killings between the police—but particularly ROTA—and the PCC showed that, despite periods of apparent restabilization, there was always a fair share of unpredictability. With the spike in chacinas and resistências toward the end of the year, including the rumored killing of the mother of a PCC member in a neighboring city, police detectives talked about a shift in the tide. The truculence of police—on and off duty—they said, was forcing the PCC away from confrontation and assassinations. "They are carrying bibles whenever they leave the house," once detective told me as we drove to a murder scene one morning. They did so, he said, in an attempt to exorcise—at least superficially—the bandido identity that defines them. Embedded in his suggestion (however likely it was) was a third possibility: asymmetric or guerillalike violence. If members of the PCC consciously defy the kinds of markers that signify being a bandido—the same markers that are signposts for detectives and police—they seek to further conceal themselves within the general population of innocent *trabalhadores*. This would not necessarily weaken the PCC system, but, rather, further embed it and obscure it in local populations, throwing into disarray well-established notions and practices of deservedness of violence.

PART THREE

Debate

CHAPTER 7

The Powerful?

By December the explosion in violence had led to more than just police and PCC casualties. The governor, Geraldo Alckmin, had sacked his secretary of public security, as well as the head of the Military Police and the head of the Civil Police. As I was preparing to return home, and having viewed the scenes of dead police and dead citizens multiple times a day, I decided to use my position to add an underheard perspective to the increasing cacophony of voices questioning public security policymakers and demanding change. In December 2012, I published an op-ed in the *New York Times* that outlined what some of the structural and institutional failures of the public security system looked like "from the inside." I did so in the hope that citizens would be more informed about their police, the nature of the violence, its key protagonists and losers, and the absence of political leadership in substantive questions.

Police—both the detectives of the Civil Police and the beat cops of the Military Police—are rarely, if ever, public voices in debates about their own work and livelihoods. While Military Police are denied the right to speak out because of their subservience to military discipline and tight regulation of insubordination, Civil Police typically distrust those among them who speak out. This distrust manifests from organizational, historical, and normative positions within the police. It also comes from top levels and political defensiveness. Some Civil Police detectives have been summarily fired for voicing opinions critical of politicians. Police advance in their careers according to bureaucratic rules but also by patronage and political connectedness. To openly criticize or support a particular political leader or figure—of a given patronage or not—is to show one's hand and expose oneself to serious vulnerabilities. At minimum, to speak out against political leaders is to put one's career at a disadvantage and at risk of having certain barriers placed in the path to promotion. This appears true, even—and perhaps particularly—in the Internet age, where police have increasingly found a voice (under their own name or a pseudonym) in blogs, on Facebook, and in other places like YouTube discussion forums.[1]

What has emerged, instead, is a new kind of vocal criticism of the top from the top. The recent election of former members of the ROTA to political office in São Paulo state is shaping an overtly public discourse of police and policing. These new elected officials, such as ROTA's former commander known widely as "Coronel Telhada," are creating a strong and public voice for hard-line policing and security policies that increasingly protect police by advocating for more leniency for police who kill perceived criminals. But this is a one-sided kind of "democratic" advocacy, which privileges the right to kill over the right to life. In doing so, it also privileges the most lethal police over those expected to do diligent and cautious investigation. This seems a democratic paradox—democratic representation of the interests of police seeks to formally enshrine the use of routine and deadly violence by police within democratic institutions. In other words, the most democratically vocal claims for security are coming from a very particular kind of police—one that finds its constituents in support of an unapologetically deadly police. This configuration of democratic claim-making for greater security stares directly at the contestation between two major theoretical positions about the formation of states—security versus democracy—and how, exactly, extreme violence may eventually be centralized in states under a democratic paradigm.[2]

There is also a resistance to police speaking out from the "middle." While union-backed collective action and strikes have been common in recent years, they are typically only for reasons of pay and job security. Rarely do these mobilizations surround claims against the generalized failure of the public security system—in which police themselves are of course implicated. Instead, strikes have often appeared scattered in terms of their organizing logic and message. This can be attributed at least in part to the fact that no single union represents Civil Police employees. Rather, the CP is large enough that there are unions for almost all of the occupations within it. Even if these unions agree on job action, the outcome is often highly fragmented in terms of message. In the most recent strike, the action gained attention for a different reason. When the Civil Police strikers marched on the government palace to voice their discontent, the governor sent the Military Police Riot Squad—*Choque*—to the gates to meet them. Mayhem ensued. The Riot Squad proceeded to relentlessly tear gas the strikers, who briefly returned the favor with live gunfire. The live televised event did little more than reinforce public perception that these two disorganized and often antagonistic police forces are responsible for the state of insecurity and violence in the city.

There are also many barriers at the bottom for colleagues who consider speaking out. The most prominent barrier are other police—colleagues—opposed to the suggestion of having their untoward activities exposed. When a police detective mused openly one afternoon about being interested in writing a memoir about everything that he had seen and done as a detective—something he believed would make him extremely rich and reveal a great many important things—he was roundly panned by the others in the room. He would be seen as a traitor and hated by everyone, they said. And, perhaps worse, he might end up dead. The intimation was clear. If he ever managed to get the book out, he might as well go into hiding.

The multidirectional embargo on police voices in public debates about police reform and public security has substantial consequences for what we know and believe about police, not just in public life but in academic debates. Much of this is mirrored in conventional expectations about police today in São Paulo, as, indeed, across much of the Global South. Under formal democratic rule, but with little representative democratic voice themselves, the police are the subject of widespread, mostly negative presumptions on the part of the general public: their unsavory working conditions, their moral outlooks, their propensity for illegality and ugly systemic attributes—*all* police kill and extort—are widely regarded as true. By and large, any convincing counterpoint to that opinion has been absent.

Indeed, this problem was an initial spark for my early stage research in 2009. I was concerned with the logical fallacies embedded in our knowledge—or, rather, assumptions—about police in the South. It seemed to me that this gap had not just emerged from the methodological limitations of scholarly debates, but more important, was a result of how little we know—especially from police themselves—about who police are, what they do, and what they think about the changing world around them. In the absence of such knowledge, police have become defined much more by the research on people *around* them and what they think police do and why.

My position within the police, then, was somewhat exceptional. Not only did I see what police were like in personal and occupational terms over the years, I was able to see, from the inside, how acutely and structurally fallible the system is—especially in the midst of a violent crisis such at that of 2012. Over the course of my research I witnessed a wide spectrum of occupational hazards stemming from the products and by-products of violence that police routinely confront both on and off the job. These ranged from dead police, those dead from police, police who wanted nothing more than to go on temporary leave but were restrained by the promise of a pension, and more barren, police who simply walked off the job in order to remove themselves from such risk and to be with their families. Indeed, many did (and do) just that—hundreds quit their jobs in the midst of the 2012 crisis.[3] But even in spite of all the strategies being employed by the tens of thousands of police to deal with insecurity, it didn't really surprise me that one of the strategies *wasn't* to speak out. Very little, if anything, was being said—by police or anyone—about where "regular" police (not those who go out looking to kill or extort) were located in the midst of this escalating urban violence.

Before I submitted the article (and not knowing if it would fly), I shopped the idea with the detectives that I was seeing every day. The response was decidedly hot and cold. Some detectives thought the prospect was very important and implored me to "tell their side of the story." Others, while not completely against the prospect, began to act differently around me in noticeable ways. One police officer in particular caught himself mid-sentence while discussing the "tolls" (*pedágio*) collected, pooled, and distributed at local police stations from arrested people, businesses, and other rentable sources. He was suddenly worried I would quote him personally in the search for a salacious, scandalous, or expository story.[4] With his tongue halfway into his cheek, another said that I looked like I could be an Iraq-styled US private security contractor—something that those who have seen and known me would probably find a rather remote possibility. Despite the spectrum of responses I received, I decided to push forward knowing that the outcome could change my ability to ever come back or be welcome among police.

Posted on the *New York Times* web site simultaneously in Portuguese and English, the op-ed landed heavily in Brazil.[5] Major daily newspapers in São Paulo, national television channels and magazines, and major online news web sites picked it up, reprinting parts or nearly all of the text. Major blogs, including the blog of a Civil Police detective fired for speaking out, posted the text in full, generating hundreds of comments.[6] At the apex of the debate about the article the following day, the National Radio Channel asked the governor, who was leaving a meeting in Brasília, about the article. He did not acknowledge the question or provide a response. Meanwhile, as the story moved swiftly through social media, police from around Brazil that I had never met were e-mailing me and asking me to meet them personally so they could tell their story. Others wanted to add me as a "friend" on Facebook. I don't know how many people read the article. In an e-mail, a representative from the *New York Times* declined to give me statistics for visits to the two versions of the article, but did note that "it did well" and was "shared widely on social media," especially the Portuguese version.

The waves from the article did not subside for some time. Some weeks later I reluctantly did an interview for the largest online news site in São Paulo. A journalist from *Universo On-Line*, known more simply as "UOL," had sought me out relentlessly for weeks with e-mails, Twitter messages, and calls to an organization I was affiliated with. After the reporter eventually explained to me that they were working on a story about police salaries throughout Brazil, I agreed to speak with her. She explained that the interview would be part of a larger analysis about the working conditions of police. For some reason, this made me feel more at ease. As a result, I spoke candidly about the challenges of policing and organized crime, and included some of the findings from my 2006 research in a PCC community about the PCC having contributed to decreases in violence and crime, especially from the point of view of local residents. I expected that a few points—sound bites, at the least—would be used to inform the research on police salaries that they were advancing. But I was wrong and naïve, and fell into the same trap that police themselves are savvy to avoid in their interactions with the media.

What they produced was vastly different than what I had anticipated, bordering on the salacious. On December 19, they published the interview, under the headline, "For Those Living in the Periphery, the PCC Reduced Crime, Says Canadian Studying Violence in São Paulo."[7] It was an article of its own, printed in a question and answer format—something that I had never expected nor presumed would even be possible without, at minimum, asking for my permission. Not only that, they placed it as the lead article on the homepage, where it generated considerable attention and more than a thousand "likes" on Facebook and hundreds of comments beneath the article. That the article generated discussion wasn't surprising considering it included many of the boundary pushing statements I had intended as background:

Q: *Regarding the lack of order in police work, did you come to any conclusions?*

A: The police on the street, the investigator, the soldado or the cabo live a much different reality from police up the chain, from who makes orders. It is rare that the police in charge, who manage policy, who are closest to the Governor, know the reality of the street. These people have never lived in a favela, have never lived in a situation where they are making $300 [USD equiv.] a month, where they need to moonlight at three or four other jobs in order to pay for their daughter's schooling. So it is because the police on the street can never reach that level or become Chief. . . . This is worse in the Military Police. The military structure leaves no space for innovation or dialogue, you can't suggest anything to your superior, you're totally subordinated under the system. Your ideas don't matter, it's only the ideas of those in charge that matter. But those in charge have no understanding of the street.

This caught the attention and raised the ire of those at the top of the public security system itself. The following day UOL published a rebuttal via the spokesman for the Public Security Secretariat, linking and referencing the original article.

> With regard to the interview with Canadian Doctoral Student Graham Denyer Willis, published by UOL on the 19th of December, we have the following clarifications:
> It is lamentable that a student should use the name of such a respected institution like the Massachusetts Institute of Technology [MIT], to lend strength to claims that are far from scientific. Apart from repeating the argument of another "expert," which simplistically uses the PCC name to explain any criminal phenomenon in the State of São Paulo, the suggestion that a criminal faction is responsible for the homicide rate reduction in São Paulo is a fallacy.
> In actual fact, these "experts," like this Canadian student Willis, confuse more than they explain. Rather than producing knowledge that helps the State to combat crime, they end up creating myths, supposedly backed up by respected academic institutions.
> Everyone knows that the rate of homicides in São Paulo has fallen significantly. Since the end of the 1990s, the State has reduced crimes against life by 72%, moving from a rate of 35.27 cases per 100,000 residents in 1999 to 10.0 per 100,000 in 2011.

This reduction is multifactorial, but it is much more correct to attribute it to government investments in public security than to the activity of a criminal faction that seems to fascinate some academics such as this Canadian.

The UN [United Nations] has recognized the actions that have made this conquest possible. São Paulo's positive experience was recognized in a UN's global study of homicide in 207 countries.

Other Latin American cities, like Bogotá, Medellin and Cali, all in Colombia, each have much higher homicide rates, at 23/100 thousand, 94.5/100 thousand and 82.4/100 thousand respectively. São Paulo's rate is much better than Brazil's, which is 22.3 per 100 thousand residents.

To throw all of this work into the mud just to glamorize a criminal faction, seems, at the least, strange.

Office of the Spokesman for the Public Security Secretary
(UOL 2012b).

At the bottom of the web page in the comment section was a single, solitary note from one reader:

Well, the worst kind of blindness is the unwillingness to see. . . . I live in the periphery and know well what happens when you kill someone without the permission of the PCC . . . any fool knows that if it wasn't for this whomever wants to kill would never care about said government "investments." I don't know why there are these attacks on the Canadian, since he's only told the truth and nothing more . . . even though it hurts, the truth needs to be said . . . even though this really is nothing new . . . the worst part is that the government pretends not to know, or, worst still, actually doesn't know. (UOL 2012b)

Reading all of this at home for Christmas in Canada I felt happy to be far away—something no ordinary Brazilian in the same circumstance could be. Between the lines of the spokespersons note were all sorts of attempts at character assassination. More important, though, were the suggestions of an infatuation with the PCC—essentially pigeonholing me as a bandido sympathizer. This was a rather typical response used to label those studying the PCC or issues surrounding it—such as Gabriel Feltran, the "expert" that I had referred to in my interview and who they pointed to in the response. And yet the note was so full of logical holes and so lacking in evidence and substance that it left itself open to being picked apart by the words of one poignant but personally connected lay reader.

I didn't know how the people that I had been doing research on for the last few years would react to this kind of press that problematized their work and could be seen to cast a shadow on any sense of prestige or institutional self-worth that they may have had. As more interview requests appeared I resolved to remove myself from the limelight and let the situation blow over a little bit. A couple of months later I spoke with a delegada I had known for years about what had transpired surrounding and following the article and the secretary's rebuttal note. She had plenty to say on the matter. Many police followed the back and forth, and she felt, were glad to see some of their problems and even their dirty laundry aired publicly. "Most police agree with you," she said, "and those who don't agree can't because they are close to power and don't want to lose their status or their position . . . they were just defending themselves."

When I eventually went back for a brief visit to see the homicide detectives, the response was even warmer. I was greeted with hugs, stories, and jokes about "royalty payments." What was I going to write about next? Was I going to become an international correspondent bigwig? Contrary to what I had thought, the articles, which were at times quite sharply critical of the police, had opened the door to a different kind of rapport, as though I had finally proved—fully and completely—that I could be trusted. There was a sense that I had exposed myself enough that I no longer needed to wear a bulletproof vest either.

Even so, my visit back was overshadowed by a number of major changes that had landed in the Homicide Division. Early in 2013 the public security secretary made significant policy changes and procedural reorganizations. Some of these sought to strengthen the integrity of homicide investigation as a means to restrain the recent explosion of resistências and chacinas suspected widely to be linked to police. The first of these measures was a quite dramatic effort to address one of the primary focuses of this book, the resistencia. A January 2013 resolution from the secretary extinguished the formal category of the resistência and outlined a new understanding for classifying and investigating deaths at the hands of police, as well as new procedures outlining what needed to happen in the immediate aftermath of a police shooting.[8]

Under this new regulatory frame, police killings of citizens would no longer be called "resistências seguida de morte." Rather, they would be categorized as "death following police intervention"—*morte decorrente de intervenção policial*. This marked an analytical shift, declaring that police shootings are homicides to be investigated with the emphasis on criminal defense and a demand for justification on the part of police. The resolution also attempted to make logical and systematic how these killings are understood and investigated by the Civil Police, shifting the blame from the dead or dying "suspect" and placing it on the police officer(s) involved, thus requiring police to face a burden of evidence that their actions were merited in order for these actions to be exonerated.

More noteworthy, though, was a new and complementary requirement for the investigation of these deaths by the homicide police. The resolution also made it illegal for police to personally transport those that they had shot to the hospital—a widespread practice known to obstruct and obscure investigations and destroy evidence. Instead, under this new policy police would need to call the public ambulance, known as SAMU, after shooting someone and await its arrival at the scene. In the meantime, they became obligated to keep the scene entirely intact, defending it—in effect—from themselves. No longer would police be able to move bodies under the guise that a person was still alive, nor would they be able to take the "long road" to the hospital to ensure the finality of death. Old, assumed, and acknowledged practices like "not shooting in the head" so that the person wouldn't die immediately—a façade for moderate use of force—as one detective once explained, or transplanting a body to a different location, became more obvious and deeply scrutinized under these new reforms. This powerful top-down reform, itself a modification of a reform suggested by the National Public Security Secretariat (SENASP) months earlier, threatened to throw light into the shadows that have defined the practice of police killings of citizens for decades.

There can be little doubt that these new policies show that the secretary was deeply concerned about the broad license to kill that police wielded, especially under the de facto policy of the routine resistência model. In an additional step, his policymakers pushed to further restrict this violence by driving a wedge between on-duty and off-duty violence or retired police. Under the resistência model, off-duty and retired police could both be recognized as representatives of the public administration. Any action by them, while on duty or off duty, against apparent "criminals" constituted a resistência. But under this new policy the secretary applied a more strict reading of the law. Off-duty and retired police would no longer be deemed agents of the public administration as defined by the Penal Code. As private citizens, a killing by an off-duty or retired police officer, like the police officer Miguel who was awakened in his home by a robbery outside his window, would be deemed a homicide just like any other. These police would no longer garner special treatment nor benefit—formally speaking, at least—from the kinds of presumptions and prefabricated justifications about why they did what they did.

But this move came with at least one hitch. Since in these instances the shooter is by definition known, these cases were removed from the jurisdiction of the central Homicide Division. Like all other homicides where the suspect is known, these became the responsibility of the local precinct—which are more obscured from public view and lack the investigative specialty of the Homicide Division. Further from centralized, specialized, and professionalized investigation, the policy shift allows for other influences to "bleed in." Therein lies a counterintuitive point: though the obvious expectation embedded in this new policy is that police need to be more tightly regulated in their use of violence, these cases are being pushed even further away from the centrally recognized authority entrusted to investigate and solve homicides—what is sold to the public as an "elite" unit of the police.

In April 2013, the governor announced another policy change relevant to homicide investigation. A rash of killings known as latrocínios—armed robberies in which the victims were also killed—had hit the city in the last year or so. These latrocínios often appeared to be a byproduct of PCC-police violence. A series of latrocínio cases made big news because of the apparent cold bloodedness of the aggressors. One incident in particular caused outrage when the aggressor later said publicly of the fifteen-year-old girl he had killed, "That's what happens to those who resist" (É o que acontece com quem reage).[9] This was almost the exact same phrase used by São Paulo's governor to describe an encounter in which eight PCC members were killed in a chacina involving ROTA in August 2012. "Those who didn't resist are alive," he said (Quem nao reagiu esta vivo) (Estado 2012). Believed to be analytically distinct because of a motivation to rob, as opposed to a desire to kill, these deaths have subsisted against the odds as a distinct category of violent death since the end of the dictatorship in 1985. Since the creation of the Homicide Division in 1986, latrocínios have been the investigative work of a specific specialty subgroup in the Homicide Division.

This simmering and perceived analytic difference between "murder" and "murder occurring during a robbery" was the primary motivation for the governor's relocation of this subgroup of crime to the Organized Crime Division (DEIC). Said the governor at the time, "A latrocínio is very different than a homicide. Those are crimes of passion, bar fights, or retribution killings. A latrocínio is a robbery and the special unit for robbery is DEIC, which has all of the tools for investigating robberies" (Jornal do Brasil 2013).

Prior to being investigated by the Homicide Division, pre-1985, latrocínios were the realm of DEIC and its dictatorship precursor the Department for Political and Social Order—DOPS. This was a time when bank robberies were undertaken by political subversives and were a defining characteristic of political violence in São Paulo and other Brazilian cities. Robberies of banks and other high-value targets, which were often followed by death, were indeed orchestrated and understood to be forms of revenue for those with political motivations—those actively subverting government and the social and political order. A detailed and meticulous investigation of latrocínios was a key feature of counterrevolutionary policing. Solving these crimes showed how to disarticulate the work of political subversives at the heart of dictatorship policing—in which DOPS and DEIC was most deeply ensconced.

Today though, latrocínios reflect a different but nonetheless deep subtext about a prototypically *urban* violence. In many ways, cross-class violence has become the enemy of the state. Killing across social position, particularly when that killing indicates a disdain or hatred for another's social class—a desire to take from the wealthy, for example—is a different kind of subversion that merits a special kind of treatment. Whether one can legitimately claim that this violence is "organized" is another question. Connecting the dots between "everyday" street-level robbers and the PCC—likely the closest mode of criminal organization—would be difficult, to say the least. Legitimate questions can be raised about why the motivation to rob should supersede a homicidal outcome, defining the boundaries of jurisdiction as a result.

These new policies in the realm of homicide investigation appear to be rather schizophrenic. On one side they attempt to better synchronize, centralize, and strengthen the investigation of killing. They also seek to concentrate the authority to regulate killing in the hands of homicide detectives and to limit the ability of police to kill without "just" cause. And yet the effect is somewhat the opposite. The authority to regulate death has been increasingly fragmented into vastly different organizational and geographical pockets of the public security system. With the displacement of latrocínios to DEIC, these killings disappear into a moral system concerned more with counter-class warfare and rent-seeking connections with the PCC than with investigating human life. Letting the homicides committed by off-duty and retired police be soaked up by local precincts banishes these cases into police stations that are defined by resource constraints, criminal influences, and limited transparency.[10]

Not only that—and perhaps much more important—the transfer of these cases away from the Homicide Division is a kind of statistical sleight of hand that decreases the categorical number of police killings while also suggesting that more homicides are being solved since the perpetrators are by definition known. This despite the fact that neither of these assertions are true.

How these policy shifts are playing out empirically for the homicide detectives is starting to become more apparent. When I spoke with homicide detectives, they said that there were indeed fewer resistências occurring. An open letter published by Human Rights Watch (HRW) in July provided some confirmation of this fact. The HRW analysis of official statistics showed that the number of police killings of citizens in the first three months of 2013 dropped by 34 percent in comparison with 2012 (HRW 2013). Exactly why this drop has occurred is likely more complex. Police were being forced to heed the demand to not take those that they shot to hospital—a factor that one might think would lead to more deaths due to the time between incident and emergency treatment. Homicide detectives reported that on a few occasions, family members had rushed their kin to hospital themselves with the police car in front clearing traffic. But the reorganization of jurisdictions, new policies, and the possibility of police violence occurring in other forms—such as chacinas—are all possible explanatory factors for the dropping rates and consequences of the policy change.

The increase in chacinas, however, could be a powerful indicator of many things. In the first three and half months of 2013 nearly half of the total number of chacinas that occurred during the entire year prior had already come to pass—thirty-seven dead versus eighty-one in all of 2012. General suspicion among detectives is that chacinas are the work of police extermination groups, savvy in their knowledge of the extent and approach of investigators and the identities of those involved in the drug trade. According to an analysis done by one of São Paulo's two largest newspapers, chacinas had been in decline since 2007 when twenty-two occurred, resulting in 89 killed. In 2011, only twelve cases occurred with forty-one dead. But in 2012, double that number occurred. Little is known, however, about who exactly has been behind chacinas in recent years. At the end of 2012, only one of the twenty-four chacinas that occurred that year had been resolved. In that case, six Military Police were arrested for killing three youths. Overall, there is a great deal of consensus that chacinas are increasing and little agreement about why.

There are alternative hypotheses for this violence too. As I have discussed, chacinas became much less common as a form of killing as the PCC became a force governing death in the periphery of São Paulo. Chacinas are particularly indicative of feuding and retribution, something that the organization does not allow. Calculation and weighing when a killing is "just" is a hallmark of the PCC's form of power and its legitimacy among members and its constituent communities. If the rise in chacinas is not a reflection of police turning ever more commonly to extralegal measures, it could be a reflection of a break down in the PCC's monopoly over the right to kill. Such a turn would be indicative of a new trajectory in São Paulo's experience with violence, and an ominous one in terms of how many people may be made especially insecure in the years to come.

While it largely remains an open question how these policy reformulations will play out long term, there has been at least one obvious and horrifying side effect of one of the policy changes. The new rule restricting police from taking individuals to hospitals has spawned a genre of cell phone video. Now, while police wait for the ambulance to arrive following a shooting, some have taken advantage of not being able to "help" to film their bloodied and injured victims dying, often while pleading for help, bleeding to death, and coughing up blood and, more often than not, while surrounded by groups of people or crowds. These videos have become routine fare on certain web sites and social media circuits, as posted and shared on Facebook pages. They circulate widely and quickly to an avid following. News media sometimes catch on to particular cases. On at least one occasion the Public Security Secretariat has promised to hold those responsible for filming three men as they lay dying after a shooting.

This video, filmed in April of 2014, captures a shocking scene and reflects in raw imagery, an utter hatred between some police and real or perceived criminals. The video begins with a police officer walking and talking, while filming three men on the ground, piled partially on top of each other. One man appears to be almost dead, his face yellowed and mouth open. He moves only slightly, in order to gasp. His eyes stare upward emptily. Another man rests his head on the dying man's side, having also been shot multiple times. He twitches and groans. The Military Police officer—who later came forward to admit that he filmed and circulated the video—circles up above. He starts speaking:

Military Police: "You're going to be famous, you thief, dying here now."

Dying man [twitching and groaning]: "My . . . kids. I work."

Voice from the background: "Are you going to take long, man? . . . to die?"

There is little dialogue. But little dialogue is needed. The imagery and the few words spoken leave many viewers speechless.

This video was posted to a web site named almost identically to the formal name of the police. The difference between the two is negligible—Polícia do Estado de São Paulo versus Polícia Militar do Estado de São Paulo. It is certainly close enough that an educated individual could mistake the difference. In the span of two days, the video was shared more than seven hundred times and commented on hundreds of times—the majority of which credited the police, in a wide variation of ways, for effectively removing three more bandidos from social circulation. But what is particularly striking is how the Secretariat for Public Security responded, with an official statement and a promise for an investigation:

> The Military Police would like to clarify that the Facebook profile "Polícia do Estado de São Paulo," which contains some improper content, is not one of the official profiles of the Institution. For this reason, there is an investigation in place on this profile, its content, and its administrators.
>
> In the case in question, the Internal Affairs Division of the Military Police is investigating whether Military Police participated in the recording and circulation of the images, and, if true, this could result in the punishment of those responsible.
>
> It is important to recall that any Military Police officer, as any citizen, can post what they choose on social networks, while being subject to civil, criminal and administrative sanctions in cases where such postings offend people, institutions, are against the law or suggest an affront to human dignity.

At least two significant points can be drawn out of the statement, considered both as a response to a specific instance and as a broader political stance. First, the Public Security Secretariat was only compelled to respond to the emergence of this genre of videos when they encroached on the formal institution. That is, a response is merited when it needs to be clarified that there is a distinction—unclear what or how much—between the formal and the informal policies and practices of the police. No mention is made of how normal, important, or wrong the shooting (and killing) of real or perceived criminals is. Rather, what is considered to be wrong—if implied—is that the informal but normal practices of killing and filming were not held at an appropriate arm's length from the formal party line.

Second, the statement walks a line between appeasing two different constituencies—police and citizens attuned to accountability. For the former, because the statement makes no mention of the deadly practices that led to the possibility of such a video being filmed, it sanctions a certain kind of behavior. Implied is a position that the violence is okay, as long as it is not visible or promoted. The statement also maintains an equivocal position about the "possibility" of punishment for someone in this circumstance, refraining from making a bold (or even strong) statement that the individual in question *will be* held to account, much less, for that matter, stating that any individual caught making these films in the future will be disciplined. For police reading this statement, there is a great deal of leeway and room for interpretation.

And yet for the latter, the statement suggests action and acknowledges that there was wrongdoing. It does so in a language intelligible to a particular part of the population. To advance a feeling that something will be done, the statement cites a number of different mechanisms at its disposal—civil, criminal, and administrative laws—before concluding with a decisive point that draws directly from the world of human rights as though extracted directly from one of the United Nations' international conventions: "human dignity" need be protected.

Except, of course, the video and the statement take for granted that police routinely violate the right to life. Ultimately, what makes the video shocking is that this violence is suddenly visible, and not obscured or hidden on the margins in the periphery of the city, nor occurring within the guarded confines of a police vehicle on the slow road to the hospital—where is it quite possible many worse things occur.

To anyone who cares spend one minute watching a video on Facebook, it allows them to transcend moral and institutional boundaries and assumptions about what police do—to see in visceral detail something that is otherwise presumed and totally mundane, even if nonetheless horrifying. After all, these kinds of killings and violence happen at a rate of 1.6 times per day at the best of times. The only real difference is that there is an objection to it being seen, filmed, and accessed more widely.

Make no mistake, this video—and the tens of others like it—are encapsulated visual renderings of how security and democracy are colliding. They are possible because of new technologies and platforms that police (and almost everyone else) are using to relate their circumstances. This is a new way that police are speaking out—from the "side"—via the Internet, on underregulated media that allows small and fragmented communities to connect. But the Internet and social media are no panacea for policing. Rather, it seems that the police who are the most violent—and/or who support violence—are most vocal and apparent in the online world and in new forms of "speaking out." That this has been made acutely visible in videos of people dying is certainly an unintended side effect of the new policy of nonremoval of suspects from a crime scene by police. But even as it destabilizes the viewer with such shocking imageries and words (however few), it allows us to peer into a world and a practice that has existed for decades. Which begs the question: *Is it better to see this violence than to let it continue unseen in the cars of the police?* This is to say, when police speak out, whether the words are ugly or not, we learn something new about what they do, what the result is, and why and how the larger moral system sanctions it. If anything can be learned in the early stages of these 2013 reforms, particularly vis-à-vis the Internet as a new platform for communication, it is that a diversity of perspectives is needed. We need to consistently pull apart a discourse dominated by the loudest and the most brazen, whether they be social media savvy or democratically elected.

My decision to write the *New York Times* op-ed can be seen in this light. But given the theoretical questions at play in this book—security and state formation versus democracy and accountability, it may seem to readers that I am acting in the interest of the former. They are right. How does one personally prefer violence, having grown up in a secure context? My own instincts are to see political leaders lead and for these representatives to diligently tackle a public security configuration that is detrimental to almost every citizen. Moreover, I'm inclined to think that most who are faced with the decision of having (a) an instant and relative absence of violence but an indeterminably fragile security punctuated by crisis, or (b) prolonged and bloody violence but a more durable security would take the latter. To do otherwise would fly in the face of the dominant normative system at play in the world, one that is backed up by notions of democracy and rights as a solution and platform for nearly everything—and especially things related to governance. If readers find that my own motivation and decision to "do something" doesn't square well with the larger questions and actions at play in these pages, they may be right. But just as there is no morally simple way to find sense in Sao Paulo's violence, there is likely no simple solution to its resolution either. This begs a larger question about what can really be done when such major pressures collide, not to mention what this means for the trajectory of the state and the exercise of sovereign power more broadly. What prospect is there, really, that the Brazilian state will ever "form" the way discourses about "ideal" states suggest it should?

CHAPTER 8

Toward an Ideal Subordination?

Is there sense to be made of São Paulo's senseless violence? If so, the world of homicide detectives can help us get there. But the social and occupational paradigm at the heart of the state's regulatory mechanisms for life and death is not what we might have thought it was. Where we have supposed that these detectives are the apex of elite police, they are not. Where they should be safe from violence, they are not. If we believed that their colleagues defer to their authority, they do not. If we expected homicide detectives to protect life by punishing those that take it away, they do not—usually. It is far past time to reconsider, wholesale, our assumptions of these police and other police like them. These are simply ~~d less~~ not like the police that we have known and researched so widely so far. And they have not made sense as a result.

The security arrangement in São Paulo is slippery and evolving even as it becomes a little clearer on closer inspection. Violence is still a moving target, particularly when viewed through the lens of the "ideal" state with its more or less stable sovereign authority—presumed as it often is. Ultimately, though, some larger and more conceptual questions hang ominously in the balance. These are future looking and of deep and enduring theoretical relevance: How much will the shared configuration of sovereignty evolve in this city? Will it evolve much at all? Will our "third wave democracies" ever get to a place where they can be appropriately evaluated by the hegemonic ideals of the North? In other words, is our notion of the ideal state and its ideal form of citizen subordination to law still useful in its ideals vis-à-vis the everyday experiences of many police? Can we—should we—dispose of the ideal state as a normative, prescriptive, and analytical apparatus?

The work of well-respected theorists of democracy suggest that there is a more or less natural process for us to get there still.[1] Violence is formative, and democratic processes will do the work. The thing that we call the "modern" or "ideal" state, a geographical entity with sovereign control over the terms of violence, defended from external threats by a military force and controlled internally by police, will come to pass as citizens demand it. The presence of violence in the daily lives of democratic citizens will eventually lead them to make substantive claims on their governments to provide better public security services. Crime victimization will lead to greater political participation, more civil activism, and greater engagement between the rulers and the ruled, establishing reciprocal relations of trust.[2] Stronger relations between citizens and their state should, in turn, lead to the development of better and more responsive public security institutions and policies. Concurrently, human rights are a vehicle to help us get there. They are a valuable set of principles *and a framework of objectives* through which demands can be made and will be heard in a democratic society.

Some significant empirical patterns test this dominant logic. First, mounting evidence suggests that democracy is not the predominant rationale for many social mobilizations these days. Security is. When people want to change their security situation, they are just as likely to do it themselves with their own hands, dollars, pitchforks, and/or guns. The real or perceived failure of democratically elected governments in places like Latin America, particularly to contain violence since the end of Cold War, has led many citizens to believe that the best way to achieve what they need—effective security—is not to demand it from the state or to claim that states must better defend their right to life. It is much more productive to find local ways to bring about security *in spite* of democratically elected and historically inequitable governments. These are, by nature, grassroots solutions. And these mobilizations run the gamut, serving as both responses to the real or perceived perpetrators of violence, as well as the responses to those responses, and the responses to the responses to the responses (and so on . . .). After all, security is considered by many to be a primeval and necessary "public good." Where it is not provided by a recognized or central "authority," evidence from the contemporary world increasingly shows that authority(ies) will emerge on their own terms.[3] Since these efforts for security have come about in spite of the state—and sometimes *because of it* in the case of violent police and wrongheaded policy—they are not so easily folded into a democratic rubric for security reform.

Second, human rights as a legitimating discourse has sowed discord rather than accord. Rights are very much welded to a particular configuration of the state where a certain foundational basis of security already exists. This is often overlooked. Rights are to be guaranteed by states. And yet we use the rhetoric of rights as a platform for trying to bring about the state we envision, sidestepping the fact that states—all states—are entirely *defined* by the violence that rights decry. In ideal states that violence is largely historical and taken for granted, even as it is indelibly inscribed in the formation and development of accountable state institutions. Applied to police reform in contexts of consensual sovereignty, rights based reforms create a problematic and nearly unintelligible amalgam of police messages and practices. A police force can create a public image in a rights-based mold while engaging in practices that simultaneously put that image to shame. Pretty web sites, PowerPoint presentations, participatory security councils, and press officers can depict images of calm and incremental reform, complete with brick-and-mortar community police stations, specialized training in human rights at the academy, and precincts open to international inspection missions. But all of this is distant from the humdrum routine of 1.6 police killings per day. Far beyond Brazil the dissonance between discourse and empirical demands plays out in two camps forever at each other's throat—those who promote rights at any cost and those who are only to happy to abuse them in pursuit of some other goal.

Third, even if increased participation comes from victimization, there are different modes of participation. Violence—and usually violent actors—emerge from the margins of society, particularly in cities. These are places that have rarely, if ever, been on the political map in any meaningful way. These communities are unmistakably defined by long histories of being off of the literal and figurative map of public services. They are the "slums," the barrios, the townships, and the *colonias* that governments (and their societies) have been all too happy to leave to their own devices. And they are, of course, deeply racialized, increasingly criminalized and resoundingly penalized.

These constituencies are huge in both spatial scale and population. They often comprise a significant plurality—if not a majority—of urban dwellers, usually located far from politically important centers of power. To suddenly begin to serve these long-marginalized communities in meaningful ways—that is, enough to engage citizens *and* dislocate the now well-established violent actors emergent from them—is a significant jump from the empirical conditions of today. Inroads may be possible, if only in a deeply contentious and uncertain process.[4]

Fourth, when it comes to violence there is a difficult incongruence between what is often good for politics and what is good for the creation of "modern" states with singular systems of law and subordination. Politicians are accountable to citizens, while their police and citizens on the margins often feel accountable to organized crime. São Paulo is one case of politicians being able to benefit from comparatively low levels of violence owing to no real policy doing of their own. Short election terms, an aversion to being associated with rising levels of perceived uncontrolled violence, the advocacy of local and international human rights organizations, and geopolitical pressures have made organized state violence a political nonstarter. The assumption that reduced levels of violence are necessarily good—both because they speciously suggest a condition of peace and a governance of effective political action- has meant that dealing with alternative sources of violence in meaningful ways does not fit nicely with the political calculations of democratic governance. As long as the victims of the everyday violence that lies beneath statistical declines in homicide and false sensations of security are on the margins, little concerted effort to dismantle these alternative regimes of violence is likely.

For the most part, imperfect short-term solutions for peace and homicide reduction typically rule the day. Increasingly common examples are the direct or indirect agreements between violent groups and formal governments or their emissaries. When violence is the product of a specific victim-perpetrator complex, making deals with that complex can make sense. The *mareros* of Central America have proven particularly stubborn in their use of violence and also in resistance to policy efforts to minimize their influence. In El Salvador, this led to the brokering of a truce between the two rival marero groups in 2012 by the Organization of American States via a local Catholic Church bishop (Dudley 2013). With the Salvadoran government active behind the scenes—but wary of visibly engaging—homicide statistics dropped overnight, suggesting a new era of relative peace premised on agreement. Maintaining this truce has been one thing, and many questions remain about the displacement of those homicides and an increase in disappearances. The decline has since started to reverse as well. Superseding the exact statistics, the Salvadoran experience is indicative of a circular pattern of violence that is increasingly evident in many places.

But if São Paulo and El Salvador are two examples of a similar phenomenon, they come at it from opposite angles in terms of the normalcy and exceptionality of violence. El Salvador is an example of agreement as a solution for long-standing violence undeterred by policy. Marero violence constituted a "normal" circumstance, not an exceptional one. São Paulo, by contrast, is a place where paralyzing violence has been comparatively abnormal since the 1990s. Here, agreement has been the norm and not the exception—even as it has also been important as a means of reestablishing a condition of normalcy during exceptional moments. These are two cases are represent two sides of the same analytical coin, where the norm can become the exception and the exception can become the norm, and one is very much defined in opposition to the other.

There is one very important example in the same analytical vein as São Paulo that seems to suggest which of these two patterns is more "normal" for some states in the contemporary world. The explosion of violence in Mexico around 2007 reflects two things about the configuration of sovereignty in that country in recent times. First, President Felipe Calderón's attempt to disrupt longstanding implicit and/or explicit agreements between cartels and the various levels of the Mexican state by cracking down on drug trafficking was essentially an effort to shrink the definition of life and death and to trace—unilaterally—a new geography of state authority. The destabilization of long-standing actual or implied agreements would be part of the process in the move toward centralized control over violence within the state, while removing the ability of cartels to kill with impunity would accelerate that change. Only partially successful, this government effort resulted in a dramatic fragmentation of the cartel landscape, and an attempt by new cartel forms to reestablish predictability and assert order amidst disorder. This laid waste to tens of thousands of lives. More important politically was the widespread impression that violence was totally out of the state's control. And this was *because* of a policy. High rates of violence became a fatal political liability.

When election time arrived and violence was a prominent and national issue on the political docket, it came as little surprise to many that one of the first things the new president, Enrique Peña Nieto, did was (re)expand the definition of appropriate life and death.[5] This new "policy" to step away from a militarized approach to drug cartels has been significant, if somewhat politically predictable. It is counterintuitive in many ways though. An expanded definition means that fewer people can die in uncontested ways on the part of drug traffickers or vigilantes without a response from the state. However, the central thrust in Peña Nieto's policy was to reduce violence, something his administration seeks to achieve by giving up the state's active attempt to centralize violence—bloody an effort as it has been. The intimation of Peña Nieto's move is that violence can occur, as long as it is quieter, less shocking, and not as politically destabilizing.

What we are witnessing as a result of the government stepping back from violently asserting authority is a new proliferation of violent actors who have emerged to occupy this new moral territory with anticartel and self defense mobilization. These are community patrols, vigilante squads, and extermination groups (some of which may maintain quiet ties to the state). Violence has decreased substantially, which is of course far from any indication that cartels are less relevant, either in political terms or in the everyday lives of millions of people. Mexico has done almost entirely the opposite of what democratic theorists might suggest. It has chosen a short-term solution that has allowed alternative forms of violence to emerge, institutionalize, and establish direct and indirect agreements with the state, even as they remain more or less autonomous actors practicing their own definition of life and death that is nonetheless subsumed under the new and broader definition.

São Paulo's circular pattern of violence may be an example of consequence to come for Mexico. It remains to be seen quite how, but the agreements that define this configuration of sovereignty will ultimately have moments of rupture and disagreement—just as they have so far. In Peña Nieto's choice to implicitly return to a world before 2007, we're left staring back at a certain kind of "normal" configuration of violence and a similarly normal structure of power.

There are, of course, a whole cohort of states today that are dealing with the same sorts of issues. The majority of these states and the rapidly growing cities that define their current-day violence are coping in ways that are very similar to Mexico and São Paulo. As alternative forms of violence emerge from their urban margins, empowered by drug and other illicit economies, the democratic rules of the game suggest a certain suite of tolerable responses. The most common of these do not substantively test the sorts of normative concepts evident in Western democracy, human rights, and global development discourses, upon which things like loan packages and bilateral aid are routinely conditioned.

These states are coming of age in a peculiar historical moment. Unlike in the formative period of our "ideal" states, they are governed both by demands to minimize violence within them *and* to be responsive to their citizenry. This operates in a mishmash of top-down and bottom-up pressures. Given the context, the ways that these states are dealing with violence is unsurprising. This moment defies any feasible comparison with the periods and ways that states of the Global North came of age in terms of violence. As Charles Tilly (1985) has deftly shown, many of those "ideal" states came about in the midst of war, plunder, and empires with kings-as-sovereign. This violence was neither internal nor particularly urban. In the condition of war, and far from any notion of political accountability or democracy, violence was not subject to any of the kinds of normative constraints or checks and balances in play today. The rules of the game were much different. Genocide was possible as a logic for conquest, and did occur. Under those historical circumstances, populations who contested or were seen as incongruent with advancing frontiers or civilizing tides could be (and often were) simply wiped out, any possibility of systemic dissention extinguished. In this sense, the circumstance of the United States and its indigenous hunting squads is little different.

But there are examples, even then, of the shared exercise of sovereign power to augment control of the margins. The difference between a "privateer" and a "pirate" was based on whether they were seen to have acted under the mandate of the sovereign or not.[6] But for many reasons, both purposeful and not, the boundary between these two was fuzzy. The English crown could claim moral, economic, and political distance from "pirates," who ostensibly acted outside of sovereign authority, even though it was generally accepted that the relationship between crown and pirates was mutually beneficial. And even while privateers expanded the influence of the crown in expected or coordinated ways, their pirate alter egos often destabilized the English imperial project, stepping into and out of the unclear realms of legitimate and illegitimate violence and plunder.

So sovereignty by consensus is not historically novel, nor static. But neither is it novel in the Global North today, nor necessarily dynamic. Italy and Russia are two obvious examples of functional states and economies with a pattern of shared sovereignty within their territories—and beyond (Blok 1974). But mafia scholars have frowned on the idea of thinking about mafias—Russian, Italian, Japanese, and others—and their provision of protection as being statelike. As Varese (2001, 5) puts it:

> When it offers and promotes its services, the mafia disregards the law: this qualifies it as a set of illegal and violent organizations. It never supplies "protection" as a public good, in the way the modern liberal-democratic state does (or aspires to do). It does not recognize citizens' rights. For this reason, one should resist the temptation to call the mafia "a state-within-the-state" unless one strips the state of any appeal to justice, as noted by St. Augustine in his treatise *De civitate Dei*. Mafia groups operate as very peculiar "firms," in no way constrained by the legal rules that bind ordinary firms in the market economy.

There are at least two important things to note from the conceptual boundaries drawn by Varese. First, is there such a thing as the provision of protection that is absent of a notion of what is "just"? Even if mafias are simply "firms," they still need to have some predictable means of deciding who gets protected and who does not. This is, as Max Weber might say, a foundation for economic exchange. If this way of deciding is by the simple calculus of whether someone paid for protection (or not), this still reflects a delineation of who belongs and who does not, and who is right and who is wrong. This need not be codified in legal tropes, formal affidavits, or (even) informal affirmations. It can just as easily be implied, as long as there is some collective sense and predictability of what it means.

Second, the provision of public goods—like security—is not a necessary quality of empirically existing states (much less the recognition of citizens rights). This is, though, a necessary quality of theoretically existing states—at least in hegemonic understanding. That there is such an empirical mixing of the everyday regulation of security on the part of state and mafia renders definitions of appropriateness based on notions of state legality (and democracy) moot. The mafia only qualifies as an illegal organization according to the law on the books, which is derived from a hegemonic understanding of what law *should* be, and as is made by empirically existing states. In practice, though, mafias are part of a system of social control and de facto law that is often accepted by the state, both by the omission of response and in the multiple levels of everyday practice that link its agents with agents of mafias. They do not "infringe" on the normative territory of the state so much as expand it in empirically accepted ways. What is interesting, in other words, is not the de jure state, but the de facto state within which mafias exist, sub-

sumed within larger practices and structures of governance—moral and
otherwise.

This is, of course, the same terrain as in São Paulo. What exactly the
patterns of exchange, deference, and agreement are between police and
Italy's mafias is not well known. But surely, after more than a century of
existence alongside the Italian state, there is a complex relationship with
its own checks and balances. The point being: Italy's pattern of sovereign authority is much too far gone to try to reconfigure. To attempt
to exorcise its mafias and their control over life and death in parts of
the country would lead to explosive consequences. The agreement(s) that
bind the state and these groups together are certainly far too well institutionalized to attempt to detach them in any meaningful way. To do so
would no doubt disrupt the Italian and potentially the EU economy, not
to mention result in a great deal of violence. The political calculus for
inaction has few meaningful detractors—so why bother?

This calculus is becoming rather similar for many states like Brazil
and Mexico. Much more than "narco-states," these states with violent
cities have similar political configurations that are very much defined by
the current geopolitical moment. Almost certainly the relationship between state and organized crime is not anywhere near as well established
or institutionalized in these places as in Italy, however. The stability of
their relationships with the state is still very much in flux. The relative
newness of many of these organized crime groups—decades old as opposed to more than a century—means that much doubt remains about
what groups will evolve into, how they may be dealt with by formal systems of government, and whether (and how) multiple groups can continue to exist in some cities.

There is no guarantee that sovereignty by consensus will go away. And
what if it doesn't? If state formation for the "ideal" state is the centralization of violence, might there be a process of "formation" for states
that share sovereign authority? This may be disturbing normative terrain. It bears consideration that agreement between states and organized
crime groups is the de facto "normal" in places like São Paulo. But here
sovereignty by consensus is neither stable nor institutionalized at this
stage of the game, as is evidenced by the cyclical pattern of violence. Could
it be that the weakness of such institutions is the reason that periods of
disagreement and agreement still occur and are so visible and prominent?
As relations become more stable, the terms of agreement evermore assumed, a certain paradigm of checks and balances established, and institutions of mutual governance codified in semipermanent and de jure

institutional forms—to such a point that they are taken for granted—we might expect the consolidation of a different kind of state. This format of authority could make us reconsider whether a state like Italy is abnormal at all.

To be clear, the idea of fully "formed" states of consensual sovereignty is not something I advocate as a point of policy. Nor do I necessarily advocate for the "ideal" state with its singular sovereignty and centralized violence with its (often forgotten) history of violence. Rather, I seek a degree of pragmatism given the structural forces at play in the world today—forces that are so different from those in previous historical moments of state formation. The ways that states try to avoid violence, for reasons of democracy, human rights, and the ugliness of bloodshed, may well lead us down a particular road, where shared and mutually constituted institutions become a more or less unquestioned and accepted part of everyday governance, with their own modes of subordination and marginality. My objective here is to advocate for a new analysis of this different set of rules, existent in some states and megacities today, but with a trajectory toward institutionalization in many others. Let us put aside the ideal state and its baggage and move toward an understanding of other structural conditions of violence today and how those conditions order social action in ways that defy hegemonic interpretations and prescriptions. If the circumstances of homicide detectives can tell us anything about the world today, it is that pressures and demands for security and democracy are shaping the world in contrasting ways. The promotion of democracy is uncritical of "peace" and what a so-called absence of violence obscures. Peace at any cost is costly. How we arrive there and what lies beneath is just as important as the state of being "peaceful."

Notes

1. To maintain anonymity, all names and some other identifying details are pseudonyms. In some cases I have made adaptations to stories or the characteristics of individuals as a way to ensure anonymity.

2. Across political and social thinking, the idea that the sovereign has the right to kill its own citizens is hegemonic. Death is a matter of sovereign power. The state's ability to kill, punish, and discipline lays the foundation for a state's legitimacy to govern, constructed often via a tax-for-protection arrangement with citizens, that must be unwavering in the face of dissent. Or so goes the theory. Hobbes's (1660) *Leviathan* of citizen subservience to a single order of violence in exchange for safety is the prototypical example. But many other conceptual iterations speak to the same point. Max Weber (1962) asserts that there are territorial dimensions to the legitimate use of violence. Schmitt (1985) speaks of sovereign power in the language of control over the definition of the "normal" via the unique ability to choose and respond to what is exceptional. Benjamin's (1996) use of the concepts of *law-making* and *law preserving* violence speak to the processes and maintenance of subordination with violence, and to expand control. Foucault's notion of biopolitics (1975) references a transformation in sovereign control over life (and death). The "ancient right" of the sovereign to take life gave way to a need to foster life and to marginalize lesser versions of it to the point of near extinction. In societies where this turn in the configuration of sovereign power has taken place—which I suggest is not entirely the case in Brazil—death is biopolitical, evading and obscured from the public eye. In a revision of Foucault's thesis, Agamben (2005) notes the gradations of (un)worthy life. There are "zones of indistinction" where some lives are deemed expendable, stripped of their political existence to a "bare" state of life. These same

themes are also prominent in the work of Arendt (1970), and the "necropolitics" of Mbembe (2003).

3. In their edited volume *States of Violence*, Sarat and Culbert (2009) take apart a number contemporary practices of violence on the part of states. Stepputat (2014) also advances these questions in important ways. Noteworthy also are Scheper-Hughes (1993), Ignatieff (2013), and Wacquant (2008b).

4. The scholarship on police broadly agrees that police do little if not reinforce social order. For some varying perspectives on how and why this happens see Ericson (1990), Bayley (1995), and Fassin (2013). David Garland (1996) has tried to push back against the idea that Northern states are sovereign or that there is such a thing as a "monopoly" on violence. Yet his argument hinges on the idea that there is no sovereign control of crime—not violence. For other important points, see Bittner (1970).

5. Since this manuscript is about the failure and struggle for a broadly "public" security, I will sometimes speak of police generically to refer to their mutual position as part of a defined system and position of supposed authority. When I speak about "police," I am speaking about aspects common to all police bodies. There are, of course, many important divisions and types of police as I discuss in depth and make clear throughout these pages. I discuss the differences between these two institutions in great depth in another publication as well (Denyer Willis 2014a). When not, I use "beat cops," "patrolling police," or "Military Police" to refer to the former and "detectives," "investigators," or "Civil police" to denote the latter. Also, in order to further protect the identities of my informants I have chosen to refer to all Civil Police officers as "detectives." Given the size of the Homicide Division, I cannot adequately discuss and manage these occupations in depth while also safeguarding the identities of research subjects. I will do so in future publications.

6. The work of Martin Innes (2003) is an obvious reference point for such an analysis of homicide detectives. Innes's examination does show many common practices in detective work. Chief among these is the drive to build a narrative of how a given crime occurred. It is true in Brazil as well that detectives must often trust their hunches as a way to pull out viable scenarios for investigation. In Brazil, however, detectives rely almost entirely on their hunches and intuition because of a lack of technology and its nonmandatory use. One could say that the discretionary space of detectives in Brazil is substantially larger than that of other homicide detectives studied to date. This also underscores a key difference vis-à-vis research on detectives by Sanders (1977), Ericson (1993), and Hobbs (1988), who point out the "entrepreneurial" and creative nature of detectives in the search for information. Brazilian detectives are similarly proactive in high-profile cases, but otherwise, do not seek information as aggressively.

7. Detectives have not been as widely studied as other police, even as they hold greater influence over high-profile investigations. Past work on homicide detectives shows a vastly different terrain of investigation and regulation over life and death. In addition to Innes (2003), Robert Jackall (2005) spent a considerable about of time accompanying detectives in different units in New York City. Jennifer Hunt's depiction (2010) is another telling example of the inquisi-

tive (and sometimes inquisitional) world of detectives. All of these portray environments where detectives have much more authority than other police.

8. David Simon (2006) is among the few other researchers to spend a prolonged period of time alongside homicide detectives. His vivid and detailed description of detectives in Baltimore became the basis for two critically acclaimed television series—*Homicide* and *The Wire*.

9. The on-duty detective—*delegado de plantão*—in the local precinct makes the initial decision about jurisdiction based on a visit to the scene and/or a narrative given by the Military Police. Where the aggressor is known—as in domestic homicides, "caught red handed" incidents, and when there is overwhelming evidence—the local precinct retains jurisdiction.

10. I follow Lipsky's (1983) epistemic tradition of "street-level bureaucrats" to understand the dilemmas and empirics of public service provision.

11. I don't intend to suggest that this process is unproblematic. The bureaucracy is complex, as is the relationship between political power and those who make and enforce the rules.

12. There is an abundance of important literature on these topics. In São Paulo, Teresa Caldeira (2000) and James Holston (2008) have produced insightful and compelling accounts of the ways that these patterns have shaped both social relations and the slow progress of democratic reform. Anthony Leeds's (1973) pioneering work on social relations in new urban settlements is an invaluable historical reference, as is Janice Perlman's *The Myth of Marginality* (1972). The work of Roy (2009) and Auyero and Swistun (2009) advance our understandings of how the "unplanned" is mixed up in contemporary processes of accumulation and is a source of lessons for planners and policymakers. For a comparative perspective on the social construction of the "slum," see also Whyte (1955) and Gans (1962).

13. Exactly what the discourses are and how they are appropriated by violent groups is a point of some debate, as Holston (2009) examines. Also, Ashforth (2005).

14. For an overview, see Davis and Denyer Willis (2011). For examples, see Goldstein (2005); Godoy (2006).

15. From a critical position, many scholars have understood the violence of cities as an unintended outcome of disruptive neoliberal structural adjustments. Neoliberalism is often understood, then, as an ideological perspective and a practice, in which "human well-being can best be advanced by liberating individual entrepreneurial freedoms and skills" (Harvey in Thomas, O'Neill, and Offit 2011). The streamlining of economic flows and the decentralization of state services to increase their "client" efficiency has also reshaped nonstate services. All of these are indicative of a global deepening of capitalist rationales and a related emphasis on accumulation and deregulation.

Research in cities of the Global South has overwhelmingly demonstrated the ways that this ideology and practice of removing social safety nets, slimming public programs to free up state efficiencies, and enticing global investment at the expense of local industry have cut particularly sharply into the well-being of the urban poor. From new free trade agreements that privilege corporations over citizens and the privatization of public services, including health care and urban transportation, scholars argue that neoliberal reforms have dramatically altered the way states relate to their citizens. The consequences of market-oriented reform are particularly deep, some say, for public security and cities.

In terms of violence, the outbreak of insecurity is often understood as a two-fold manifestation of neoliberal transformation. It is both symptom and solution. It is at once a reaction to the withdrawal of a more tightly controlled security system shocked by drastic and decidedly unparticipatory policies that often led to a great deal of deprivation. At the same time, however, Vadim Volkov (2002) and others have argued that neoliberalism is also manifested in the forms and patterns of violence that emerge, many of which reflect neoliberal rationales in their "innovative and entrepreneurial" trappings. The forms of violence that we see emerging, they argue, are appropriating these neoliberal reforms and recommissioning their substance with "parallel modes of production and profiteering, sometimes even of governance and taxation" (Comaroff and Comaroff 2006, 5).

16. For those scholars emphasizing the importance of democracy, the focus has often (if implicitly) been on what has *not* changed vis-à-vis expectations for the way political systems should work in "third wave" democracies. Efforts to make sense of democratic shortcomings often hinge on the idea that fragile, failing, or nascent democratic institutions of newly (re)democratizing countries have struggled mightily to overcome and reform the inequitable, enduring, and historically rooted patterns of clientelistic and concentrated power. As Arias and Goldstein (2010) find, this is particularly true when it comes to democracy's "incompleteness" and discussions of urban violence. In terms of the ever greater prominence of violence, a great deal of emphasis has been put on the "un"rule of law and the failure of basic legal measures. The inability or unwillingness of states to assure that law is fairly applied, and thus failing to guarantee citizenship and other civil rights across a more or less equitable plane has lead to an outpouring of so-called "rule of law reforms" (see O'Donnell 2004; Trubek 2006). Indeed, the absence of rights that is made so obvious by police killings of citizens, of rampant urban homicide rates, and out-of-control economic crime, has lead many scholars to push for democratic and rights-based reforms that envision rights and public accountability as a stepping stone towards a consolidated and *democratic* rule of law.

Put differently, what many scholars see in urban violence is the frailty of democracy and the intransigence of past forms of undemocratic governance. Politicians are seen to be deeply clientelistic and engaged in unholy deals with elites and drug trafficking groups, often securing votes in exchange for piecemeal benefits and spin-offs. Even under a new democracy the urban poor must continue to make do in spite of public policies that blatantly benefit the powerful over the relatively powerless, just as in decades past. For their part, police in the Global South continue to be violent, relying on practices of repression that harken to the way things were done during authoritarian government. Torture, extortion, and police killings continue seemingly unabated, while prisons have become spaces where rights are systemically violated as they overflow their capacity. Democratic citizenship, it seems, it a far-fetched ideal that history simply refuses to cede. For more, see Ahnen (2007); Barcellos (1992); Brinks (2007); Call (2002); Chevigny (1999); and Hinton (2006).

17. Martha Huggins (1991, 2000, 2003) has been a key figure in detailing the connection between (and in spite of) politics, regime change, and policing.

18. This definition builds on the work of Paoli (2002) and Tilly (1985).

19. This dynamic is on display in El Salvador where the two dominant transnational *maras* have agreed, on the condition of receiving better accommodation for their imprisoned leaders, to a ceasefire. In the span of one year, the homicide rate has declined by around 60 percent—no small feat for a place where as recently as 2009, 14 per day died in homicides. In Medellin under Don Berna following Operation Orion, the centralization of violence had a similar effect (Civico 2012). Eliminating rival groups, or uniting fractured armed groups under one banner, almost irrespective of how nefarious the banner, render null the economic, spatial, and identity rivalries that typically contribute to civil-war-scale homicide rates. But, not subsumed or regulated by the state, these pacts form and break apart in cyclical fashion, causing shockwaves of violence and creating otherwise baffling statistical spikes.

20. This is in keeping with Charles Tilly's enduring work, clear in his 1985 article "War Making and State Making as Organized Crime." Building on the work of Gambetta (1993) and Schelling (1963), Varese argues that this is not what most organized crime does. They may monopolize certain commodities, but Mafias alone provide "private" protection. Yet mafias differ from "states" because they do not have an "appeal" of justice. This position suggests that protection need not have a notion of right and wrong, and that protection can exist in a "pure" economic form—something that is not borne out in the empirics of this work, nor in much of the work on mafias, which note other deep identity, kin, religious and criminal cleavages that underpin notions of acceptance, belonging and "codes" of proper conduct, as Gambetta (2009) shows in part.

21. Marginality has a long and rich theoretical lineage that can be traced back to the Chicago School of urban sociology. Robert Park's foray in 1927 on the "minds of marginal men" enshrined the concept as a point of debate about cities, particularly for urban sociologists. The debate continues at the heart of American sociology, in the work of scholars like Robert Sampson, William Julius Wilson, and Sudhir Venkatesh. But the causes, reproduction, and significance of marginality has become a major cross-disciplinary topic uniting anthropologists, sociologists, urban theorists, and urban planners, among others. For some noteworthy examples see Young (2004), Perlman (1979, 2007), and Das and Poole (2004).

22. For more see Agamben (2005), Wacquant (2008b), Wacquant and Bourdieu (2002), Scheper-Hughes (1993), and Auyero, Bourgois, and Scheper-Hughes (2014). For more on Brazil, see Mitchell and Wood (1999).

23. Das and Poole (2004) come within a hair of making the argument made here. They state, "What the consideration of margins enables us to see is how economic citizenship, rent extraction, and multiple regulatory regimes are necessary parts of the functioning of the state, much as the exception is necessary for the understanding of law" (2004, 21). To this I add that the *regulation of violence* by other regimes is also a necessary part of the functioning of the state—which leads to a larger conceptual order than the state, consensual sovereignty.

24. For an outstanding overview see Hansen and Stepputat (2006).

25. There is a great deal of work on related topics done by scholars such as Hansen and Stepputat (2014), Buur (2006), Rodgers (2006), and Davis (2009b).

26. Hansen and Stepputat (2006).

27. Latham (2000); Comaroff and Comaroff (2006).

28. The exception is not possible without a normal. Agamben's "bare life" is not possible without the *polis*. The formal city is not without the informal city. There is a great deal of symmetry—stated or implied—in the theory in this regard. And yet few have noted that the impossibility of pulling apart the included and the excluded is also true in terms of the exercise of violence and the regulation of life and death. As we know well from the gangs of Chicago to the paramilitaries of Colombia, the victims and perpetrators of violence collide, eliminating each other in ways often deemed productive for the larger system of social control. "Let them kill each other" is a common refrain (Dicken 2005, 310). For the most part, though, the "productivity" of this killing has remained disorganized, following the rather individualistic idea of personal honor that is often so deeply embedded in the "code of the street" (Anderson 2000). Sao Paulo, and to a lesser extent cities like Rio de Janeiro, are examples of increasingly organized killing within "excluded" populations. These are examples of where the severity and perpetuity of victimhood has led to the establishment of caps on the power of perpetrators. The creation of limitations on the use of violence—by entities existing in spite of the state—is made digestible because the victims are at once the perpetrators who see the value of decreased violence in their own immediately personal way and are willing to succumb to a trusted authority that understands this same logic of victimhood and violence.

29. Wedel (2003, 9).

30. Some have attempted to massage democratic theory to fit the empirics of violence and perceived corruption. Arias and Goldstein's (2010) concept of "violent pluralism" is one noteworthy example. The work of Markus Müller (2011) on "negotiated states" also advances thinking about the possibility of categorically different empirically existing states that struggle perpetually with violence. See also Clunan and Trinkunas (2010) and Newburn (1999).

31. Three concepts are prominent in this discourse: the rule of law, human rights, and public accountability. Each of these concepts aims to diminish the capacity of police to (ab)use power in their own way, but the logic of each is parallel. Namely, if you have (a) a stable rule of law, (b) respect for human rights, or (c) accountable public institutions, police abuses of power will be mitigated, police behavior will be more responsible, and as a result, *democracy will thrive*. For more, see Bayley and the National Institute of Justice (2001).

32. Didier Fassin's (2013) revealing ethnographic text on policing, processes of urban violence, and civil unrest in Paris provides a remarkable comparison in this regard.

33. Parts of this work were published as a chapter in the 2009 book *Youth Violence in Latin America: Gangs and Juvenile Justice in Comparative Perspective*.

34. I discuss the document in some depth in an article for the *Boston Review*. For more details, see Denyer Willis (2014b).

CHAPTER 1

1. Classic examples and discussion have been advanced by work such as Stokes (1962), Eckstein (1990), Caldeira (2000), Gilbert (2007), and Holston (1989).

2. The accepted measure for homicide comparisons is the number per 100,000 residents. This is intended to serve as a standardized unit useful across cities (and towns) of different sizes. To the extent that these statistics are accurate because of their dependence on local administration and investigation, the UNODC has produced multiple studies of global comparison. The recent *Global Study on Homicide* (UNODC 2011) is one example, which gives the rates of a number of cities, such as Cape Town (41), New York (6.4), Bogota (18), Rio de Janeiro (36), and São Paulo (11).

3. Crowe and Ferreira (2006).

4. Manso (2013).

5. Unless otherwise specified, I use primarily the statistics from the Public Security Secretariat of São Paulo. I am intimately familiar with the deeply problematic construction of those statistics, thus will employ these only for supplementary and illustrative purposes. I outline the problems and gaps with these statistics at several points in this book.

CHAPTER 2

1. In January 2013, a number of reforms were introduced that reshaped the rationale of investigation and introduced some conditions on procedure. As I detail in the final section, resistências ceased to exist by that name and were instead given the denomination of "death occurring as a result of police action" (*morte decorrente de intervenção policial*). In addition, new rules required the police involved in the shooting to immediately call 190, the number of the emergency responders, to evacuate the injured to a hospital. This replaced a system in which the police themselves would take the body to the hospital, raising questions about the integrity of the crime scene, the likelihood of survival, and what might actually happen in a police vehicle on the way to medical attention.

2. This line of analysis follows the work of Schelling (1963) and others like Park (1927) and Scheff (1967), who argue that formal communication is not a premise for agreement or mutual recognition—especially between complex institutions. See also Arantes (1996).

3. This is precisely how Schelling saw the constitution of boundaries in the Korean War. I have used his formulation almost exactly, substituting "killing" for "Yalu River" and "police" and "PCC" for the "we" and "the Chinese":

> If the Yalu River is to be viewed as a limit in the Korean War that was recognized on both sides, its force and authority is to be analyzed not in terms of the joint unilateral recognition of it by both sides of the conflict—not as something that we and the Chinese recognized unilaterally and simultaneously—but as something that we "mutually recognized." It was not just that we recognized it and they recognized it, but that we recognized that they recognized it, they recognized that we recognized it, we recognized that they recognized that we recognized it, and so on. It was a shared expectation. To that extent, it was a somewhat undeniable expectation. (Schelling 1959, 40–41)

4. There is an enormous body of knowledge surrounding police in the Global North that dates back to the 1950s. The work transcends methodological and disciplinary boundaries. Many of the foundational concerns about police in places like Brazil have had decades of research done on them by researchers in other contexts. And yet, the near hegemonic knowledge on police in the North routinely falls short in its effort to explain the world of police in the Global South.

5. In an attempt to streamline service some types of reports can now be filed online. These include everything from a missing person, to lost documents, or armed carjacking.

6. Michel Misse (2011) has done important work in this regard, particularly in Rio de Janeiro.

7. A 2012 *O Estado de São Paulo* newspaper article by Andre Caramante reported that between 2006 and 2010, police in São Paulo State killed more people than were killed in "justified homicides" in the United States over the same period. It also pointed out that the rate of police killings of citizens per 100,000 were 5.51 and 0.63, respectfully.

8. Both of these massacres are consequential for the PCC. The Castelinho killings were shown by subsequent medical examinations to have been execution style. According to Jozino (2009), though the twelve dead prisoners had been shot sixty-one times between them, none of their guns had blood on them, indicating the likelihood that they were planted. In addition, only three of the twelve dead tested positive for gunpowder residue on their hands. To make matters more clear, in November 2014 the police involved in the incident were found not guilty for the murders in question.

9. *Jornal Flit Paralisante* (2012a). There are many examples of journalists sanctioned or fired for criticizing police, police use of violence, or detailing certain cases of violence.

10. Apocalipser767567476 (2013).

11. The distinction between the municipality of São Paulo and greater São Paulo is significant. The municipality itself has 11,370,000 residents according to the 2010 census. The boundaries of Greater São Paulo, almost double that number to 19,973,000, according to the national and state statistics institute IBGE and SEADE.

12. Detectives are occasionally compelled to investigate if they are having a slow day, if they see some benefit to doing so, or if they desire a specific end for the case in question—like doing justice for a colleague involved or injured.

13. There are some contrasting opinions. Camila Dias (2013) argues that some origin myths have become central to the organization's own idea of its roots.

14. Drauzio Varella was a prison doctor and later wrote the book *Estação Carandiru*, which describes, via both experience and interviews, what life was like in the prison before and immediately following the massacre. This book also later became the award winning film *Carandiru*.

15. Novaes and Magalhães (2013).

16. Moran, Gill, and Conlan (2013) have been examining the spaces within and around prisons, including their reformation in terms of built form. Many have done work in this vein without referring to it in geographical terms. Wacquant's (2008a) "hyper-ghetto" is one example.

17. Biondi (2010); Sinhoretto, Silvestre, and Lins de Melo (2013).

18. Denyer Willis (2009); SEADE (2012).

19. Denyer Willis and Tierney (2012).

20. Ventura (2013).

21. This is the estimation of Cavallaro and Dodge (2007).

22. Such dismissals of the PCC's existence have been common. One such incident occurred during a question-and-answer session with a well-known Brazilian academic during a public presentation at a major American university.

CHAPTER 3

1. Andreas and Greenhill (2010) lay out many of the ways that statistics can be consumed, appropriated, and uncritically circulated in the public sphere.

2. Lima (2008).

3. Maia (1999).

4. Peres et al. (2011).

5. Goertzel and Kahn (2009).

6. UOL (2012a).

7. Feltran (2011); Dias (2013); Biondi (2010).

8. Dias (2013); Biondi (2010); Telles and Hirata (2010).

9. For more see Denyer Willis (2014b).

10. The PCC admits new members by "baptism." Though the ceremony is not well known, the documents and my discussions with police revealed that two baptized members preside. Their names are formally recorded, and they become inseparable from those they have baptized. They become responsible for them not only as "godfathers"—*padrinhos*—but are also responsible if their "godson" runs afoul of the rules. In a single case, both godfather and godson can be punished, if it can be shown that the godfather has not guided his protégé well enough. This structure of accountability evokes an organized and hierarchical system in which almost everyone is implicated and connected.

11. The following are the original documents. I have attempted to stay as true to them as possible in my translation and formatting.

12. According to some documents, it is still possible to return to the organization after being expelled. The parameters and requirements of returning are unclear, however.

13. Feltran (2011).

14. As a throwback to the tightly centralized governments of eras past, every Brazilian is required to have their fingerprints taken and recorded on their national ID card, the *Registro Geral*. Though it takes time to find matches these records are combined with prison records. Anyone who has ever been arrested can be easily tracked down, at least in identity.

15. Waiselfisz (2012).

CHAPTER 4

1. These statistics come from the internal affairs bureaus of the Civil and the Military Police. See Corregedoria (2013).

2. For a great deal more on and around the bandido, see Leeds (1996), Caldeira (2000), Goldstein (2003), Arias (2006), Holston (2008), Perlman (2007), Penglase (2009), and Roth-Gordon (2009).

3. Eric Hobsbawm (1959; 1969) focuses on the rural aspects of the "bandit," whom he sees as an apolitical type.

4. Cano and Alvadia's (2008) report looks at medical records of the individuals killed by gunshots during this period.

5. For more see Denyer Willis (2009) and Feltran (2011).

6. There is an important distinction between arrests of individuals caught in the act and those arrested following an investigation. The latter, known as *flagrante*, is the most common type of arrest. I examine the distinction between these types of arrest more deeply in Denyer Willis (2014a).

7. This is according to the official human resources pay scale of the Civil Police (Recursos Humanos 2012).

8. These are all second professions of real police that I met while doing research.

9. These videos are only as shocking as the comments beneath them, which often devolve into a war of words between police officers and those who support them, and PCC members and those who stand behind them. For examples see: http://www.youtube.com/watch?v=kalcxLjh4ts and http://www.youtube.com/watch?v=jgtyFEbu2kE.

10. This video was hosted on YouTube.com (Paulinhopittbull 2012).

11. Not that this is the fault of those immediately responsible for supervision. These supervisors are functionaries of those above them. My point is that violent death is *structurally* devalued. For those at the top of the public security system, control over death isn't a source of great political capital. Except in certain cases of *repercussão*—repercussion—it doesn't much matter how well detectives do their job, since it is the police that are doing the killing. It is precisely this fact that has created an opening for the PCC to exert control over death and to leverage an identity of persecution.

CHAPTER 5

1. Denyer Willis (2009).

2. Parts of this data have also appeared in a post at opendemocracy.net: http://www.opendemocracy.net/opensecurity/graham-denyer-willis/são-paulo-insecure-citizens-all-of-them.

3. Brazilian law allows for non–maximum security prisoners to leave prison to celebrate holidays and important dates with their families. This temporary release is conditional on their return to prison of their own free will. This program is highly divisive and the source of much debate.

4. Newburn (1999) and Punch (1985).

5. Dal Bó, Dal Bó, and Di Tella (2006).

6. The literature on policing understands deviance largely by the notion of the "abuse of power" for reasons of either money or power. I am not arguing that there is no abuse of power for these two reasons, but rather, being motivated by violence creates a different form of "deviance" that needs a more fine-grained analysis.

7. Feltran (2011).

8. Denyer Willis and Tierney (2012).

CHAPTER 6

1. Prisons in Brazil are defined by warehousing in more than just the neoliberal sense. The open confinement regime is one where prisoners are free to mingle openly and to take control of their own affairs. Prison guards rarely intervene, save to bring someone out or to put someone in.

2. I use "supermaximum" to denote the most restrictive prison type in Brazil, known as *regime disciplinar diferenciado* (RDD). Designed to cut ties between imprisoned organized crime leaders and the outside world, RDD confines prisoners for twenty-two hours a day, with up to two hours of solitary fresh air time per day and a maximum of two visitors per week. They are allowed no television, newspaper, or radio access.

3. Cavallaro and Dodge (2007).

4. Caramante (2012).

5. Owing to protectionist importation policies that seek to incentivize national industry, imported vehicles are exceptionally expensive in Brazil. A modest car such a Honda Fit, which retails for about $15,000 dollars in the United States, retails for around R$68,000 Brazilian Reais—roughly $30,000 USD. A Toyota Hilux is a monumentally expensive vehicle by local standards with a retail price of greater than $85,000 USD. It is a striking marker of status. In a system defined by acute incapacity and generalized insufficiency, this one police agency, which happens to be known for its lethality, is set definitively apart.

6. This might be a reference to a certain kind of torture that the Civil Police were known to use during the dictatorship—the *Pau de Arara* (parrot's perch). There is no evidence that this is still used, but evoking the imagery of this practice is nonetheless powerful.

CHAPTER 7

1. Blogs have become an important venue for both kinds of police to voice their discord about their circumstances. But police recognize that these blogs need be both anonymous and tempered. One of the most widely read blogs, flitpara silante.wordpress.com, maintained by a Civil Police delegado, became the source of great consternation in 2011 when the delegado was fired by a decree directly from the governor, for his "representation of the Public Security Secretary" (*Jornal Flit Paralisante* 2011).

2. How this plays out is very much an open question that strikes to the very heart of everyday tropes like the "war on drugs."

3. During the height of the violence there were some reports that police were quitting in record numbers. One media report suggested that police were dropping out at numbers only matched twelve years prior, when violence in the city was at its height (UOL 2012a).

4. There is no shortage of these kinds of stories, as I hope this manuscript has shown. But the search for the salacious above all else is part of the problem of why we know so little about police—and why they are so reticent to talk.

5. Denyer Willis (2012).

6. Jornal Flit Paralisante (2012b).

7. Granjeia (2012).

8. DOSP (2013).

9. Bergamin (2012).

10. For a detailed discussion of some of these dynamics see Mingardi (1992) and Denyer Willis (2014a).

CHAPTER 8

1. Desmond Arias and Daniel Goldstein's (2010) book, "Violent Democracies in Latin America," contains a long and valuable discussion of what the authors call the "Democratization School." For more, see also Denyer Willis (2014a); Collier (2000); Kingstone and Power (2008); Marks and Goldsmith (2013).

2. Regina Bateson (2012) has written a thorough and award-winning essay on this topic.

3. David Skarbek (2014) has shown that much of the California prison system is governed by different prison gangs in a nuanced balance that allows for routine economic exchange and a prevailing sense of security and predictability in everyday life on the inside.

4. One very notable example in this sense is the Police Pacification Units (UPP) in Rio de Janeiro. This policy does many of these things—but only in certain parts of the city. Like any policy in this direction, the UPP is slowly redrawing the conditions of belonging and state-society relations in the city. This is, of course, a very long-term project whose violence regularly stands in contrast with the city's democratically oriented civil society. It is unlikely, though, that the UPP project will manage to bring in all of the margins. Instead, it will install a new notion of marginality in the city, built on perceptions of who deserves this project and who does not.

5. Herein lies an important counterintuitive. In this case, an expanded definition means that fewer people can die in uncontested ways without a response from the state. However, the central thrust in Peña Nieto's policy was to reduce violence, something that it is hoped was achieved by giving up the state's attempt to centralize sovereign authority.

6. Fuchs (2000).

Bibliography

Adorno, Sérgio. 2002. "Exclusão socio-economica e violência urbana." *Sociologias* 4 (8): 84–135.

Agamben, Giorgio. 2005. *States of Exception.* Chicago: University of Chicago Press.

Agência Estado. 2012. "Confronto entre PCC e Rota faz governo federal ampliar alerta contra o crime." *Último Segundo*, September 28. Retrieved from http://ultimosegundo.ig.com.br/brasil/sp/2012-09-28/confronto-entre-pcc-e-rota-faz-governo-federal-ampliar-alerta-contra-o-crime.html.

Ahnen, Ronald. E. 2007. "The Politics of Police Violence in Democratic Brazil." *Latin American Politics and Society* 49 (1): 141–64.

Alpert, Geoffrey, John MacDonald, and Roger Dunham. 2005. "Police Suspicion and Discretionary Decision Making during Citizen Stops." *Criminology* 43 (2): 407–34.

Anderson, Elijah. 1990. *Streetwise: Race, Class, and Change in an Urban Community.* Chicago: University of Chicago Press.

———. (2000). *Code of the Street: Decency, Violence, and the Moral Life of the Inner City.* New York: Norton & Company.

Andreas, Peter, and Kelly Greenhill. 2010. *Sex, Drugs, and Body Counts: The Politics of Numbers in Global Crime and Conflict.* Ithaca, NY: Cornell University Press.

Antaki, Mark, and Coel Kirby. 2009. "The Lethality of the Canadian State's (Re)cognition of Indigenous Peoples." In *States of Violence: War, Capital Punishment, and Letting Die*, edited by Austin Sarat and Jennifer L. Culbert, 192–228. Cambridge: Cambridge University Press.

Apocalipser767567476. 2013. "ROTA chumbo quente!" Retrieved from http://www.youtube.com/watch?v=vHLEqK_stS8.

Arendt, Hannah. 1970. *On Violence.* New York: Houghton Mifflin.

Arantes, Antonio. 1996. "The War of Places: Symbolic Boundaries and Liminalities in Urban Space." *Theory, Culture and Society*, 13: 81–92.

Arias, Enrique D. 2006. *Drugs and Democracy in Rio de Janeiro: Trafficking, Social Networks and Public Security*. Chapel Hill: University of North Carolina Press.

Arias, Enrique D., and Daniel Goldstein. 2010. *Violent Democracies in Latin America*. Durham, NC: Duke University Press.

Arns, Paulo. E. 1985. *Brasil: nunca mais*. Petropolis: Vozes.

Ashforth, Adam. 2005. *Witchcraft, Violence and Democracy in South Africa*. Chicago: University of Chicago Press.

Augustoqm5. 2013. "Tribunal do Crime—PCC—Justiça paralela." Retrieved from http://www.youtube.com/watch?v=XVs9y1lXfZQ.

Auyero, Javier. 2007. *Routine Politics and Violence in Argentina: The Gray Zone of State Power*. New York: Cambridge University Press.

———. 2012. *Patients of the State: The Politics of Waiting in Argentina*. Durham, NC: Duke University Press.

Auyero, Javier, Phillipe Bourgois, and Nancy Scheper-Hughes. 2014. *Violence at the Urban Margins*. New York: Oxford University Press.

Auyero, Javier, and Deborah Swistun. 2009. *Flammable: Environmental Suffering in an Argentine Shantytown*. New York: Oxford University Press.

Bailey, John, and Lucía Dammert. 2005. *Public Security and Police Reform in the Americas*. Pittsburgh: University of Pittsburgh Press.

Baltrusis, Nelson, and Maria C. L. D'Ottaviano. 2009. "Ricos e pobres, cada qual em seu lugar: a desigualdade socio-espacial na metrópole paulistana." *Caderno CRH*, 22 (55): 135–49.

Barcellos, Caco. 1992. *Rota 66: A história da polícia que mata*. São Paulo: Record.

Bateson, Regina. 2012. "Crime Victimization and Political Participation." *American Political Science Review* 106 (3): 570–87.

Bayley, David. 1995. "A Foreign Policy for Democratic Policing." *Policing and Society: An International Journal of Research and Policy* 5 (2): 79–93.

Bayley, David, and James Garofalo. 1989. "The Management of Violence by Police Patrol Officers." *Criminology* 27 (1): 1–26.

Bayley, David, and the National Institute of Justice. 2001. *Democratizing the Police Abroad: What to Do and How to Do It*. Washington, DC: US Government Printing Office.

Benford, Robert D., and David A. Snow. 2000. "Framing Processes and Social Movements: An Overview and Assessment." *Annual Review of Sociology* 26: 611–39.

Benjamin, Walter. 1996. "Critique of Violence." In *Walter Benjamin: Selected Writings, Vol. 1, 1913–1926*, edited by Marcus Bullock and Michael W. Jennings. Cambridge, MA: Belknap.

Bergemin, Gima. 2012. "'É o que acontece com quem reage,' diz ladrão que matou garota." *Folha.com.br*, October 22. Retrieved from http://www1.folha.uol.com.br/cotidiano/2012/10/1172954-e-o-que-acontece-com-quem-reage-diz-ladrao-que-matou-garota.shtml

Binder, Arnold, and Peter Scharf. 1980. "The Violent Police-Citizen Encounter." *The ANNALS of the American Academy of Political and Social Science* 452 (1): 111–21.

Biondi, Karina. 2010. *Junto e Misturado—Uma etnografia do PCC.* São Paulo: Terceiro Nome.

Bittner, Egon. 1970. *The Functions of the Police in Modern Society.* Cambridge: Oelgeschlager, Gunn & Hain.

Blok, Anton. 1974. *The Mafia of a Sicilian Village, 1860–1960.* Cambridge: Waveland Press.

Bourdieu, Pierre, and Loïc J. Wacquant, eds. 1992. *An Invitation to Reflexive Sociology.* Chicago: University of Chicago Press.

Brinks, Daniel. 2007. *The Judicial Response to Police Violence in Latin America: Inequality and the Rule of Law.* Cambridge: Cambridge University Press.

Budds, Jessica, and Paulo Teixeira. 2005. "Ensuring the Right to the City: Pro-Poor Housing, Urban Development, and Tenure Legalization in São Paulo, Brazil." *Environment and Urbanization* 17 (1): 89–114.

Buur, Lars. 2006. "Reordering Society: Vigilantism and Expressions of Sovereignty in Port Elizabeth's Townships." *Development and Change* 37 (4): 735–57.

Caldeira, Teresa. 1986. "Electoral Struggles in a Neighborhood on the Periphery of São Paulo." *Politics & Society* 15 (1): 43–66.

———. 2000. *City of Walls: Crime, Segregation and Citizenship in São Paulo.* Berkeley: University of California Press.

Caldeira, Teresa, and James Holston. 1999. "Democracy and Violence in Brazil." *Comparative Studies in Society and History* 41: 691–729.

Call, Charles. 2002. "War Transitions and the New Civilian Security in Latin America." *Comparative Politics* 35 (1): 1–20.

Campos, Candido M. 2004. "Construção e Deconstrução de Centro Paulistano." *Ciência e Cultura* 56 (2): 33–37.

Cano, Ignácio, and Alberto Alvadia. 2008. *Análise dos Impactos dos ataques do PCC em São Paulo em Maio de 2006.* Laboratório de Análise da Violência (LAV-UERJ). Retrieved from http://www.observatoriodeseguranca.org/files /AtaquesPCC_IgCano.pdf.

Caramante, André. 2012. "Mortes cometidas por policiais da Rota sobem 45%." *Folha de São Paulo,* July 5. Retrieved from http://www1.folha.uol.com.br/fsp /cotidiano/52816-mortes-cometidas-por-policiais-da-rota-sobem-45.shtml.

Caramante, André, Giba Bergamim, and Afonso Benites. 2012. "PM de SP mata mais que a polícia dos EUA." *Folha de São Paulo,* July 22. Retrieved from http://www1.folha.uol.com.br/fsp/cotidiano/55888-pm-de-sp-mata-mais-que -a-policia-dos-eua.shtml.

Cardia, Nancy, and Sueli Schiffer. 2002. "Violência e desigualdade social." *Ciência e Cultura* 54 (1): 25–31.

Cavallaro, James. 1996. *Brazil: Fighting Violence with Violence: Human Right Abuses and Criminality in Rio de Janeiro.* New York: Human Rights Watch/ Americas Watch Report.

Cavallaro, James, and Raquel Dodge. 2007. "Understanding the São Paulo Attacks." *Revista*. David Rockefeller Center for Latin American Studies. Cambridge, MA: Harvard University.

Chevigny, Paul. 1999. *Edge of the Knife: Police Violence in the Americas*. New York: New Press.

Civico, Aldo. 2012. "We Are Illegal, but not Illegitimate: Modes of Policing in Medellin, Colombia." *PoLAR: Political and Legal Anthropology Review* 35 (1): 77–93.

Clunan, Anne, and Harold Trinkunas, eds. 2010. *Ungoverned Spaces: Alternatives to State Authority in an Era of Softened Sovereignty*. Stanford, CA: Stanford Security Studies.

Collier, Paul M. 2000. "Calling the Police to Account: The Role of Management in Constructing a Shared Frame of Reference for the Operation of and Accountability for Policing." Working Paper 0016, Aston Business School.

Comaroff, Jean, and John L. Comaroff, eds. 2006. *Law and Disorder in the Postcolony*. Chicago: University of Chicago Press.

Cordeiro, Ricardo, and Maria R. C. Donalisio. 2001. "Homicídios masculinos na Região Metropolitana de São Paulo entre 1979 e 1998: uma abordagem pictórica." *Caderno de Saúde Pública* 17 (3): 669–77.

Corrêa, Astorige. 2005. *Correinha, Caçador de Bandidos. Líder do Verdadeiro Esquadrão da Morte*. Retrieved from http://www.ebooksbrasil.org/eLibris/correinha.html.

Corregedorias da Policia Civil e Militar. 2013. *Dados dos mortos e feridos na polícia civil e militar em 2012*. São Paolo.

Coy, Martin. 2003. "Tendências Atuais de Fragmentação nas Cidades Latino-Americanas e Desafios para a Política Urbana e o Planejamento Urbano." *Iberoamericana* 3 (11): 111–28.

CPI-Câmara dos Deputados. 2006. *Transcrição ipsis verbis: Depoente Marcos Willians Herbas Camacho, CPI—Tráfico de armas*. Brasília. Retrieved from http://www1.folha.uol.com.br/folha/cotidiano/20060708-marcos_camacho.pdf.

————. 2009. *CPI do Sistema Carcerário*. Brasília. Retrieved from http://bd.camara.gov.br/bd/bitstream/handle/bdcamara/2701/cpi_sistema_carcerario.pdf.

Crowe, Jaime P., and Sergio L. Ferreira. 2006. "Jardim Ângela: em defesa da vida." *Divulgação em Saúde para Debate* 35: 85–91.

Dal Bó, Ernesto, Pedro Dal Bó, and Rafael Di Tella. 2006. "'Plata o Plomo?' Bribe and Punishment in a Theory of Political Influence." *American Political Science Review* 1: 41–53.

Darlington, Shasta. 2012. "Brazil Gang's Slaughter of Police Sparks Fightback." *CNN*. Retrieved from http://www.cnn.com/2012/11/19/world/americas/brazil-police-killed.

Das, Veena, and Deborah Poole. 2004. *Anthropology in the Margins of the State*. Santa Fe, NM: School for Advanced Research.

Davis, Diane. E. 2004. "Conflict, Cooperation, and Convergence: Globalization and the Politics of Downtown Development in Mexico City." *Research in Political Sociology* 15: 143–78.

————. 2006. "Undermining the Rule of Law: Democratization and the Dark Side of Police Reform in Mexico." *Latin American Politics and Society* 48 (1): 55–86.

————. 2009a. "Urban Violence, Quality of Life, and the Future of Latin American Cities: The Dismal Record So Far and the Search for New Analytical Frameworks to Sustain the Bias towards Hope." In *Global Urban Poverty: Setting the Agenda*, edited by Alison M. Garland, Mejgan Massoumi, and Blair A. Ruble, 57–87. Washington, DC: Woodrow Wilson International Center for Scholars.

————. 2009b. "Non-State Armed Actors, New Imagined Communities and Shifting Patterns of Sovereignty and Insecurity in the Modern World." *Contemporary Security Policy* 3 (2): 221–45.

————. 2013. "Zero-Tolerance Policing, Stealth Real Estate Development, and the Transformation of Public Space: Evidence from Mexico City." *Latin American Perspectives* 40 (2): 53–76.

Davis, Diane E., and Graham Denyer Willis. 2011. "Anti-Crime Social Movements in Latin America." In *Blackwell Encyclopedia of Social and Political Movements*, edited by David A. Snow, Donatella Della Porta, Bert Klandermans, and Doug McAdam, 1–3. Oxford: Blackwell Publishing.

Davis, Mike. 1990. *City of Quartz: Excavating the Future in Los Angeles*. New York: Verso.

————. 2006. *Planet of Slums*. New York: Verso.

Denyer Willis, Graham. 2009. "Deadly Symbiosis? The PCC, the State, and the Institutionalization of Violence in São Paulo." In *Youth Violence in Latin America*, edited by Gareth A. Jones and Dennis Rodgers, 167–82. New York: Palgrave.

————. 2012. "What's Killing Brazil's Police?" *New York Times Sunday Review*, December 2. Retrieved from http://www.nytimes.com/2012/12/02/opinion /sunday/in-brazil-poverty-is-deadly-for-police-officers.html.

————. 2014a. "Antagonistic Authorities and the Civil Police in São Paulo, Brazil." *Latin American Research Review* 49 (1): 3–22.

————. 2014b. "The Gun library: An Ethic of Crime in São Paulo." *Boston Review*, April 4. Retrieved from: http://www.bostonreview.net/world/graham -denyer-willis-pcc-gun-library-sao-paulo-prisons-crime.

Denyer Willis, Graham, and Julia Tierney. 2012. *Urban Resilience in Situations of Chronic Violence: A Case Study of São Paulo, Brazil*. Retrieved from http:// www.urcvproject.org/uploads/SãoPaulo_URCV.pdf.

Dias, Camila C. N. 2013. *PCC—Hegemonia Nas Prisões e Monopólio da Violência*. São Paulo: Saraiva.

Dicken, Bulent. 2005. "City of God." *City* 9 (3): 307–20.

DOSP. 2013. Executivo. *Diário Oficial do Estado de São Paulo*, January 8.

Dowdney, Luke. 2006. *Neither War nor Peace: International Comparisons of Children and Youth in Organised Armed Violence*. Rio de Janeiro: 7Letras.

Drybread, Kristen. 2009. "Sleeping with One Eye Open." In *Violence: Ethnographic Encounters*, edited by Parvis Gassem-Fachandi, 79–96. New York: Berg.

Dudley, Steven. 2013. *The El Salvador Gang Truce and the Church: What Was the Role of the Catholic Church?* CLALS WHITE PAPER, No. 1. Washington: American University. Retrieved from http://www.american.edu/clals/upload /CLALS_White_Paper_Series_No-_1_The_El_Salvador_Gang_Truce_and _the_Church.pdf.

Eckstein, Susan. 1990. "Urbanization Revisited: Inner-city Slum of Hope and Squatter Settlement of Despair." *World Development* 18 (2): 165–81.

Ericson, Richard. V. 1990. *Reproducing Order: A Study of Police Patrol Work.* Toronto: University of Toronto Press.

———. 1993. *Making Crime: A Study of Detective Work.* Toronto: University of Toronto Press.

Esser, Daniel. 2004. "The City as Arena, Hub, and Prey Patterns of Violence in Kabul and Karachi." *Environment and Urbanization* 16 (2): 31–38.

Estado de São Paulo. 2012a. "Vítimas de homicídios tiveram ficha criminal consultada, diz delegado-geral." *Estadão.com.br*, November 22. Retrieved at: http://www.estadao.com.br/noticias/cidades,vitimas-de-homicidios-tiveram -ficha-criminal-consultada-diz-delegado-geral,963643,0.htm.

———. 2012b. "Em 11 meses, 106 policiais foram mortos por bandidos no Estado." *Estadão.com.br*, December 28. Retrieved from http://www.estadao.com .br/noticias/impresso,em-11-meses-106-policiais-foram-mortos-por -bandidos-no-estado-,978309,0.htm.

Eze, Uwom, Effiong Akang, and William Odesanmi. 2011. "Pattern of Homicide Coroner's Autopsies at University College Hospital, Ibadan, Nigeria: 1997–2006." *Medicine Science and the Law* 51 (1): 43–48.

Fassin, Didier. 2013. *Enforcing Order: An Ethnography of Urban Policing.* Malden, MA: Polity Press.

Feltran, Gabriel. 2010. "Crime e castigo na cidade: os repertórios da justiça e a questão do homicídio nas periferias de São Paulo." *Caderno CRH* 23 (58): 59–73.

———. 2011. *Fronteiras de Tensão: Política e Violência nas Periferias de São Paulo.* São Paulo: UNESP.

Ferguson, James. 2005. "Seeing Like an Oil Company: Space, Security, and Global Capital in Neo-liberal Africa." *American Anthropologist* 107 (3): 377–82.

Fernandes, Heloisa R. 1991. "Violencia e Modos de Vida: 'Os Justiceiros.'" *Revista Crítica de Ciências Sociais* 33: 135–44.

Folha de São Paulo. 2012a. "Mortos tiveram ficha criminal checada antes de crimes, diz delegado." *Folha de São Paulo*, December 22. Retrieved from http:// www1.folha.uol.com.br/cotidiano/1189393-mortos-tiveram-ficha-criminal -checada-antes-de-crimes-diz-delegado.shtml.

———. 2012b. "'NYT' relaciona morte de PMs em SP a falta de apoio baixos salaries." *Folha de São Paulo*, December 2. Retrieved from http://www1.folha .uol.com.br/cotidiano/1194760-nyt-relaciona-morte-de-pms-em-sp-a-falta -de-apoio-e-baixos-salarios.shtml.

Foucault, Michel. 1975. *Discipline and Punish: The Birth of the Prison.* New York: Random House.

———. 1990. *The History of Sexuality. Vol. 1. An Introduction.* New York: Random House.

Fruhling, Hugo. 2009. "Research on Latin American Police: Where Do We Go from Here?" *Police Practice and Research* 10 (5–6): 465–81.

Fuchs, Barbara. 2000. "Faithless Empires: Pirates, Renegadoes, and the English Nation." *ELH* 67 (1): 45–69.

Fyfe, James. 1988. "Police Use of Deadly Force: Research and Reform." *Justice Quarterly* 5 (2): 165–205.

Gambetta, Diego. 1993. *The Sicilian Mafia: The Business of Private Protection.* Cambridge, MA: Harvard University Press.

———. 2009. *Codes of the Underworld: How Criminals Communicate.* Princeton, NJ: Princeton University Press.

Gans, Herbert. 1962. *The Urban Villagers: Group and Class in the Life of Italian Americans.* New York: Free Press.

Garcia, Marcos. R. V. 2009. "Identity as 'Patchwork': Aspects of Identity Among Low-Income Brazilian *Travestis.*" *Culture, Health, and Sexuality* 11 (6): 611–23.

Garfinkel, Harold. 1949. "Research Note on Inter- and Intra-Racial Homicides." *Social Forces* 27 (4): 369–81.

Garland, David. 1996. "The Limits of the Sovereign State: Strategies of Crime Control in Contemporary Society." *British Journal of Criminology* 36 (4): 445–71.

Gawryszewski, Vilma P., and Luciana Costa. 2005. "Homicídios e desigualdades sociais no Município de São Paulo." *Revista de Saúde Pública* 39 (2): 191–97.

Gay, Robert. 1990a. "Neighborhood Associations and Political Change in Rio de Janeiro." *Latin American Research Review* 25 (1): 102–18.

———. 1990b. "Community Organization and Clientelist Politics in Contemporary Brazil: A Case Study from Suburban Rio de Janeiro." *International Journal of Urban and Regional Research* 14 (4): 648–66.

———. 1994. *Popular Organization and Democracy in Rio de Janeiro: A Tale of Two Favelas.* Philadelphia: Temple University Press.

Gilbert, Alan. 2007. "The Return of the Slum: Does Language Matter?" *International Journal of Urban and Regional Research* 31 (4): 697–713.

Globo. 2012. "'Deixo meus filhos tensos por estar trabalhando' diz PM." *Globo,* November 11. Retrieved from http://g1.globo.com/fantastico/noticia/2012/11/deixo-meus-filhos-tensos-por-estar-trabalhando-diz-pm.html.

Godoy, Angelina S. 2006. *Popular Injustice: Violence, Community, and Law in Latin America.* Stanford, CA: Stanford University Press.

Goertzel, Ted, and Túlio Khan. 2009. "The Great São Paulo Homicide Drop." *Homicide Studies* 13 (4): 398–410.

Goffman, Erving. 1959. *Presentation of Self in Everyday Life.* Garden City, NY: Anchor Books.

Goldstein, Donna. 2003. *Laughter Out of Place: Race, Class, Violence, and Sexuality in a Rio Shantytown.* Berkeley: University of California Press.

Goldstein, Daniel. 2005. "Flexible Justice: Neo-liberal Violence and 'Self-Help' Security in Bolivia." *Critical Anthropology* 25 (4): 389–411.

Gonsaga, Ricardo A. T., Caroline F. Rimoli, Eduardo A. Pires, Fernando S. Zogheib, Marcos V. T. Fujino, and Milena B. Cunha. 2012. "Avaliação da mortalidade por causas externas." *Revista do Colégio Brasileiro de Cirur-giões* 39 (4): 263–67.

Granjeia, Juliana. 2012. "Na visão da periferia, PCC reduziu crimes, diz canadense que estuda violência em São Paulo." *UOL Notícias*, December 20. Retrieved from http://noticias.uol.com.br/cotidiano/ultimas-noticias/2012/12/19/policial -nao-se-sente-parte-do-estado-afirma-pesquisador-canadense-que-estuda-a -criminalidade-em-sp.htm.

Gutierres, Marcelo. 2008. "Maluf retoma bordão de 'Rota na rua' durante campanha à Prefeitura de SP." *Folha de São Paulo*, July 15. Retrieved from http:// www1.folha.uol.com.br/folha/brasil/ult96u422564.shtml.

Hagopian, Frances. 1990. "'Democracy by Undemocratic Means?' Elites, Political Pacts, and Regime Transition in Brazil." *Comparative Political Studies* 23 (2): 147–70.

Hansen, Thomas B., and Finn Steputtat. 2006. "Sovereignty Revisited." *Annual Review of Anthropology* 35: 16.1–16.21.

Harvey, David. 2003. "The Right to the City." *International Journal of Urban and Regional Research* 27 (4): 939–41.

Herbert, Steve. 1996. "The Normative Ordering of Police Territoriality: Making and Marking Space with the Los Angeles Police Department." *Annals of the Association of American Geographers* 86 (3): 567–82.

Hills, Alice. 2014. "Somalia Works: Police Development as State Building." *African Affairs* 113 (450): 88–107.

Hinton, Mercedes S. 2006. *The State on the Streets: Police and Politics in Argentina and Brazil*. Boulder, CO: Lynne Rienners.

Hinton, Mercedes, and Tim Newburn. 2009. *Policing Developing Democracies*. New York: Routledge.

Hobbes, Thomas. 1981 (1660). *The Leviathan*. Penguin.

Hobbs, Dick. 1988. *Doing the Business: Entrepreneurship, the Working Class, and Detectives in the East End of London*. New York: Oxford.

Hobsbawm, Eric. 1959. *Primitive Rebels: Studies of Archaic Forms of Social Movement in the 19th and 20th Centuries*. Manchester: Manchester University Press.

———. 1969. *Bandits*. New York: Delacourt.

Holloway, Thomas. 1993. *Policing Rio de Janeiro: Repression and Resistance in a 19th Century City*. Stanford, CA: Stanford University Press.

Holston, James. 1989. *The Modernist City: An Anthropological Critique of Brasília*. Chicago: University of Chicago Press.

———. 2008. *Insurgent Citizenship: Disjunctions of Democracy and Modernity in Brazil*. Princeton, NJ: Princeton University Press.

———. 2009. "Dangerous Spaces of Citizenship: Gang Talk, Rights Talk, and Rule of Law in Brazil." *Planning Theory* 8 (1): 12–31.

Huggins, Martha K., ed. 1991. *Vigilantism and the State in Modern Latin America: Essays on Extra-Legal Violence*. New York: Praeger.

———. 1998. *Political Policing: The United States and Latin America*. Durham, NC: Duke University Press.

———. 2000. "Legacies of Authoritarianism: Brazilian Torturers' and Murderers' Reformulation of Memory." *Latin American Perspectives* 27 (57): 57–78.

————. 2003. "Moral Universes of Brazilian Torturers." *Albany Law Review* 67: 527.

Huggins, Martha K., Mika Haritos-Fatouros, and Philip G. Zimbardo. 2002. *Violence Workers: Police Torturers and Murderers Reconstruct Brazilian Atrocities*. Berkeley: University of California Press.

Hughes, Pedro J. A. 2004. "Segregação socioespacial e violência na cidade de São Paulo: referências para a formulação de políticas públicas." *São Paulo em Perspectiva* 18 (4): 93–102.

Human Rights Watch (HRW). 2009. *Lethal Force: Police Violence and Public Security in Rio de Janeiro and São Paulo*. New York: Human Rights Watch.

————. 2013. *Brasil: Execuções, Acobertamentos Pela Polícia*. Retrieved from http://www.hrw.org/news/2013/07/29/letter-governor-alckmin-and-attorney -general-marcio-rosa-about-police-violence.

Hunt, Jennifer. 2010. *Seven Shots: An NYPD Raid on a Terrorist Cell and its Aftermath*. Chicago: University of Chicago Press.

Ignatieff, Michael. 2013. *The Lesser Evil: Political Ethics in an Age of Terror*. Princeton, NJ: Princeton University Press.

Innes, Martin. 2003. *Investigating Murder: Detective Work and the Police Response to Criminal Homicide*. New York: Oxford University Press.

Jackall, Robert. 2005. *Street Stories: The World of Police Detectives*. Cambridge, MA: Harvard University Press.

Jornal do Brasil. 2013. "Alckmin anuncia medidas de combate à violência em São Paulo." *Jornal do Brasil*, May 22. Retrieved from http://www.jb.com.br /pais/noticias/2013/05/22/alckmin-anuncia-medidas-de-combate-a-violencia -em-São-paulo/.

Jornal Flit Paralisante. 2011. "Roberto Conde Guerra não pertence mais aos quadros da Polícia Civil . . . Foi demitido em razão das postagens neste blog e comentários sobre a tentatives de desvio de verbas reservadas no caso divulgado pela Rede Globo e protagonizado pelo então director do DIRD—Ternos viram caso de polícia." *Jornal Flit Paralisante*, May 3. Retrieved from http:// flitparalisante.wordpress.com/2011/05/03/roberto-conde-guerra-nao-pertence -mais-aos-quadros-da-policia-civil-foi-demitido-em-razao-das-postagens-neste- blog-e-comentarios-sobre-a-tentativa-de-desvio-de-verbas-reservadas-no-caso -divulgado-pe/.

————. 2012a. "Jornalista André Caramante é vítima de ódio do ex-chefe da ROTA." *Jornal Flit Paralistante*, July 21. Retrieved from http://flitparalisante .wordpress.com/2012/07/21/jornalista-andre-caramante-e-vitima-de-odio -do-ex-chefe-da-rota-andre-caramante-notorio-defensor-de-bandidos-na- pm-quando-o-servidor-nao-presta-e-demitido-ja-na-folha-quando-nao -presta/.

————. 2012b. "The *New York Times*: What's Killing Brazil's Police? (O Que Está Matando a Polícia Brasileira?)—by Graham Denyer Willis." *Jornal Flit Paralisante*, December 2. Retrieved from http://flitparalisante.wordpress.com /2012/12/02/the-new-york-times-whats-killing-brazils-police-o-que-esta -matando-a-policia-brasileira-by-graham-denyer-willis/.

Jozino, Josmar. 2009. "IC não acha indício de confronto e indica execução na Castelinho." *Estado.com.br*, May 11. Retrieved from http://www.estadao.com

.br/noticias/impresso,ic-nao-acha-indicio-de-confronto-e-indica-execucao
-na-castelinho,368753,0.htm.

———. 2013. "Polícia só esclarece 1 das 24 chacinas do ano passado." *Folha de São Paulo*, January 7. Retrieved from http://www1.folha.uol.com.br/fsp /cotidiano/87433-policia-so-esclarece-1-das-24-chacinas-do-ano-passado.shtml.

Kingstone, Peter R., and Timothy Power, eds. 2008. *Democratic Brazil Revisited*. Pittsburgh: University of Pittsburgh Press.

Koonings, Kees, and Dirk Kruijt, eds. 1999. *Societies of Fear: The Legacy of Civil War, Violence, and Terror in Latin America*. London: Zed Books.

———, eds. 2004. *Armed Actors, Organized Violence, and State Failure in Latin America*. London: Zed Books.

———, eds. 2007. *Fractured Cities: Social Exclusion, Urban Violence, and Contested Spaces in Latin America*. London: Zed Books.

Kurtz, Markus J., and Sarah M. Brooks. 2008. "Embedding Neoliberal Reform in Latin America." *World Politics* 60 (2): 231–80.

Latham, Robert. 2000. "Social Sovereignty." *Theory, Culture & Society* 17 (4): 1–18.

Leahy, Joe. 2012. "Spiraling Drug War Envelops São Paulo." *Financial Times*, December 20. Retrieved from http://www.ft.com/cms/s/0/ee7b50c0-4ab0-11e2 -968a-00144feab49a.html.

Leeds, Anthony. 1973. "Political, Economic, and Social Effects of Producer and Consumer Orientations Toward Housing in Brazil and Peru: A Systems Analysis." *Latin American urban research* 3: 181–216.

Leeds, Elizabeth. 1996. "Cocaine and Parallel Polities in the Brazilian Urban Periphery: Constraints on Local-Level Democratization." *Latin American Research Review* 31 (3): 47–83.

Lemanski, Charlotte. 2004. "A New Apartheid? The Spatial Implications of Fear of Crime in South Africa." *Environment and Urbanization* 16 (2): 101–12.

Lemgruber, Julita. 2004. "Violência, omissão e insegurança pública: o pão nosso de cada dia." *Center for Studies on Public Security and Citizenship*. Retrieved from http://www.fireball.com.br/demo/cesec/wp-content/uploads/2011/06 /Julita_Associacao_Brasileira_de_Ciencias1.pdf.

Libertun de Duren, Nora R. 2009. "Urban Planning and State Reform From Industrial Suburbs to Gated Communities." *Journal of Planning Education and Research* 28 (3): 310–22.

de Lima, Roberto Kant. 1994. *A polícia da cidade do Rio de Janeiro: seus dilemas e paradoxos*. Rio de Janeiro: Forense.

Lima, Renato S. D. 2008. "A produção da opacidade: estatísticas criminais e segurança pública no Brasil." *Novos Estudos-CEBRAP* 80: 65–69.

Lipsky, Michael. 1983. *Street-Level Bureaucracy: Dilemmas of the Individual in Public Services*. New York: Russell Sage Foundation.

Machado, Leandro, and Afonso Benites. 2013. "Sem estrutura, IML da zona leste de SP marca corpos a caneta." *Folha de São Paulo*, January 19. Retrieved from http://www1.folha.uol.com.br/cotidiano/1217330-sem-estrutura-iml-da-zona -leste-de-sp-marca-corpos-a-caneta.shtml.

Maia, Paulo B. 1999. "Vinte anos de homicídios no Estado de São Paulo." *São Paulo em Perspectiva* 13 (4): 121–29.

Manso, Bruno. 1999. "Os bandidos da chacina." *Revista Veja*, September 8. Retrieved from http://veja.abril.com.br/080999/p_042.html.

———. 2000. "Por que tanto se mata na periferia de São Paulo?: *Braudel Papers* 26, Instituto Fernando Braudel de Economia Mundial. Retrieved from http://pt.braudel.org.br/publicacoes/braudel-papers/downloads/portugues /bp26_pt.pdf.

———. 2013. "Crecismento e Queda dos Homicidios entre 1960 e 2010: Uma Análise Situacional." Retrieved from http://www.fflch.usp.br/dcp/assets/docs /III_SD_2013/Mesa_7.1_-_Bruno_Paes_Manso_III_SD2013.pdf.

Marcuse, Peter. 1997. "The Enclave, the Citadel, and the Ghetto: What Has Changed in the Post-Fordist U.S. City." *Urban Affairs Review* 33 (2): 228–64.

Marks, Monique, and Andrew Goldsmith. 2013. "The State, the People of Democratic Policing: The Case of South Africa." In *Democracy, Society and the Governance of Security*, edited by J. Wood and B. Dupont, 139–64. Cambridge: Cambridge University Press.

Massey, Douglas. 1990. "American Apartheid." *American Journal of Sociology* 96 (2): 329–57.

Mbembe, Achille. 2003. "Necropolitics." *Public Culture* 15 (1): 11–40.

Melo, Markus C. 1995. "State Retreat, Governance and Metropolitan Restructuring in Brazil." *International Journal of Urban and Regional Research* 19 (3): 342–57.

Mendez, Juan E., Guillermo O'Donnell, and Paulo S. Pinheiro, eds. 1999. *The (un)Rule of Law and the Underprivileged in Latin America*. Notre Dame, IN: University of Notre Dame Press.

Midgal, Joel S. 1988. *Strong Societies and Weak States: State-Society Relations and State Capabilities in the Third World*. Princeton, NJ: Princeton University Press.

Mingardi, Guaracy. 1992. *Tiros, gansos e trutas: Coitidiano e reforma na Polícia Civil*. São Paulo: Scritta Editorial.

Miraglia, Paula. 2008. *Safe Spaces in São Paulo*. Retrieved from http://vo.urban -age.net/o_downloads/archive/_SA/16_NewsPaper_Essay_Miraglia.pdf.

Misse, Michel. 1999. *Malandros, marginais e vagabundos: Acao social da violencia no Rio de Janeiro*. PhD diss., Instituto de Pesquisas State University of Rio de Janeiro, Rio de Janeiro, Brazil.

———. 2010. "Crime, sujeito e sujeição criminal Aspectos de uma contribuição analítica sobre a categoria 'bandido.'" *Lua Nova* 79: 15–38.

———. 2011. "'Autos de Resistência': Uma Análise dos Homicídios Cometidos port Policiais na Cidade do Rio de Janeiro (2001–2011)." Retrieved from http://www.necvu.ifcs.ufrj.br/images/Relatorio%20final%20Autos%20 de%20Resistência.pdf.

Mitchell, Michael, and Charles Wood. 1999. "Ironies of Citizenship: Skin Color, Police Brutality, and the Challenge to Democracy in Brazil." *Social Forces* 77 (3): 1001–20.

Moran, Dominique, Dierdre Conlon, and Nick Gill, eds. 2013. *Carceral spaces: Mobility and agency in imprisonment and migrant detention*. Surrey: Ashgate Publishing.

Moser, Caroline. 2004. "Urban Violence and Insecurity: An Introductory Road-map." *Environment and Urbanization* 16 (2): 3–16.

Müller, Markus. 2011. *Public Security in the Negotiated State: Policing in Latin America and Beyond*. New York: Palgrave.

Newburn, T. 1999. *Understanding and Preventing Police Corruption: Lessons from the Literature*. Police Research Series Paper 110. London: Home Office.

North, Douglas C. 2005. *Understanding the Process of Economic Change*. Princeton, NJ: Princeton University Press.

Novaes, Marina, and Vagner Magalhães. 2013. "'Fiquei com sangue até o meio da canela,' diz perito do Carandiru." *Terra Brasil*, April 6. Retrieved from http://noticias.terra.com.br/brasil/policia/fiquei-com-sangue-ate-o-meio-da -canela-diz-perito-do-carandiru,eodc5afed16dd310VgnVCM4000009bcceb oaRCRD.html.

O'Donnell, Guillermo. 1993. "On the State, Democratization, and Some Conceptual Problems: A Latin American View with Glances at Some Postcommunist Countries." *World Development* 21 (8): 1355–69.

———. 2004. "Why the Rule of Law Matters." *Journal of Democracy* 15 (4): 32–46.

O'Neill, Kevin L. 2010. "The Reckless Will: Prison Chaplaincy and the Problem of Mara Salvatrucha." *Public Culture* 22 (1): 67–88.

———. 2011. "Delinquent Realities: Christianity, Formality, and Security in the Americas." *American Quarterly* 63 (2): 337–65.

O'Neill, Kevin L., and Kendron Thomas, eds. 2011. *Securing the City: Neoliberalism, Space, and Insecurity in Postwar Guatemala*. Durham, NC: Duke University Press.

Paes Machado, E., and Ceci V. Noronha. 2002. "A polícia dos pobres: violência policial em classes populares urbanas." *Sociologias* 4 (7): 188–221.

Paoli, Letizia. 2002. "The Paradox of Organized Crime." *Crime, Law & Social Change* 37: 51–97.

Park, Robert. 1927. "Human Nature and Collective Behavior." *American Journal of Sociology* 32 (5): 733–41.

Paulinhopittbull. 2012. "PM mata assaltante em hotel em São Paulo." Retrieved from http://www.youtube.com/watch?v=4Bwx4GzUz10.

Penglase, Benjamin. 2009. "States of Insecurity: Everyday Emergencies, Public Secrets and Drug Trafficker Power in a Brazilian Favela." *PoLAR: Political and Legal Anthropology Review* 32 (1): 47–63.

Percival, Val, and Thomas Homer-Dixon. 1998. "Environmental Scarcity and Violent Conflict: The Case of South Africa." *Journal of Peace Research* 35 (3): 279–98.

Pereira, Anthony. 2000. "An Ugly Democracy? State Violence and the Rule of Law in Brazil Postauthoritarian Brazil." In *Democratic Brazil: Actors, Institutions, and Processes*, edited by P. R. Kingstone and T. Power, 217–35. Pittsburgh: University of Pittsburgh Press.

Peres, Maria F. T., Juliana F. de Almeida, Diego Vicentin, Magdalena Cerda, Nancy Cardia, and Sergio Adorno. 2011. "Fall in Homicides in the City of São Paulo: An Exploratory Analysis of Possible Determinants." *Brazilian Journal of Epidemiology* 14 (4): 709–21.

Perez, Louis A. 2005. *To Die in Cuba: Suicide and Society.* Chapel Hill: University of North Carolina Press.

Perlman, Janice. 1979. *The Myth of Marginality: Urban Poverty and Politics in Rio de Janeiro.* Berkeley: University of California Press.

———. 2007. "Marginality, From Myth to Reality: The Favelas of Rio de Janeiro 1968–2005." Retrieved from http://advantronsample2.com/Marginality _from_Myth_to_Reality.pdf.

Pimentel, Spensy. 2013. "Tempo de Terror no Rosana." *A Pública.* Retrieved from http://www.apublica.org/2013/02/tempo-de-terror-rosana/.

Pine, Adrienne. 2008. *Working Hard, Drinking Hard: On Violence and Survival in Honduras.* Berkeley: University of California Press.

Pinheiro, Paulo S. 1997. "Violência, crime e sistemas policiais em países de novas democracias." *Tempo Social* 9 (1): 43–52.

Pinheiro, Paulo S., and Sergio Adorno. 1993. "Violência Contra Crianças e Adolescentes, Violência Social e Estado de Direito." *São Paulo em Perspectiva* 7 (1): 106–17.

Portes, Alejandro, and Kelly Hoffman. 2003. "Latin American Class Structures: Their Composition and Change During the Neoliberal Era." *Latin American Research Review* 38 (1): 41–82.

Preti, Antonio, and Paula Miotto. 2000. "Death by Homicide in Italy, 1980–94: Age and Gender Differences among Victims." *Medicine Science and the Law* 40 (3): 233–40.

Punch, Maurice. 1985. *Conduct Unbecoming: The Social Construction of Police Deviance and Control.* London: Tavistock.

Purcell, Mark. 2003. "Citizenship and the Right to the Global City: Reimagining the Capitalist World Order." *International Journal of Urban and Regional Research* 27 (3): 564–90.

R7. 2012. "Mortes de policiais podem ter sido motivadas por vingança, diz PM." *R7.* Retrieved from http://noticias.r7.com/São-paulo/noticias/mortes -de-policiais-podem-ter-sido-motivadas-por-vinganca-diz-pm-20120621 .html.

———. 2013. "Número de chacinas aumenta na Grande SP em 2013." *R7.* Retrieved from http://noticias.r7.com/São-paulo/numero-de-chacinas-aumenta -na-grande-sp-em-2013-19042013.

Recursos Humanos. 2012. "Retribuição mensal." Retrieved from http://www .recursoshumanos.sp.gov.br/retribuicao_mensal/area%20policial/pol%20 civil.pdf.

Reichenheim, Michael E., Edinilsa R. Souza, Claudia L. Moraes, Maria H. Jorge, Maria Cosme P. da Silva, and Maria C. S. Minayo. 2011. "Violence and Injuries in Brazil: The Effect, Progress Made, and Challenges Ahead." *Lancet* 377: 1962–75.

Ribeiro, Luiz C., and Luciana C. D. Lago. 1995. "Restructuring in Large Brazilian Cities: The Centre/Periphery Model." *International Journal of Urban and Regional Research* 19 (3): 369–82.

Roberto, Eduardo, and Gabriel Vituri. 2012. "Being a Brazilian Policeman Sucks." *Vice.* Retrieved from http://www.vice.com/read/pcc-police-São-paolo-gang-crime.

Roberts, Bryan R. 2005. "The Social Context of Citizenship in Latin America." *International Journal of Urban and Regional Research* 1 (1): 38–65.

Rodgers, Dennis. 2004. "Disembedding the City: Crime, Insecurity, and Spatial Organization in Managua, Nicaragua." *Environment and Urbanization* 16 (2): 113–24.

———. 2006. "The State as a Gang: Conceptualizing the Governmentality of Violence in Contemporary Nicaragua." *Critique of Anthropology* 26 (3): 315–30.

Rodrigues, Artur, Marcelo Godoy, and William Cardoso. 2012. "PM encontra em Paraisópolis lista de 40 policiais marcados para morrer." *Estado de São Paulo*, October 31. Retrieved from http://www.estadao.com.br/noticias /impresso,pm-encontra-em-paraisopolis-lista-de-40-policiais-marcados-para -morrer,953618,0.htm.

Rolnik, Raquel. n.d. *São Paulo: Crise e Mudanca*. São Paulo: Brasiliense.

———. 1999. "Exclusão Territorial e Violência." *São Paulo em Perspectiva* 13 (4): 100–111.

———. 2000. "Exclusão Territorial e Violência: O caso do Estado de São Paulo." *Cadernos de Textos* 2: 173–96.

Romero, Simon. 2012. "Alarm Grows in São Paulo as More Police Officers Are Murdered." *New York Times*, October 2. Retrieved from http://www.nytimes .com/2012/10/03/world/americas/spike-in-police-officer-deaths-alarms-São -paulo.html.

Rotberg, Robert I. 2002. "The New Nature of Nation-State Failure." *Washington Quarterly* 25 (3): 85–96.

Roth-Gordon, Jennifer. 2009. "The Language that Came Down the Hill: Slang, Crime, and Citizenship in Rio de Janeiro." *American Anthropologist* 111 (1): 57–68.

Rotker, Susan, ed. 2002. *Citizens of Fear: Urban Violence in Latin America*. Piscataway, NJ: Rutgers University Press.

Roy, Ananya. 2009. "Why India Cannot Plan its Cities: Informality, Insurgence and the Idiom of Urbanization." *Planning Theory* 8(1): 76–87.

Rozema, Ralph. 2008. "Urban DDR-Processes: Paramilitaries and Criminal Networks in Medellın, Colombia." *Journal of Latin American Studies* 40 (3): 423–52.

Rudra, Nita. 2002. "Globalization and the Decline of the Welfare State in Less-Developed Countries." *International Organizations* 56: 411–45.

Sanders, William. 1977. *Detective work: A study of criminal investigations*. New York: Free Press.

Sarat, Austin, and Jennifer L. Culbert, eds. 2009. *States of Violence: War, Capital Punishment, and Letting Die*. Cambridge: Cambridge University Press.

SBT. 2012. "Polícia Acredita que PCC esteja envolvido na morte de Cabo Bruno." *SBT Television*. Retrieved from http://www.sbt.com.br/jornalismo/noticias /24906/Policia-acredita-que-PCC-esteja-envolvido-na-morte-do-Cabo -Bruno.html.

Scharf, Peter, and Arnold Binder. 1983. *The Badge and the Bullet: Police Use of Deadly Force*. New York: Praeger.

Scheff, Thomas J. 1967. "Toward a Sociological Model of Consensus." *American Sociological Review* 32 (1): 32–46.

Schelling, Thomas C. 1959. *Toward a Theory of Strategy for International Conflict*. Rand Publication No. P-1648. Washington, DC: Rand.

———. 1963. *The Strategy of Conflict*. New York: Oxford University Press.

Scheper-Hughes, Nancy. 1993. *Death without Weeping: The Violence of Everyday Life in Brazil*. Berkeley: University of California Press.

Schmitt, Carl. 1985. *Political Theology*. Cambridge, MA: MIT Press.

Scott, James. 1999. *Seeing like a State*. New Haven, CT: Yale University Press.

———. 2009. *The Art of Not Being Governed: An Anarchist History of Upland Southeast Asia*. New Haven, CT: Yale University Press.

Seade. 2012. "Sistema Estadual de Análise de Dados." Retrieved from http://www.Seade.gov.br/produtos/distritos/index.php?page=consulta&action=var_list&busca=Saude.

Simon, David. 2006. *Homicide: A Year on the Killing Streets*. New York: Picador.

Sinhoretto, Jaqueline, Giane Silvestre, and Felipe A. L. Melo. 2013. "O encarceramento em massa em São Paulo." *Tempo Social* 25 (1): 83–106.

Skaperdas, Stergios, Rodrigo Soares, Alys Willman, and Stephen Miller. 2009. *The Costs of Violence*. Social Development Department, World Bank. Retrieved from http://siteresources.worldbank.org/EXTSOCIALDEVELOPMENT/Resources/244362-1239390842422/6012763-1239905793229/costs_of_violence.pdf.

Skarbek, David. 2014. *The Social Order of the Underworld: How Prison Gangs Govern the American Penal System*. New York: Oxford.

Soja, Edward. 1996. *Thirdspace: Journeys to Los Angeles and Other Real-and-Imagined Places*. Oxford: Basil Blackwell.

Souza, Fátima 2007. *PCC, a facção*. São Paulo: Editora Record.

Stepputat, Finn. 2014. *Governing the Dead: Sovereignty and the Politics of Dead Bodies*. Manchester: University of Manchester Press.

Stokes, Charles. 1962. "A Theory of Slums." *Land Economics* 8: 187–97.

Subprefeitura de Cidade Tiradentes. 2013. *Histórico*. Retrieved from http://www.prefeitura.sp.gov.br/cidade/secretarias/subprefeituras/cidade_tiradentes/historico/index.php?p=94.

Tardiff, Kenneth, Peter M. Marzuk, Andrew C. Leon, Charles S. Hirsch, Marina Stajic, Laura Portera, and Nancy Hartwell. 1994. "Homicide in New York City: Cocaine Use and Firearms." *Journal of the American Medical Association* 272 (1): 43–46.

Taussig, Michael. 2003. *Law in a Lawless Land: Diary of a Limpieza in Colombia*. New York: The New Press.

Telles, Vera, and Daniel Hirata. 2007. "Cidade e práticas urbanas: nas fronteiras incertas entre o ilegal, o informal e o ilícito." *Estudos Avançados* 21 (61): 173–91.

———. 2010. "Illegalismos e jogos de poder em São Paulo." *Tempo Social* 22 (2): 39–59.

Ticktin, Miriam. 2011. *Casualties of Care: Immigration and the Politics of Humanitarianism in France*. Berkeley: University of California Press.

Tilly, Charles. 1985. "War Making and State Making as Organized Crime." In *Bringing the State Back In,* edited by Peter Evans, Dietrich Rueschemeyer, and Theda Skocpol, 169–86. Cambridge: Cambridge University Press.

Thomas, Kendron, Kevin L. O'Neill, and Thomas Offit. 2011. "An Introduction." In *Securing the City: Neoliberalism, Space, and Insecurity in Postwar Guatemala,* edited by Kevin Lewis O'Neill and Kendron Thomas, 1–24. Durham, NC: Duke University Press.

Tomasz, Kleber. 2012. "Rota Mata Suspeito de Chefiar Tráfico na Favela Paraisópolis." *Globo,* November 3. Retrieved from http://g1.globo.com/São-paulo /noticia/2012/11/suspeito-de-trafico-de-drogas-e-morto-pela-rota-em-São -paulo-diz-coronel.html.

Torres, Haroldo G., Eduardo Marques, Maria P. Ferreira, and Sandra Bitar. 2003. "Pobreza e Espaço: Padrões de Segregação em São Paulo." *Estudos Avancados* 17 (43): 97–128.

Trubek, David. 2006. "The Rule of Law in Development Assistance: Past, Present and Future." In *The New Law and Economic Development: A Critical Appraisal,* edited by David Trubek and Alvaro Santos, 74–94. Cambridge: Cambridge University Press.

Tulchin, Joseph S., and Meg Ruthenburg. 2006. *Towards a Society under Law: Citizens and Their Police in Latin America.* Washington, DC: Woodrow Wilson Center Press.

Uildriks, Neils, ed. 2010. *Mexico's Unrule of Law.* Lanham, MD: Lexington Books.

Ungar, Mark. 2008. "The Privatization of Citizen Security in Latin America." *Social Justice* 34 (3–4): 20–37.

———. 2009. "Police Reform in Argentina: Public Security versus Human Rights." In *Policing Insecurity,* edited by Neils Uildriks, 169–96. Lanham, MD: Lexington Books.

United Nations Office on Drugs and Crime (UNODC). 2011. *Global Study on Homicide: Trends, Contexts, Data. UNODC.* Retrieved from http://www .unodc.org/documents/data-and-analysis/statistics/Homicide/Globa_study _on_homicide_2011_web.pdf.

UOL Notícias. 2012a. "Jovens desistem da carreira de policial temendo represálias." *UOL Notícias,* December 14. Retrieved from http://mais.uol.com .br/view/jinmcnm98vmk/jovens-desistem-da-carreira-de-policial-temendo-re presalias-04020E1C326AC8914326?types=A&.

———. 2012b. "Em nota, Estado diz que queda da violência está relacionada aos investimentos do governo." *UOL Notícias,* December 21. Retrieved from http://noticias.uol.com.br/cotidiano/ultimas-noticias/2012/12/21/queda-da -violencia-esta-relacionada-aos-investimentos-do-governo-diz-estado.htm.

Vale, Larry J. 2009. *From the Puritans to the Projects.* Cambridge, MA: Harvard University Press.

Van Maanen, John. 1984. "Making Rank Becoming an American Police Sergeant." *Journal of Contemporary Ethnography* 13 (2): 155–76.

———. 1988. *Tales of the Field: On Writing Ethnography.* Chicago: University of Chicago Press.

Varese, Frederico. 2001. "The Russian Mafia: Private Protection in a New Market Economy." New York: Oxford.

Venkatesh, Sudhir. 2002. *American Project: The Rise and Fall of a Modern Ghetto.* Cambridge, MA: Harvard University Press.

Ventura, Felipe. 2013. "Após presídio em SP ativar bloqueador de celular, detentos tentam reclamar com operadoras." *Gizmodo*, January 14. Retrieved from http://gizmodo.uol.com.br/apos-presidio-ativar-bloqueador-de-celular-detentos-tentam-reclamar-com-operadoras/.

Volkov, Vadim. 2002. *Violent Entrepreneurs: The Use of Force in the Making of Russian Capitalism.* Ithaca, NY: Cornell University Press.

Voltaire. 1817. *Œuvres complètes de Voltaire: Dictionnaire philosophique.* Paris: Chez Th. Desoer.

Wacquant, Loïc. 2001. "Deadly Symbiosis: When Ghetto and Prison Meet and Mesh." *Punishment and Society* 3 (1): 95–133.

———. 2008a. "The Militarization of Urban Marginality: Lessons from the Brazilian Metropolis." *International Political Sociology* 2: 56–74.

———. 2008b. *Urban Outcasts.* Malden, MA: Polity Press.

Wacquant, Loïc, and Pierre Bourdieu. 2002. *An Invitation to Reflexive Sociology.* Chicago: University of Chicago Press.

Waiselfisz, Julio J. 2010. *Mapa da violência 2010: anatomia dos homicídios no Brasil.* São Paulo: Instituto Sangari.

———. 2012. *Mapa da violência 2012: Os novos padrões da violência homicida no Brasil.* São Paulo: Instituto Sangari.

Weber, Max. 1962. *Basic Concepts in Sociology.* New York: Philosophical Library.

Wedel, Janine. 2003. "Corruption and Organized Crime in Post-Communist States: New Ways of Manifesting Old Patterns." *Trends in Organized Crime* 7 (1): 3–61.

Weingast, Barry. 2010. "Why Developing Countries Prove So Resistant to the Rule of Law." In *Global Perspectives on the Rule of Law*, edited by James Heckman, Robert Nelson, and Lee Cabatingan, 28–51. New York: Routledge.

Westley, William. A. 1970. *Violence and the Police: A Sociological Study of Law, Custom, and Morality.* Cambridge, MA: MIT Press.

Whyte, William F. 1955. *Street Corner Society.* Chicago: University of Chicago Press.

Williams, Bryan C. 2011. "The Challenge of the Slums: Looking for Democratic Inclusion in the Squatter Settlements of Rio de Janeiro, Brazil (1995–2000)." *Proceedings from LASA 2011: Latin American Studies Association Conference on Social Movement Governance, Poverty and the New Politics of the Americas.* Tampa, FL.

Wilson, William J. 1987. *The Truly Disadvantaged: The Inner City, the Underclass, and Public Policy.* Chicago: University of Chicago Press.

World Bank. 2011. "Violence in the City: Understanding and Supporting Community Responses to Urban Violence." Social Development Department, Conflict, Crimena d Violence Team. Retrieved from http://siteresources.worldbank

.org/EXTSOCIALDEVELOPMENT/Resources/244362-1164107274725 /Violence_in_the_City.pdf.

Young, Alfred. 2004. *The Minds of Marginalized Black Men*. Princeton, NJ: Princeton University Press.

Zaverucha, Jorge. 1997. "The 1998 Brazilian Constitution and its Authoritarian Legacy: Formalizing Democracy while Gutting its Essence." *Journal of Third World Studies* 15 (1): 105–24.

Zedner, Lucia. 2006. "Policing Before and After the Police: Historical Antecedents of Contemporary Crime Control." *British Journal of Criminology* 46 (1): 78–96.

Index

CPSIA information can be obtained
at www.ICGtesting.com
Printed in the USA
LVOW07s0757210817
545781LV00001B/4/P